THE
HISTORY
OF RUSSIA

ADVISORY BOARD

THE HISTORY OF RUSSIA

SECOND EDITION

CHARLES E. ZIEGLER

The Greenwood Histories of the Modern Nations
Frank W. Thackeray and John E. Findling, Series Editors

GREENWOOD PRESS
An Imprint of ABC-CLIO, LLC

A B C ☰ C L I O

Santa Barbara, California • Denver, Colorado • Oxford, England

Library of Congress Cataloging-in-Publication Data

Ziegler, Charles E.
  The history of Russia / Charles E. Ziegler.—2nd ed.
    p. cm. — (The Greenwood histories of the modern nations)
  Includes bibliographical references and index.
  ISBN 978-0-313-36307-8 (paper : alk. paper)—ISBN 978-0-313-36308-5 (ebook) 1. Russia—History. 2. Soviet Union—History. 3. Russia (Federation)—History—1991- I. Title.
  DK40.Z54 2009
  947—dc22   2009028949

13 12 11 10 09   1 2 3 4 5

This book is also available on the World Wide Web as an eBook.
Visit www.abc-clio.com for details.

ABC-CLIO, LLC
130 Cremona Drive, P.O. Box 1911
Santa Barbara, California 93116–1911

This book is printed on acid-free paper ∞
Manufactured in the United States of America

To Janna and Alan

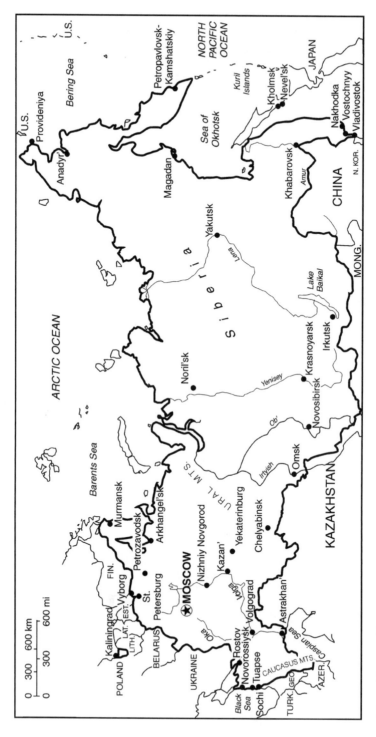

Map of Russia. [Cartography by Bookcomp, Inc.]

Contents

A photo essay follows page 122

Series Foreword

The Greenwood Histories of the Modern Nations series is intended to provide students and interested laypeople with up-to-date, concise, and analytical histories of many of the nations of the contemporary world. Not since the 1960s has there been a systematic attempt to publish a series of national histories, and as series advisors, we believe that this series will prove to be a valuable contribution to our understanding of other countries in our increasingly interdependent world.

Some 40 years ago, at the end of the 1960s, the Cold War was an accepted reality of global politics. The process of decolonization was still in progress, the idea of a unified Europe with a single currency was unheard of, the United States was mired in a war in Vietnam, and the economic boom in Asia was still years in the future. Richard Nixon was president of the United States, Mao Tse-tung (not yet Mao Zedong) ruled China, Leonid Brezhnev guided the Soviet Union, and Harold Wilson was prime minister of the United Kingdom. Authoritarian dictators still controlled most of Latin America, the Middle East was reeling in the wake of the Six-Day War, and Shah Mohammad Reza Pahlavi was at the height of his power in Iran.

Since then, the Cold War has ended, the Soviet Union has vanished, leaving 15 independent republics in its wake, the advent of the computer age has radically transformed global communications, the rising demand for oil makes the Middle East still a dangerous flashpoint, and the rise of new economic powers like the People's Republic of China and India threatens to bring about a new world order. All of these developments have had a dramatic impact on the recent history of every nation of the world.

For this series, which was launched in 1998, we first selected nations whose political, economic, and socio-cultural affairs marked them as among the most important of our time. For each nation, we found an author who was recognized as a specialist in the history of that nation. These authors worked cooperatively with us and with Greenwood Press to produce volumes that reflected current research on their nations and that are interesting and informative to their readers. In the first decade of the series, more than 40 volumes were published, and as of 2008, some are moving into second editions.

The success of the series has encouraged us to broaden our scope to include additional nations, whose histories have had significant effects on their regions, if not on the entire world. In addition, geopolitical changes have elevated other nations into positions of greater importance in world affairs and, so, we have chosen to include them in this series as well. The importance of a series such as this cannot be underestimated. As a superpower whose influence is felt all over the world, the United States can claim a "special" relationship with almost every other nation. Yet many Americans know very little about the histories of nations with which the United States relates. How did they get to be the way they are? What kind of political systems have evolved there? What kind of influence do they have on their own regions? What are the dominant political, religious, and cultural forces that move their leaders? These and many other questions are answered in the volumes of this series. The authors who contribute to this series write comprehensive histories of their nations, dating back, in some instances, to prehistoric times. Each of them, however, has devoted a significant portion of their book to events of the past 40 years because the modern era has contributed the most to contemporary issues that have an impact on U.S. policy. Authors make every effort to be as up-to-date as possible so that readers can benefit from discussion and analysis of recent events.

In addition to the historical narrative, each volume contains an introductory chapter giving an overview of that country's geography, political institutions, economic structure, and cultural attributes. This is meant to give readers a snapshot of the nation as it exists in the contemporary world. Each history also includes supplementary information following the narrative, which may include a timeline that represents a succinct chronology of the nation's historical evolution, biographical sketches of the nation's most important historical figures, and a glossary of important terms or concepts that are usually expressed in a foreign language. Finally, each author prepares a comprehensive bibliography for readers who wish to pursue the subject further.

Readers of these volumes will find them fascinating and well written. More importantly, they will come away with a better understanding of the contemporary world and the nations that comprise it. As series advisors, we hope that this series will contribute to a heightened sense of global understanding as we move through the early years of the twenty-first century.

Frank W. Thackeray and John E. Findling
Indiana University Southeast

Preface

Russia is a very large country with a long and complex history. This book provides a brief, accurate introduction to Russian, Soviet, and post-Soviet history in a readable format that will be of use to high school students, college students, teachers, and nonspecialists. It includes major social, cultural, and economic developments so that readers new to the subject will come away with a good general understanding of this fascinating and troubled country. For those who wish further reading, the bibliographic essay includes some of the better known accessible works.

For those who grew up in the post–World War II United States, Russia (or more accurately, the Soviet Union) was a constant source of fear and attention. Secretive leaders in the Kremlin, the massive stone fortress in the heart of Moscow, had sworn to spread communism across the globe. At any time they might rain thousands of nuclear warheads on America. School children in the 1950s learned to "duck and cover"—to hide under their desks and put their hands over their heads in the event of a nuclear attack. U.S. taxpayers spent billions and then trillions of dollars on bombers, missiles, fighter aircraft, submarines, aircraft carriers, troops, tanks, and the other war paraphernalia to defend against the communist threat. Leftists and communist sympathizers were hounded and persecuted by Senator Joseph McCarthy's House Un-American Activities Committee in the 1950s. The United States lost 58,000 men and rent itself apart trying to stop the spread of communism in Vietnam in the 1960s and early 1970s. In the 1980s, President Ronald Reagan swept into office on a strong anticommunist platform, pledging to build a space shield that would provide a comprehensive missile defense for America.

Few experts or government officials expected the Soviet communist government to collapse in 1991. When it did, Americans were overjoyed, expecting that once Russians had rejected dictatorship and socialist economics, they would quickly learn the ways of democracy and market capitalism. Russians likewise expected that within a few years they would be as affluent as the West Europeans, Japanese, or Americans. After all, Russia was a highly educated nation with talented people and vast natural resources. Sadly, as the 20th century drew to a close, these expectations had still not been borne out. Russia's economy had shrunk nearly every year since 1991. The government was deeply in debt, joblessness was rising, and crime was rampant. Russia had managed to hold several rounds of relatively free presidential and parliamentary elections, but the country's new democracy was still quite fragile. Moreover, democratic Russia had had only one president, Boris Yeltsin, and he was frequently sick and unable to govern.

Americans seem to have lost interest in Russia now that it is no longer communist and seems to pose no threat to the United States or its allies. Russia, however, is still a major nuclear power, and its leaders are determined that it will be influential and respected around the world. And Russia may some day extricate itself from the economic morass into which it has sunk. If that happens, Russia will indeed once again be a power to reckon with.

A brief note on transliteration and pronunciation: Russian names are written in Cyrillic, and so must be transliterated into the Latin alphabet. This means that occasionally the same word will be rendered by two different spellings: for example, tsar and czar. In most cases, I have followed the Library of Congress transliteration style used in the United States, with a few minor modifications for common usage (Trotsky instead of Trotskii). In Russian words and names, unlike French, all the letters should be pronounced.

Readers should also be aware that until the 20th century, Russia followed the old, Julian calendar abandoned by Europeans in 1582. The Julian calendar was inaccurate, so in Russia dates were 12 days behind the modern Gregorian calendar in the 19th century and 13 days behind in the 20th century. The Bolsheviks adopted the Gregorian calendar in February 1918, but the Russian Orthodox Church still celebrates its holidays according to the older calendar. Different dates for events in Russian history therefore are often referred to as "Old Style" or "New Style," depending on which calendar was in effect.

Chapter 8 draws in part from Charles E. Ziegler, "The Collapse of the Soviet Union, 1985–1991: Interpretive Essay," in *Events That Changed the World in the*

Twentieth Century, edited by Frank W. Thackeray and John E. Findling (Westport, CT: Greenwood Press, 1995).

I would like to thank Bruce Adams of the History Department at the University of Louisville for his helpful comments on various chapters. Frank Thackeray, one of the series' general editors, also gave me useful feedback on the manuscript. I am grateful to Dianne O'Regan for compiling the index and to Justine Ziegler who helped with the proofreading. My greatest debt of gratitude, however, is to my wife Janna Tajibaeva, whose many insights and suggestions from her years inside the Soviet Union made the book much better. Her tolerance and encouragement are deeply appreciated, and it is to her that I dedicate this book.

Preface to the Second Edition

When this book went to press in 1999, Russia was still struggling with the transition from communist dictatorship toward a new political and economic order. The 1990s had been a period of political anarchy, with President Boris Yeltsin presiding over the dismantling of the planned economy, and newly rich oligarchs amassing huge fortunes from the privatization of government-owned assets. The country was not a stable democracy, but at least elections were held on schedule, dozens of political parties competed for votes, the media were relatively free to criticize government officials, and Russians were free to travel and worship as they wished.

Yet many believed the costs of political and economic liberalization were too high. More than a third of Russians were living in poverty, crime had soared, disease and alcoholism had contributed to a gradual decline in population, and the nation seemed to be going through a spiritual crisis. Russia was no longer a respected world power; instead, the Americans and Europeans ignored Russian national interests and humiliated the nation, while China's rise in the east presented a long-term threat.

Vladimir Putin's popularity can only be fully understood within this context. His eight years as president saw record economic growth, the stabilization of everyday life, and the restoration of Russia as a powerful state respected on the world stage. Much of this success had little to do with Putin's governance (the country's economic performance was due mostly to record high oil and gas prices, for example), but Putin did restore order in Russia, largely through authoritarian measures that eroded the country's chances for developing into a working democracy. He leveraged Russia's natural resource wealth into considerable foreign policy influence, at least along the periphery, if not globally. And Putin made Russians proud of their country once again. But Russian nationalism resurgent had a dark side, too, in the form of bellicose anti-American rhetoric and skinhead attacks on foreigners.

Chapter 10 takes the reader through the Putin era and into early 2009. I have also updated the list of notable people, the glossary of terms, and the bibliographic essay, and have added a list of Web sites for those interested in keeping current with Russian politics. Once again, I would like to thank Frank Thackeray for his support and his helpful comments on revising the manuscript. Special thanks, and the dedication, go to Janna Tajibaeva and Alan Taj Ziegler.

Timeline of Historical Events

1000–700 B.C.	Cimmerians rule southern Russia
700–200 B.C.	Scythians occupy southern Russia
200 B.C.–A.D. 200	Sarmatians rule southern Russia, region had close links to Greek world
200–370	Goths control Russian steppe
370–453	Rule of Huns
fifth–ninth centuries	Various Turkic peoples inhabit southern Russia
862	Riurik of Varangians (Scandinavian tribe) establishes Riurikid dynasty
980–1015	Vladimir, Grand Prince of Kiev
988	Official conversion of Kievan Rus to Orthodox Christianity
1132–1136	Emergence of Novgorod city-state
1147	First mention of Moscow in the chronicles
1237–1240	Mongol conquest of Russian lands

1242	Aleksandr Nevskii defeats Teutonic Knights
1327–1341	Ivan I (Moneybag), Grand Prince of Moscow
1337	Holy Trinity–Saint Sergius Monastery founded
1367	Stone fortress (*kreml*) constructed in Moscow
1462–1505	Ivan III, Grand Prince of Moscow
1478	Moscow annexes Novgorod
1547–1584	Ivan IV (The Terrible), tsar of Russia
1552	Conquest of Kazan; construction of St. Basil's Cathedral in Moscow
1582	Ermak's conquest of western Siberia
1584–1613	Time of Troubles
1613	Mikhail Romanov elected tsar (1613–1645); start of Romanov dynasty
1645–1676	Reign of Tsar Alexis
1649	Adoption of Law Code (*Ulozhenie*)
1653–1667	Orthodox Church reforms lead to schism
1667–1671	Rebellion under Stenka Razin
1682–1725	Reign of Peter I (The Great), tsar of Russia
1689	Treaty of Nerchinsk between Russia and China
1700–1721	Sweden and Russia fight Northern War
1703	St. Petersburg founded as Peter's "Window on the West"
1709	Russian victory over Swedes at Poltava
1714	Establishment of Naval Academy in St. Petersburg
1722	Establishment of Table of Ranks
1736–1739	Russo-Turkish War
1741–1761	Reign of Tsarina Elizabeth
1755	Establishment of Moscow University
1762–1796	Reign of Catherine II (The Great)

1768–1774	Russo-Turkish War
1773–1775	Pugachev Rebellion
1781–1786	Ukraine absorbed into the Russian Empire
1787–1792	Russo-Turkish War
1793–1795	Second and Third Partitions of Poland
1796–1801	Reign of Paul
1801–1825	Reign of Aleksandr I
1801	Annexation of Georgia by Russia
1807–1811	Mikhail Speransky's reforms
1812	Napoleon's invasion of Russia
1819	St. Petersburg University established
1825	Revolt and suppression of the Decembrists
1825–1855	Reign of Nicholas I
1830–1831	Polish Rebellion
1842–1851	Construction of St. Petersburg-Moscow railway, the first rail line in Russia
1853–1856	Crimean War
1855–1881	Reign of Aleksandr II, the "Tsar Liberator"
1861	Emancipation Manifesto frees serfs
1864	Zemstvo (local government), legal, and education reforms
1865–1885	Conquest of Central Asian regions, absorption into Russian empire
1872	Publication of Karl Marx's *Das Kapital* in Russian
1877–1878	Russo-Turkish War
1881	People's Will assassinates Aleksandr II in St. Petersburg
1881–1894	Reign of Aleksandr III
1891–1892	Famine in Russia
1891–1904	Construction of Trans-Siberian railway

1894–1917	Reign of Nicholas II
1898	Founding of Russian Social Democratic Labor Party (RSDLP)
1902	Vladimir Lenin publishes *What Is to Be Done?*
1903	RSDLP splits into Bolshevik and Menshevik factions at second congress
1904–1905	Russo-Japanese War
1905–1907	Bloody Sunday massacre leads to Revolution of 1905; Duma created
1911	Assassination of Prime Minister Peter Stolypin
1914–1918	World War I
1916	Murder of Gregory Rasputin, confidant of the Royal Family
1917	February Revolution; abdication of Nicholas; rule by Provisional Government; Bolshevik coup in October
1918–1921	Civil War pits Reds against Whites; tsar and family killed at Ekaterinburg
1920	War with Poland
1921	Tenth Party Congress; ban on Party factions
1921–1928	New Economic Policy (NEP)
1922	Joseph Stalin appointed General Secretary of Communist Party
1922	Union Treaty creates Union of Soviet Socialist Republics
1924	Death of Vladimir Lenin
1928	Start of Five-Year Plans
1929	Stalin defeats the "Right Opposition," consolidates his power
1929–1939	Collectivization of agriculture
1932–1933	7.5 million die from famine
1934	Assassination of Leningrad Party Secretary Sergei Kirov
1936	Promulgation of Stalin Constitution

1936–1938	Show trials, purges
1939	Molotov-Ribbentrop Non-Aggression Pact
1940	USSR annexes Baltic states
1941–1945	Great Fatherland War (World War II)
1945–1948	Communist parties consolidate control of Eastern Europe
1946–1948	*Zhdanovshchina*, cultural repression and isolation
1949	Victory of communists under Mao Zedong in China
1949	Formation of Council for Mutual Economic Assistance
1950	Mao visits Moscow; Sino-Soviet Treaty signed; outbreak of Korean War
1953	Death of Joseph Stalin; Nikita Khrushchev becomes General Secretary
1955	Formation of Warsaw Pact military alliance
1956	Twentieth Party Congress; Khrushchev's De-Stalinization speech
1956–1962	The Thaw (period of cultural relaxation)
1956	Soviet troops crush Hungarian Revolution
1957	Anti-Party Group tries to oust Khrushchev and fails
1957	Soviet Union launches first spacecraft, *Sputnik*
1957	Creation of regional economic councils (*sovnarkhozy*)
1958	Boris Pasternak awarded Nobel Prize for *Dr. Zhivago*
1959	Sino-Soviet split becomes public
1961	Construction of Berlin Wall
1962	Publication of Aleksandr Solzhenitsyn's *One Day in the Life of Ivan Denisovich* in *Novyi Mir*
1962	Cuban Missile Crisis
1964	Khrushchev deposed; Leonid Brezhnev becomes Party General Secretary; Alexei Kosygin becomes Premier
1965–1968	Kosygin economic reforms
1966	Trial of dissidents Iulii Daniel and Andrei Siniavsky

1968	Warsaw Pact invasion of Czechoslovakia
1969	USSR and China exchange fire along Sino-Soviet border
1972	Beginning of détente: SALT I and ABM Treaties, U.S.-Soviet summitry
1975	Physicist Andrei Sakharov awarded Nobel Peace Prize
1977	Promulgation of Brezhnev Constitution
1979	SALT II Treaty
1979	Soviet troops invade Afghanistan
1980–1981	Solidarity labor movement in Poland
1982	Brezhnev dies; Iurii Andropov becomes General Secretary
1984	Andropov dies; Konstantin Chernenko becomes General Secretary
1985	Chernenko dies; Mikhail Gorbachev becomes General Secretary
1986	Explosion at Chernobyl nuclear reactor in Ukraine
1986	Nationalist demonstrations in Alma Ata, Kazakhstan
1987	Gorbachev begins economic reforms; political liberalization accelerates
1988	Nineteenth Party Conference discusses reform
1989	Elections to Congress of People's Deputies; Soviet withdrawal from Afghanistan; Eastern Europeans abandon communism; fall of Berlin Wall; conflict between Armenia and Azerbaijan over Karabagh; Gorbachev repairs Sino-Soviet relations
1990	Elections to Russian Congress of People's Deputies; Gorbachev elected President of USSR; Conventional Forces treaty in Europe
1991	Foreign Minister Eduard Shevardnadze resigns, warning of coup d'état; Boris Yeltsin elected President of Russia; conservatives attempt coup d'état in August; dissolution of USSR and formation of Commonwealth of Independent States (CIS)

1992	"Shock therapy" economic reforms adopted; Yeltsin rules by decree; new Union Treaty adopted; Viktor Chernomyrdin appointed Prime Minister
1993	National referendum of President and Parliament; Yeltsin dissolves Parliament and shells the White House; new Constitution approved in referendum; START II Treaty signed with United States
1994	Troops sent into republic of Chechnya
1995	December parliamentary elections; Communists are the largest party
1996	Yeltsin wins two rounds of presidential elections; Yevgeny Primakov appointed Minister of Foreign Affairs; Alexander Lebed negotiates cease-fire in Chechnya; Yeltsin undergoes heart surgery
1998	Collapse of ruble; Primakov appointed Prime Minister
1999	Russia critical of NATO air strikes against Serbia; Yeltsin appoints Vladimir Putin prime minister; second war in Chechnya begins; Duma institutes impeachment proceedings against Yeltsin; December parliamentary elections; Yeltsin resigns
2000	Putin elected President; *Kursk* submarine sinks.
2001	Putin pledges support for United States in war against terror
2002	Chechen militants take hostages in Dubrovka Theater
2003	Mikhail Khodorkovsky arrested; December Duma elections
2004	Putin wins re-election as President; Chechen militants take hostages at Beslan school in North Ossetia, Putin ends election of governors
2005	Mass protests over monetization of social benefits; Shanghai Cooperation Organization calls for withdrawal of U.S. troops from Central Asia
2007	Putin condemns United States at Munich security forum; United Russia wins control of Duma in December elections

2008   Putin's designated successor, Dmitrii Medvedev,
                elected President; Medvedev appoints Putin as prime
                minister; collapse of oil prices weakens Russian econ-
                omy

2009   Russian government draws down oil fund to support
                heavily indebted banks and corporations

1

Russia and Its People

Russia is a huge, complex, and extraordinarily interesting place. Straddling Europe and Asia, it is neither European nor Asian in outlook and culture. Although Russia, as the Soviet Union, shared the superpower spotlight with the United States throughout much of the 20th century, it is also very different from America. Russians today are struggling with their sense of identity, a conflict that has characterized the past three centuries of Russian history. Russia is no longer an imperial power, as it had been since the time of Peter the Great, though some have described Putin's Russia as neo-imperialist. Russia is no longer communist, as it was from 1918 to 1991. Russia is no longer an absolutist dictatorship, as it was under the tsars and the communists, but it is not yet fully democratic, either. What, then, is Russia?

Physically, the Russian Federation is the largest country in the world, even after the dissolution of the Soviet Union in 1991. It occupies about 6.6 million square miles of territory, and is nearly twice the size of the United States. From east to west, the country stretches over 5,000 miles and occupies 11 time zones. Cities in the Russian Far East, such as Khabarovsk and Yuzhno-Sakhalinsk, are closer to San Francisco than they are to Moscow. Russia has a long coastline on the Pacific, but there are few ports and only a small population in this vast region. In the north, Russia borders the Arctic Ocean; on the south, China,

Mongolia, and Kazakhstan form its boundaries. To the west, the former Baltic republics (Latvia, Lithuania, Estonia), Ukraine, and Belarus separate Russia from the rest of Europe. Russia relinquished much of its access to the Black Sea via Ukraine after the breakup of the Union of Soviet Socialist Republics (USSR). The fragmentation of the Soviet Union has left Russia more geographically isolated, smaller, and somewhat more landlocked.

The former Soviet Union had a population of nearly 290 million, and was the third-largest country in the world. Today, the Russian Federation's population is just under 141 million (and declining), making it the ninth-largest nation in the world, after China, India, the United States, Indonesia, Brazil, Pakistan, Bangladesh, and Nigeria (which although it has not conducted a census in 40 years, likely has a larger population than Russia). Over 80 percent of Russia's population is concentrated in the western quarter of the country; less than 25 million live in the vast expanses of Siberia and the Russian Far East. As one might expect, most of the roads, railways, and air routes are concentrated in the populous areas of western Russia. Siberia is extremely rich in natural resources—oil, natural gas, gold, diamonds, furs, and timber—but much of this wealth is virtually inaccessible or very costly to extract due to the country's weak transportation system.

Today, Russia is more ethnically homogeneous than imperial Russia and the former Soviet Union. Just before its collapse, the Soviet Union's population was barely 51 percent ethnic Russian, whereas the Russian Federation is about 82 percent Russian. The next-largest group is the Tatars, a Moslem Turkic people concentrated along the Volga some 400 miles east of Moscow. Tatars are the descendants of the Mongols, who conquered the Russian lands in the 13th century. They comprise just under 4 percent of Russia's population. Ukrainians, the Russians' Slavic cousins, make up another 3 percent of the population. A mix of Turkic and Caucasian peoples, together with Germans, Jews, Belorussians, and small Siberian tribes, make up the remaining 12 percent. On the whole, relations among the various ethnic groups are good, but there are sporadic outbursts of violence against non-Russians. Chechens are resented for their armed resistance to Russian rule, terrorist acts, and purported mafia connections. Under President Vladimir Putin, nationalist thugs often assaulted migrant workers from the Caucasus region, Central Asia, and China. The living conditions of the Siberian peoples are much like those encountered by Native Americans in the early United States, and they suffer from the same maladies—unemployment, marginalization, and alcoholism.

Russia as a whole lies much further north than the United States; in this sense, it is more comparable to Canada. Although Russia has an abundance of fertile agricultural land, its northern position results in short growing seasons and cold weather; consequently, many crops do not fare well. Some of the best cropland was located in Ukraine and Kazakhstan, areas that were lost after the Soviet Union dissolved. Typical Russian crops include winter wheat, rye, sugar beets, and potatoes. Soviet policies severely damaged agriculture, and this sector of the economy has not recovered in the post-communist period. In 2008, imports constituted nearly half of all food consumed in Russia.

Much of Russia is flat, and the absence of natural barriers is often said to account for the historical Russian preoccupation with secure borders. The Ural Mountains, running north to south, separate European Russia from Siberia and the Far East. The Urals are geologically old and not very high—they might be compared to the Appalachian Mountains in the United States. West of the Urals is the large European Russian plain. Directly eastward is the central Siberian plain, followed by the higher Siberian plateau. Much of this area is covered with forest; bear, elk, and deer are common, and a few Siberian tigers have survived. The northern section of Russia is comprised of the ecologically fragile arctic tundra. A large area of northern Russia is permafrost—the ground a few meters below earth is perpetually frozen. During the summer, the top layer becomes swampy, making construction difficult and costly, and causing buildings to sway drunkenly. Russia's huge land mass causes its climate to vary. Some areas of the south can be quite hot in the summer, while north-central Russia is brutally cold in the winter. Temperatures in Moscow often drop to -40° Fahrenheit; in the Siberian town of Verkhoyansk, temperatures can reach -90°!

The Russian Far East is ruggedly mountainous, and there are active volcanoes and hot springs on the Kamchatka peninsula. Russian geography is also distinguished by the huge rivers that flow northward, emptying into the Arctic Ocean—the Lena, Ob, and Enesei. The mighty Volga meanders through much of western Russia, and in the Far East, the Amur River forms a long stretch of the Russo-Chinese border. Traditionally, Russian rivers have provided a wealth of fish, including the huge sturgeon (some of which grow to be 2,000 pounds), which yields the world's best caviar. Sadly, pollution has ruined much of the Russian fishing industry. Russia is also home to many inland lakes and seas, including the magnificent Lake Baikal, the largest body of fresh water in the world. During the Soviet era, courageous writers and intellectuals lobbied hard against cellulose plants operating on Baikal's shores, managing to spare the "blue heart of Siberia" from serious ecological damage.

Overall, Russia is an urban nation, with about 70 percent of its population living in cities. Moscow, the capital, is the largest and most dynamic city, with a population of 9 million. Close to three-fourths of Western investment has been concentrated in the capital alone, and it shows. A drab and boring place in Soviet times, Moscow now boasts exotic restaurants and nightclubs, posh (and exorbitantly expensive) hotels, refurbished roads, traffic jams, and a bustling economy. Mayor Yurii Luzhkov—whose wife is Russia's richest woman, with an estimated fortune of $4.2 billion as of 2008—has parried his long career into a platform for Russian nationalism. St. Petersburg (known as Leningrad under the Soviets) is the second-largest city, at about 4 million. Its network of canals and bridges, stately Italian architecture, and green parks make Petersburg a favorite tourist destination and a source of great pride for its Russian inhabitants. The fabulous collection of artwork in the Hermitage Museum, the former Winter Palace of the tsars, is itself worth a trip to Russia. St. Petersburg, Putin's hometown, hosted the G-8 summit in 2006. It was also designated as the site for a controversial 400-meter (1,300 feet) futuristic skyscraper to house Gazprom, Russia's powerful, state-owned gas monopoly.

Many other Russian cities, unfortunately, are rather bleak settings where old Soviet industries limp along and the new market economy has yet to take off. Water and gas supplies are often sporadic in the concrete high-rise blocks of apartment buildings that date back to the Khrushchev era. There are a few success stories, however. Nizhnii Novgorod, an ancient city east of Moscow, developed a reputation as Russia's Silicon Valley in the 1990s, under the innovative leadership of its youthful governor, Boris Nemtsov. President Yeltsin later tapped him to be a financial advisor. Regional capitals, such as Perm, Irkutsk, and Yekaterinburg, made significant progress during the oil and gas boom of the early 2000s. But many cities are heavily polluted, such as those in southern Russia and northern Siberia, or they are dominated by mafia gangs and authoritarian governors, like the port city of Vladivostok in the Russian Far East.

Life in the Russian countryside was and still is far removed from the relatively cultured existence available in the major cities. Russian villages are far poorer than the cities. Some rural Russian homes still do not have indoor plumbing, and there are few, if any, cultural amenities in the villages. The countryside is backward; picturesque (but inefficient) horse-drawn carts are common there. Agricultural production was mechanized under the Soviets, and peasants were forced onto huge collectives and state farms, many of which still are operating today. But productivity is low and there are few opportunities for young people in the country. As a result, they leave for the cities in droves. This migration occurred on a large scale even under the residency restrictions of the Soviet period (urban residents had to have a *propiska*, or residence permit); now, the Russian Constitution guarantees freedom of movement, and there is no way to keep citizens down on the farm.

Russians are a highly literate, well-educated people. When the Soviet government came to power in 1917, about 55 percent of the population was illiterate. Now, literacy stands at about 97 percent, and Russian students routinely outperform Americans in math and the natural sciences. Under the Soviet regime, all schools were operated by the state. In the post-communist period, the education system has come to resemble that of the West, with private and religious schools supplementing state education. But standards have slipped somewhat, in part because state education is severely under-funded, and in part because of pervasive corruption in higher education. The new Russian elite often send their children abroad to expensive boarding schools and universities in France, Switzerland, or the United States. Young, entrepreneurial Russians quickly master English or German, languages that are both necessary in the international business world.

The communist authorities clearly failed in their attempts to eradicate religion. Recent years have witnessed the resurgence of Russian Orthodoxy, the state church of the tsars. Church buildings have been restored, and services are packed with believers of all ages. About two-thirds of the population is nominally Russian Orthodox, while about 18 percent—mostly Tatars, Chechens, Ingush, and other peoples of the Caucasus Mountains—are Muslims. Given the high birthrate of Muslims, and the very low birthrate of ethnic Russians, the religious balance is gradually shifting. There are also large numbers of Baptists, some Catholics and Buddhists, and a smattering of fringe religions, like Hare Krishnas and members of various cults, but most of the Jews have left Russia. Many government functions are now sanctioned by the presence of Russian Orthodox priests, as in pre-communist times, leading civil libertarians to worry about the reestablishment of an official state religion.

For centuries, Russia's government was a centralized, absolutist monarchy headed by the tsar (after the Roman Caesars) and organized according to rank and privilege. In the Soviet period, a more pervasive dictatorship was enacted through the Communist Party. Vladimir Lenin established the Soviet system and laid the foundation for a totalitarian dictatorship, which his successor, Joseph Stalin, developed into one of the most thoroughly repressive governments in history. Subsequent leaders of the Communist Party—Nikita Khrushchev (1953–1964) and Leonid Brezhnev (1964–1982)—tempered the most oppressive aspects of Stalinism, but preserved the basics of the party-state system. Mikhail Gorbachev (1985–1991), the first Soviet leader to undertake serious reform, set in motion a series of events that brought about the collapse of the USSR, leaving 15 newly independent states in its place.

The present Russian government is a mixed presidential-parliamentary system patterned after the French government, but with extraordinary powers delegated to the president. It is nominally federal, with political authority divided between Moscow and 84 regional governments. According to the 1993 Constitution, the President is elected for a maximum of two four-year terms; however, an amendment enacted at the end of 2008 extended this maximum to two six-year terms. The Russian President has sweeping powers in foreign policy and domestic politics. He appoints the Prime Minister, who is largely responsible for running the economy. The President also appoints his Cabinet, a National Security Council, and one-third of the justices to a 19-member Constitutional Court, which has the power of judicial review. Only a few of the President's nominees, including the Prime Minister, are subject to approval by the Parliament. The Russian Parliament, like the United States Congress, has the power to impeach the President. In the late 1990s, communist and nationalist members of Parliament frequently proposed impeachment motions against President Yeltsin, often on frivolous grounds. President Putin dominated the Parliament during his eight years in office; only the marginalized Communist Party presented any significant opposition to his initiatives.

Russia's legislature, the Federal Assembly, is divided into two chambers: the larger and more significant lower house, the Duma (450 deputies), and a smaller (168-member) Federal Council. Duma deputies must stand for election every five years. Originally, half were elected from districts, and half by party list, in a type of proportional representation system that was very similar to Germany's. In 2007, this practice was changed so that elections were based solely on party lists, with parties needing seven percent of the vote to gain representation. During Yeltsin's tenure, the Duma was controlled by parties that were vigorously critical of the President; in 1993, this opposition drew blood as the President used tanks to shell rebels in the Russian White House (the white marble edifice on the banks of the Moscow River) into submission. Members of the upper house are chosen by the executives and legislatures from the 84 territorial units of the Russian Federation; there are two from each ethnic republic or region. In a sense, the Federal Council embodies a principle of representation similar to that of the United States Senate, although under Putin, this body exercised little independent authority.

Russians are suspicious of and cynical about their government, although they are also quite patriotic. Years of broken promises under communism and by Boris Yeltsin's post-communist government engendered skepticism of all things political. Russians read many daily or weekly newspapers and watch the state and private television stations, but they believe little of what they hear. Rumor networks supplemented the censored press under communism, and even today, Russians are willing to give greater credence to a neighbor's gossip than to a reporter's story. Under Yeltsin, Russian newspapers and television stations were owned by rival corporate moguls who routinely distorted the truth to serve their political or economic interests. Putin brought all of the major television stations under state control early in his tenure, and newspaper reporters were harassed and intimidated into exercising self-censorship, ensuring that Russians would receive mostly government-approved news.

In the 1990s, the Russian economy experienced hyperinflation, unemployment and underemployment, capital flight, and growing income inequality. A burdensome and irrational tax system led most businesses to keep two sets of books, forcing the government to operate at a deficit. Wealthy entrepreneurs had connections to the criminal mafia gangs, and the great majority of

Russian businesses paid them protection money. Under Putin, the economy expanded dramatically due largely to record oil and gas prices, and many Russians believed life had returned to normal, at least until the financial crisis of 2008–09.

In public, Russians can often seem abrupt and unfriendly. In actuality, Russians are extraordinarily hospitable, taking time out of their busy schedules to escort guests around town or invite them home for a lavish feast. Many Russians are sports enthusiasts. Soccer is the most popular professional sport, and Russia has generally won more than its fair share of medals in Olympic gymnastics, ice-skating, weightlifting, and track. Russians were thrilled when the Black Sea resort of Sochi was chosen for the 2014 Winter Olympics, thanks largely to Putin's personal lobbying. For recreation, skiing, skating, hiking, hunting, and chess are popular, as are trips to the forest to gather mushrooms. City dwellers often have a dacha, or country home, where they can escape the crowded and noisy urban life and tend their vegetable or flower gardens. Occasionally a luxurious second home or, more likely, just a tiny cottage, the dacha provides a welcome summer getaway from the city's pollution and crowds.

As in most countries, men in Russia occupy more privileged positions than women. Russia is sexist—more so than the United States, but much less so than Japan. The Soviet government did at least educate women, ensure they received equal pay for equal work, and mandate that certain percentages of women must hold public positions. But men monopolized the higher-paying and more prestigious jobs. Moreover, men generally refused to do the shopping or housework, so women bore the double burden of holding down full-time jobs while taking care of the family. In the 1990s, women made up 70 percent of the unemployed; they were the first workers fired during the economic reform process. Businesses blatantly favor attractive young women for secretarial positions. Prostitution, conducted underground during the Soviet era, has soared. A women's movement has emerged in Russia, but it is fairly small and not particularly radical by Western standards.

Artistic and cultural life in Russia, especially in the big cities of Moscow and St. Petersburg, was once exceptional. The Soviet regime supported traditional forms of culture—ballet, opera, symphonies, museums—as long as they promoted socialist values. Of course, the authorities frowned on the more avant-garde pursuits, such as jazz and rock music, postmodernist theater, and abstract art. Now that cultural repression has ceased, Russians are free to experiment. But Russia's young writers and artists are more interested in making money than in being creative. Movie theaters and video stores, for example, are stocked with gangster films and pornography. Cheap detective and romance novels fill the bookstores. Talented painters produce schlock for the tourist markets. Happily, there are still Russia's magnificent museums:

the Hermitage Museum, which rivals New York's Metropolitan Museum of Art or the British Museum; Moscow's Pushkin Museum, with its excellent Impressionist exhibit; and the Russian Museum in St. Petersburg. After years of renovation, the Tretiakov Gallery in Moscow reopened in 1996. Financed by one of Russia's great 19th-century merchants, the Tretiakov boasts a superb collection of native Russian icons and paintings by such masters as Andrei Rublev and Ilya Repin.

Russia's present, like its past, is troubled, violent, and utterly fascinating. The country is only beginning to emerge from long decades of brutal repression, and is experiencing great difficulty building a viable and respected democracy. Russia's political and economic leadership has frequently behaved irresponsibly, enriching itself and exercising power with only minimal regard for the welfare of the people. Yet the country has tremendous unrealized potential. Russia boasts the world's largest reserves of natural resources, and Russians are some of the most highly educated and creative people in the world. Russia is not a captive of its history, doomed to reenact its authoritarian past, as some suggest. With some responsible leadership, and a little luck, Russia could become an affluent democracy. It would be a distinctly Russian democracy, however, quite unlike those found in the West. This brief survey should help us understand, and appreciate, Russia's distinctiveness, its absorbing past, and its turbulent present.

2

Kievan Russia and the Mongol Experience

THE RISE AND DECLINE OF KIEV

For many Russians, Ukraine, which gained its independence in 1991, along with the other 14 republics of the former USSR, is more than simply another Slavic country. The first state of the eastern Slavic peoples was centered around Kiev, Ukraine's capital. It was the Kievan state that adopted Orthodox Christianity as Russia's official religion, and it was in Kievan Russia that the Russian language acquired written form and its distinct Cyrillic alphabet. Although Moscow would emerge as the political center of Russia two centuries after the Mongol invasion, Kiev's early history is an inseparable part of Russia's historic identity.

According to the *Primary Chronicle,* a 12th-century account of early Russian history mixing fact and legend, the rise of Kiev began with the city's occupation by the shadowy Oleg, a Varangian, from 882 to his death in 913. Oleg came to Kiev from Novgorod, the ancient northern city where, according to the *Primary Chronicle,* warring tribes agreed (in 860–862) to invite princes from Scandinavia to rule over them. Of the three princes who accepted their offer, only Riurik survived to establish the first Russian dynasty. Oleg, according to this account, campaigned southward along the Dniepr River, captured strategic Kiev (the city is situated on a hill overlooking a bend of the river), and united it with Novgorod, establishing the Kievan state.

Oleg was succeeded by Prince Igor, who expanded Kievan authority and conducted a series of campaigns against Byzantium in 941–944. Igor was murdered by one of the tribes that offered tributary to Kiev, the Derevlians, and his wife Olga took his place. A rather devious figure, Olga visited cruel revenge on those who had murdered her husband. When a Derevlian delegation proposed that the new widow marry their prince, she graciously assented, invited the delegation to be carried by her servants in their boat to a splendid banquet, and then had them dropped in a huge trench and buried alive. A second delegation sent to Kiev was burned to death in a bath house. Next, Olga invited herself to the city where her husband was buried, held a huge funeral feast for her hosts (who were either very trusting or not terribly astute), and had her followers slaughter some 5,000 of the drunken revelers. She then laid siege to the Derevlians' city, burning it and imposing heavy taxes on the survivors.

Olga was the first Christian Kievan ruler. Although she converted to Christianity around 954–955, her son and successor Sviatoslav was pagan, and it was not until 988, under Vladimir (980–1015), that the Kievan state formally adopted Byzantine Christianity. Sviatoslav greatly expanded Kievan territory with his subjugation of the Viatichi, an eastern Slavic tribe, and his campaigns against the Khazars, Alans, and Bulgars. Following an unsuccessful campaign against Byzantium, Sviatoslav was killed by the Pechenegs, a fierce tribe of Central Asians. Legend has it that the chief of the Pechenegs had Sviatoslav's skull lined with gold and used it as a drinking cup.

Prince Vladimir's forcible conversion of Kievan Russia to Orthodox Christianity and his marriage to the Byzantine emperor's sister strengthened Kiev's links to Constantinople. Reportedly, Vladimir considered the pros and cons of the region's major religious influences: Christianity, Judaism, and Islam. As Nicholas Riasanovsky has pointed out, the story of how the Russians chose Orthodoxy over Islam or Judaism may be apocryphal (supposedly, Islam was unacceptable because it rejected alcohol, Judaism because it was the stateless religion of a defeated people, and Roman Catholicism because it lacked splendor), but it does indicate the range of choices that were available in this cosmopolitan environment. Historians David MacKenzie and Michael Curran note that Vladimir's emissaries were more impressed with the pageantry and glory of the Greek Orthodox ritual than with the philosophical depth of Orthodox beliefs. This preoccupation with ceremony over substance would be a constant in Russian and Soviet history.

The adoption of Orthodoxy would have a formative impact on Russian development. Geography combined with religion to isolate Russia from many of Europe's later cultural, philosophical, and political currents, most notably the Reformation and the Renaissance. In the Kievan period, however, Russia was no less advanced than Western Europe, and had close contacts with many European principalities. Kiev's location on the Dniepr River made it a critical stop on the trade route from the Varangians to the Greeks—that is, from Scandinavia to Byzantium. Much of Kiev's prominent position was due to its location astride the trade routes of this period.

By the middle of the 11th century, Kiev controlled most of the territory from the Baltic to the Black Sea, and from the Carpathian Mountains to the Oka River in the east. Prince Iaroslav the Wise (1019–1054) ruled over the Kievan state at its zenith, developing and expanding the Orthodox Church and implementing the first written Russian laws, *The Russian Justice.*

The Kievan political system was authoritarian, but much less so than its successor state, Muscovy. Many scholars have remarked on the democratic character of certain political institutions, especially the *veche* (town assembly) and the duma (council of boyars, or nobility). The *veche* was an assembly, dating from prehistoric times, of free heads of households who were called together from time to time to resolve questions of war, succession, or other major issues. The *veche* was a disorderly form of direct democracy, featuring freewheeling debates where decisions were made unanimously, rather than by majority rule.

The boyars' duma also preceded the institution of the prince, and served as his advisory and consultative body. The institution of the duma persisted through the Muscovite and Imperial periods, resurfaced as Tsar Nicholas II's concession to limited constitutional government in 1907, and was recreated in 1993 as democratic Russia's main legislative assembly.

Kiev's major political institution was the office of Prince. Typical princely Kievan functions included providing military leadership, dispensing justice, protecting the Orthodox Church, and administering the government through the *druzhina,* or military retainers. Janet Martin has argued that a well-defined political system had evolved in Kievan Russia by the 11th century, in which Kiev was the center of princely authority, legitimate rulers were those who descended from the Riurikid dynasty, and succession occurred laterally based on seniority.

Interestingly, Kievan law and punishments were relatively mild by the standards of that era. The Russian laws formulated early in the 11th century by Grand Prince Iaroslav—*The Russian Justice*—dealt largely with property crimes and assessed fines for most offenses. Iaroslav also developed a Church Statute in an effort to define the respective jurisdictions of princely, boyar, and Church authority. In supporting the Church's juridical authority, the Kievan government was able to impose Christian legal and social norms throughout the Russian lands.

Kievan society was complex and stratified. At the top was the princely class, served by the *druzhina.* Next in the hierarchy were the boyar nobility, who energetically defended their interests against princely encroachment, and the Orthodox clergy. Below the boyars and clergy were the *liudi* or free middle-class, comprised largely of urban craftsmen, the owners of blacksmith shops, tanneries, or carpentry shops, and moderately prosperous merchants and rural landowners. Urban workers and free peasants without property constituted the next level of society. The lowest classes were debtors (the half-free), and slaves.

There has been some dispute over the Kievan form of government. Soviet historians, who analyzed Kievan politics from a Marxian class perspective, described it as a European-style feudal system, with powerful landowners exploiting peasant labor and a complex hierarchy of mutual obligations. Kiev does appear to have been highly decentralized, like a feudal system, but Kiev was as much a trading state as it was agricultural. As Janet Martin points out, the Kievan peasantry were not tied to the land, like serfs, but were free landowners. They farmed and shared joint responsibilities for taxes and other obligations through the village commune. The boyar nobility owned rural estates, but, as Martin observes, they largely raised horses and livestock, and did not necessarily interfere or compete with peasant farming.

Kiev's economy revolved mainly around trade and agriculture. The writings of the Byzantine emperor Constantine Porphyrogenitus described how the Kievan princes would tour their territories collecting tributes, including boats, which they would then use to transport their exports down the broad Dniepr River to Constantinople. Kiev exported wax, honey, furs, flax, and slaves, and in turn imported wines, silks, spices, ironware, and glassware from Byzantium, Asia, and Eastern Europe.

The larger towns, like Suzdal, Novgorod, Ryazan, and Smolensk, were centers of medieval Kievan political, ecclesiastical, and commercial life. The major cities probably had 10,000 to 20,000 inhabitants; Kiev's population might have been as large as 50,000, which was roughly comparable to London in that period. Kievan Russia's houses, shops, and churches were built of wood, so fire was a common hazard. Wood was plentiful, but its extensive use for construction means that we know little about Kievan structures, as only archaeological ruins remain from that time. Various trades were practiced in Kievan towns, and the major urban centers boasted marketplaces where all manner of products were bought and sold. To protect their wealth, Russian medieval princes usually built a fortress, or kremlin, which was basically a stockade of logs fortified by towers. Later, kremlins, like those found in Moscow, would be constructed of more enduring stone and brick.

The great majority of people in medieval Kievan Russia lived in the countryside and farmed for a living. The peasants used slash and burn techniques to clear patches of forest, moving on when the soil in a particular area became depleted. Kievan agriculture consisted of cattle raising and wheat cultivation in the south, while rye, flax, hemp, barley, and oats were produced in the north. They also raised horses, pigs, sheep, goats, and chickens, fished in nearby lakes and rivers, and gathered mushrooms and wild berries to supplement their diets. Honey, beeswax, and furs were quite significant in Kievan agriculture and trade, as were metal-work and textiles. A portion of what the peasants produced was allocated to the Kievan princes as tributes or taxes, and they in turn extended their protection to the rural population.

In religious matters, Kievan culture combined early indigenous pagan Slavic beliefs with the strong influence of Byzantine Orthodox Christianity. The Church and the Kievan state cooperated in symbiotic fashion; indeed, Orthodox Christianity provided much of the cultural glue that held the decentralized Kievan principalities together. Nicolai Petro has suggested that the early relationship between church and state could be considered one of harmony, with the Church acting as the moral conscience and supporter of the state. This symbiotic relationship ended with Peter the Great's subordination of the Church to the state early in the 18th century. From then on, the Russian state dominated and regulated Church affairs; in turn, the Orthodox Church promoted the idea that the tsar was God's direct representative on earth.

Kievan culture at this time was heavily influenced by Byzantium through the Greek Orthodox Church connection. Kievan Russia accepted Byzantine Christianity uncritically. Russia's Orthodox clergy stressed the ritualistic and physical aspects of worship: the beauty of religious icons, the splendor of golden cupolas, and the joyousness of ringing bells. As James Billington notes in *The Icon and the Axe*, Russian Orthodox services feature the interdependence of sight, sound, and smell in the form of icons, religious hymns, and incense, as in pre–Vatican II Catholic rituals.

The visual nature of Russian Orthodoxy was reflected in the primary artwork of the period: Russian forms of the Byzantine icon. These two-dimensional paintings of tempera on wood depicted saints such as Boris and Gleb, Kievan princes who were cruelly murdered by their brother Sviatopolk (called "the Damned," who ruled from 1015 to 1019), and various historical and religious themes. Icons were daily reminders of the presence of God in all aspects of life; their pictorial representation of spirituality was especially important for average Russians, who could not read or write. Icons decorated the interior of every Orthodox Church and, from the earliest Christian times, Russian families kept icons on their walls or in a special corner of their houses. Many early icons have survived; some of the best examples can be found at the Russian Museum in St. Petersburg, the cathedrals of the Kremlin in Moscow, and the Holy Trinity–St. Sergius Monastery in Sergiev Posad (formerly Zagorsk) outside of Moscow.

Russian Orthodoxy differs from other branches of Christianity in that it did not develop a rational or inquisitive theology. There was, for example, no Russian counterpart to the Western Jesuit tradition of critical scholarship, and attempts at innovation were strenuously resisted by the faithful. Orthodox teachings stressed uncritical obedience to political and religious authority, and did not hold science or secular learning in high esteem. The Church's influence reinforced the strongly conservative tendencies in Russian society, and inhibited scientific and technical development.

Russian literature of the time, as in medieval Europe, was strongly religious. The introduction of a written alphabet by the Byzantine monks Cyril and Methodius, by way of what is now Bulgaria, was intended as a means of spreading Christianity to the Slavs. Written works were therefore designed to serve a purpose: to reinforce belief in God. The earliest Russian writings consisted of collections of readings from the Gospels, the lives of the saints, and sermons. Secular literature as we know it did not exist. However, some works, such the Kievan chronicles, including the *Primary Chronicle,* blended history and politics with religion and myths. These early chronicles are valuable partly as historical records, and partly for the insights they provide into the culture and political struggles of the time. Church Slavonic served as both the written and spoken language of worship for medieval Russia, and was intelligible to all worshippers, unlike the Latin that was used in Catholic masses of the same period.

One notable example of historical narrative from the late 12th century is the *Lay of the Host of Igor.* Not overtly religious, the *Lay* is an account in verse of an unsuccessful Russian campaign against the Polovtsy, a Turkic people who first invaded Kievan territory in the mid-11th century. In addition to written works, medieval Russia also possessed a strong oral tradition. Secular epic poems (*byliny*) that recounted the partly mythical, partly real adventures of ancient Russian *bogatyri* (heroic warriors) were very popular among the people. These *byliny* and other songs would be sung at festivals and weddings by bards, who would also recount magical Russian folk tales for their audience.

The most prominent examples of medieval Russian architecture were likewise religious. While most Orthodox churches built of wood did not survive, a number of impressive stone churches have been preserved. Among the most notable examples are the Cathedral of St. Sophia in Kiev, the St. Sophia Cathedral in Novgorod, and the Cathedral of the Assumption in Vladimir. Russian churches are quite different from the massive Gothic cathedrals of medieval France, England, and Germany. Some are virtually square; others may resemble a pile of building blocks of various shapes. Most are distinguished by oriental cupolas (onion domes) surmounting one or more drums, with a cross at the very peak. Mosaics, frescoes, and icons decorated the interiors. While Gothic cathedrals inspire awe, Russian churches strike the observer as whimsical and colorful on the outside, and exotic and warm on the inside.

APPANAGE RUSSIA

The half-century following the death of Iaroslav the Wise in 1054 saw a period of constant civil wars among his less able sons, Iziaslav, Sviatoslav, and Vsevolod. Next came a period of political fragmentation, decentralization, and dynastic struggle among the northern princes, which extended from about 1100 to 1237, and was called the Appanage period of Russian history. The term comes from the custom of Russian princes dividing their territories among their sons, granting each an appanage (*udel*). The Appanage period witnessed the proliferation of princely families and the boyars who served as their retainers. The immunities and privileges granted to the boyars, such as the power to collect taxes and administer justice, eroded the peasants' social and economic position. The peasantry, who had largely been free landholders during the Kievan era, were gradually transformed into renters during the Appanage period, and finally became serfs tied to the land by the end of the 16th century.

This proliferation of small principalities greatly weakened the political unity of Russia, and made the land vulnerable to foreign conquest. The Polovtsy, a Turkish people, were one of the major forces threatening the Kievan state from the latter part of the 11th century to the middle of the 13th century. Grand Prince Vladimir Monomakh, an able ruler (1113–1125), and his son Mstislav (1125–1132), fought the Polovtsy and enacted some progressive domestic measures (for example, Monomakh's social legislation to help the poor), but Kiev was clearly in decline relative to other major Russian cities by the middle of the 12th century.

Factors often cited as contributing to this decline include the weak and decentralized nature of the Kievan political system, debilitating political and social conflicts, external aggression, the decline of trade, and, perhaps most importantly, the uncertainties of princely succession. Scholars are divided on whether Kiev declined in absolute terms, or only relative to other emerging Russian city-territories, like Vladimir, Novgorod, Rostov, Suzdal, Chernigov, Periaslavl, and Smolensk. Whatever the case, the various Kievan states were unable to present a unified defense against outside forces.

Following the death of Grand Prince Iaropolk II in 1139, the Kievan state's luster faded, and two regional centers—Volyhnia and Galicia in the southwest (present-day western Ukraine and Belarus), and Vladimir-Suzdal in the northeast—emerged as prominent states in the century preceding the Mongol invasion. Prince Iaroslav Osmomysl (1153–1187) developed Galicia into a strong state to the point where he defended Kiev against the Asian nomads of the steppes. Prince Roman of Volyhnia (1197–1205) united his territory with Galicia, defending his lands against the threat of nomads, Lithuanians, Poles, and Hungarians.

The emergence of the northeast was linked in large part to the migration of peoples from the Kiev area in the 12th century. Although agriculturally less fertile, this area to the east of Moscow, between the Volga and Oka Rivers, was sufficiently removed from the feuding princes and nomadic marauders to provide a measure of security. One of the most powerful Rostov princes was Iurii Dolgorukii ("Long Arm," 1149–1157), the son of Vladimir Monomakh. Prince Iurii waged a 10-year struggle for control of Kiev, a position from which he could establish a claim to political supremacy over the south.

The city-state of Novgorod had the reputation of being prosperous, fiercely independent, and proud—its full title was "Lord Novgorod the Great." According to the *Primary Chronicle*, the Varangian Prince Riurik, founder of the Kievan dynasty, first came to Novgorod in 862. Not only was the city one of the main trading partners of Kiev, it also served as a prominent commercial link between the Scandinavian and Germanic peoples along the Baltic Sea and the Asiatic Bulgars of the Volga region. Located northwest of Moscow, at its height, Novgorod controlled a huge area from Russia's far northeast to the Ural Mountains.

Novgorod also stands out as a city-state in which strong constraints were placed on princely authority. The city's *veche* evolved into a strong institution in the late 11th/early 12th century, circumscribing the authority of the mayor (*posadnik*) and the archbishop, and asserting its right to appoint the city's prince. The *veche* frequently appointed princes who were outsiders, and then required them to reside outside the city proper. The *veche* decided issues of war and peace, mobilized the army, proclaimed laws, and levied taxes. In addition, a Council of Notables, presided over by the archbishop and consisting largely of boyars and local officials, constituted Novgorod's aristocratic assembly.

During the 12th century, there were frequent clashes between the Rostov-Suzdal princes and their boyars, who resisted the princes' costly foreign policy adventures. Iurii Dolgorukii's son, Andrei Bogoliubskii (1157–1174), sought to control the key city of Novgorod. He also attacked and overturned Kiev in 1169, decisively ending that city's central position in early Russia. Andrei chose to rule from the northern city of Vladimir, rather than Kiev. The high point of northeast rule was achieved under Andrei's younger brother, Vsevolod (1177–1212), who subordinated the southern lands to Vladimir-Suzdal rule.

The recurring conflict between boyar nobility and princes in late Kievan Russia was not unlike the disputes between King John I and the English nobility at about the same time. However, while political struggle in early 13th-century England resulted in the signing of the Magna Carta and introduced the principle of limited royal authority, in Russia, the conflict weakened the state and facilitated the Mongol conquest. Kievan Russia was not an easily defended island, like England, but a vulnerable, open territory located at the intersection of powerful military forces.

Had Russia's geographic position been more favorable, perhaps those elements of democratic government and limited authority might have been reinforced. As it was, the Mongol invasion and two centuries of foreign oppression highlighted the need for unchallenged, centralized authority and domestic repression to protect the Russian state. It was a lesson that Russia's rulers would use to justify over 700 years of authoritarian governance.

THE MONGOL CONQUEST AND RULE

In 1223, a fierce group of Asiatic warriors swept into Russia through the passes of the Caucasian Mountains, defeated a combined force of Russians and Polovtsy at the Kalka River, and then disappeared. The Mongols, or Tatars, as the Russians called them, had conquered northern China and Central Asia under the great Genghis Khan (1167–1227), and on their return to Mongolia, briefly engaged the Russians in battle. Fourteen years later, the Mongols would return to Russia, determined this time to subjugate the territory as part of their campaign to conquer Europe. From 1236 to 1238, the Mongols attacked and defeated the Volga Bulgars, destroyed Russian Ryazan, and conquered Vladimir and Suzdal. Novgorod, surrounded by dense forests and treacherous bogs, escaped annihilation, but the city was forced to pay tribute to the Mongols.

The Mongols renewed their Russian campaign in 1240–1242, conquering Kiev and subduing Hungary, Galicia, and southern Poland. Their sophisticated military tactics, highly mobile form of warfare, and extensive military experience made them a formidable foe. The Mongols trained their young men to fight from an early age through hunting. In their military campaigns, they employed an advanced system of communications, using scouts and a system of signal flags and messengers. They adroitly employed enveloping movements and feints, and readily adapted foreign technologies, such as Persian siege machines, to the Mongolian style of attack. Kievan military practices, by contrast, resembled those in Europe, and consisted largely of heavily armored cavalries (the prince and his *druzhina*) that were usually augmented by poorly armed peasant conscripts. Although the Russians fought fiercely, they were no match for the Mongols.

As many historians have noted, the constant feuding and division among Russia's principalities, and their consequent inability to unite and resist the invaders, made them easy prey. The 1236 attack on the Volga Bulgars, located directly east of Vladimir-Suzdal, should have alerted the Russian princes to the Mongol danger. Perhaps they believed that the Mongols posed no greater threat than the Pechenegs or Polovtsy, who engaged the Russians in sporadic battles along the frontier, while trading and even intermarrying with the Russians. In any case, they were woefully unprepared for the swift and thorough destruction visited upon them by the Mongol warriors.

Russia was not the Mongols' sole objective, but rather one stage in their drive to conquer Europe. However, just as the Mongols were poised to launch an assault against the rest of Europe and fulfill Genghis Khan's dream of a drive "to the last sea," the Great Khan Ogedei died in Karakorum and the campaign was called off. The feared assault on Western Europe would not be resumed. The Russian lands became the westernmost part of the Mongol empire, with Batu Khan establishing the headquarters of his Golden Horde (large tribal group) at Sarai on the lower Volga River. Sarai served as the Mongol capital of the Golden Horde to which Russian princes were obliged to make periodic journeys to pay tribute and pledge their loyalty.

Although the Mongols were skillful conquerors, they did not have enough administrators to rule Russian territories directly. Instead, the khan at Sarai granted a patent (*iarlyk*), or official appointment, to the various Russian princes, giving them the right to rule certain domains. In exchange, the princes would provide tribute to the Mongols. Initially, this was one-tenth of everything in the principality—livestock, food, and population. In this way, the Mongols obtained troops and horses for their army, along with slaves, furs, silver, and other goods. Later, as Mongol control weakened, the khans delegated primary responsibility for tax collection to the Prince of Moscow, thus elevating him to the status of Grand Prince and contributing to Moscow's emergence as the premier Russian city.

In Novgorod, Prince Aleksandr Nevskii cooperated with the Mongols, apparently reasoning that since resistance was futile, it would be better to strike a favorable arrangement with Batu Khan in the south. This would free Novgorod to consolidate its authority in the north. Aleksandr had acquired the nickname "Nevskii" when he surprised and routed a Swedish invasion fleet along the Neva River in 1240. This bold warrior conducted a series of campaigns against the Lithuanians, Swedes, and Germans, his Christian neighbors to the west. In 1242, his forces defeated the German Teutonic Knights on the ice of Lake Chud, in present-day Estonia, a battle immortalized in Sergei Eisenstein's 1938 film *Aleksandr Nevskii*. This work by the Soviet Union's greatest director was sanctioned by the dictator Joseph Stalin, who valued the film's skillful use of early Russian history to mobilize Soviet patriotism against the threat looming from Hitler's Germany. Eisenstein's film was pulled from public circulation after Germany and the USSR signed a non-aggression pact in August 1939, but was shown again after the German invasion in June 1941.

Mongol rule lasted for about one century in the western part of Russia, and for nearly two centuries in the eastern region. The impact of the Mongol invasion on Russia has been subject to dispute among scholars. Certainly, they visited enormous destruction on the Russians, laying waste to many cities and slaughtering people by the thousands. But some major cities escaped destruction (Novgorod, Tver, Iaroslavl, and Rostov), while other areas recovered fairly quickly.

Some prominent Russian observers—the 19th-century poet Aleksandr Blok, and the 20th-century historian George Vernadsky, for example—asserted that Mongol rule had a major formative impact on Russian culture. These Eurasianists, as they were called, claimed that the Mongol experience had made Russia an Asian nation, or at least a nation of mixed Asian and European characteristics. They claimed that this explained the Russian preference for a simple rural society over dehumanizing industrialization; for emotion over reason; for spiritual values over materialism. Europe was the land of reason and enlightenment, while Asia and Russia were lands of mysticism and sentimentality.

For Blok, a nobleman committed to the 1917 Bolshevik Revolution, Russia had been corrupt Europe's shield against Mongol depredations. His poem "The Scythians," penned early in 1918, derides a Europe immersed in war and celebrates the new world of socialist revolution. For emigré Eurasianists writing from Paris in the 1920s, the central Western value alien to Russia was Marxism, the philosophy of a German Jew imposed on their homeland by Lenin and the Bolsheviks. After the collapse of communism, these arguments on the national essence of Russia—was it a mainstream European country, was it a unique blend of Asia and Europe, or was it something else entirely?—would resurface as Russians searched for a post-communist identity.

Another impact of Mongol rule, as the British historian Robert Crummey has observed, was to strengthen the office of the Grand Prince and enhance the influence of Russian Orthodoxy as a source of cohesion and identity within Russia. Mongol support for Moscow's Grand Princes conferred an important advantage in the city's rivalry with Novgorod and Tver, and the Orthodox religion provided the cultural and ideological glue to bind together Russia's dispersed communities, however tenuously, until political reintegration was accomplished.

The indirect nature of Mongol administration and the tolerance and even special privileges granted to the Orthodox Church suggest that the Mongols probably did not have a lasting impact on Russia's political institutions. They were few in number, and concentrated largely in the south around Sarai. In his very readable history *The Mongols,* David Morgan points out that the Golden Horde was more generally called the Khanate of Qipchaq, in recognition of the heavy concentration of Qipchaq (or Polovtsy) Turks in the area. If the Mongols were quickly assimilated by these Turkic peoples in the region where they were most densely concentrated, as Morgan claims, it seems doubtful they would have greatly influenced the Russians in the northern and western regions, where few Mongols had settled.

Mongol rule decisively ended Kiev's position as the leading Russian principality. As the Golden Horde's grip over Russia weakened in the latter part of the 14th century and early 15th century, the northern principalities of Novgorod, Tver, and Moscow emerged as Russia's cities of consequence. Of these three, the rulers of the previously obscure principality of Moscow would assume the tasks of gathering the dispersed Russian lands, defending an expanding Russia from its external adversaries, and firmly establishing Moscow as the center of Russian political and religious authority.

3

Muscovite Russia, 1240–1613

Moscow itself is great: I take the whole town to be greater than London with the suburbs: but it is very rude, and stands without all order. Their houses are all of timber, very dangerous for fire. There is a fair castle, the walls whereof are brick, and very high: they say they are eighteen feet thick. . . The Emperor lies in the castle, wherein are nine fair Churches, and therein are religious men. . . The poor are very innumerable, and live most miserably. . . In my opinion, there are no such people under the sun for their hardness of living.

> —Captain Richard Chancellor, English explorer and trader, 1553

POLITICS AND EXPANSION

Compared with the major cities of Kievan and Appanage Russia, 12th-century Moscow was merely a small, obscure town. Moscow was not even mentioned in the chronicles until 1147, when Iurii Dolgorukii, Prince of Novgorod, reputedly established the town as a commercial and strategic center. The evolution of Moscow from a provincial town to the capital of a unified, centralized state is the result of several factors: the impact of Mongol conquest and rule, favorable geographic location, and, to an extent, luck.

Moscow's rise to preeminence in the 14th and 15th centuries involved cultivating favor with the Golden Horde, the Mongol tribe that ruled Russia from Sarai, while struggling for supremacy with the larger northern cities—most notably Tver and Novgorod. Daniel, the youngest son of Aleksandr Nevskii, became the ruler of Moscow in 1263, and the city was granted the status of a separate principality. Daniel enlarged Moscow and expanded his authority along the length of the Moscow River. After Daniel's death in 1303, his son Iurii Danilovich (1303–1325) annexed Mozhaisk in the east and fought with Prince Michael of Tver for control of Vladimir and Novgorod.

The Golden Horde supported Iurii in this struggle, granting him the title of Grand Prince and conferring upon him the right to extract tributes from all of the northeastern towns. Iurii, like his grandfather, Aleksandr Nevskii, owed his strong position in Novgorod to a businesslike acceptance of Mongol suzerainty. The Mongols, in turn, supported Moscow in the struggle against its major Russian rival—Tver—and against powerful Lithuania and the Teutonic Knights.

Novgorod's elite also contributed to Moscow's rise through their tendency to engage in self-destructive feuding. This ancient city's institutions, as we saw in Chapter 2, embodied some partially democratic ideas, most notably through the *veche,* and a strong tradition of independence. Admirable as these traits might be from a 20th-century perspective, in the climate of intrigue and factional struggle of the 14th century, they combined to weaken Novgorod's chances to dominate post-Kievan Russia.

In the first century after the Mongol invasion, Moscow benefited greatly from its location. Shielded in the forested north, the city avoided the periodic Mongol raids that threatened southern Russian cities. Moscow's location at the intersection of several major trade routes facilitated its development. Moscow also enjoyed Mongol support against its powerful neighbors. After about 1350, however, Moscow had become sufficiently powerful to challenge declining Mongol authority.

Moscow's power was greatly enhanced when the city assumed Kiev's former role as the center of Russian Orthodoxy. The city of Vladimir hosted the metropolitan, or head of the Orthodox Church, after 1300. Metropolitan Peter (1308–1326) was not on the best terms with Prince Michael of Tver, who had supported another candidate to lead the Orthodox Church. Peter developed close ties with Prince Iurii of Moscow and, after his death in 1325, with Prince Ivan I (Kalita, or "Moneybag"). When Peter died, he was buried in Moscow; his successor, a Greek bishop named Theognostus, assessed Tver's eroding position and decided to shift his permanent residence to Moscow.

Theognostus ardently supported Ivan's efforts to unify Russian lands under Moscow's control. Ivan deliberately ingratiated himself with the Golden Horde by serving as an effective tax collector. By collecting tributes from the other Russian princes, he strengthened his political position and amassed enough revenue to purchase a number of appanages, substantially expanding the territory under Moscow's control.

By the middle of the 14th century, Mongol power was declining, while that of Lithuania to the west was growing under the Jagiellonian Dynasty. A crucial event marking Russia's challenge to Mongol authority was the Battle of Kulikovo Field in 1380. Grand Prince Dmitrii Donskoi (1359–1389), aided by the farsighted Metropolitan Alexis, unified Russia's princes against the Lithuanian threat. Mongol unity had been undermined by its division into the khanates (roughly, principalities) of Kazan, Astrakhan, and Crimea, and by the struggle between Tokhtamysh (representing the Central Asian warlord Tamerlane) and Mamai, Prince of the Horde, for control of Russia. Russia had taken advantage of the opportunity this provided to challenge the Horde's right to rule and collect tribute. In response, Mamai concluded an alliance with Lithuania and engaged the Russians in battle at Kulikovo, on the upper reaches of the Don River. Dmitrii, whose cause was reportedly endorsed by the Abbot Sergius, moved before the Lithuanians could reach Mamai and inflicted a surprising defeat on the Mongols.

The Battle of Kulikovo Field destroyed the myth of Mongol invincibility and strengthened Russia's national awakening—no matter that Mamai would return to overthrow Moscow a mere two years later. As the Mongol rulers continued to war among themselves, the Golden Horde's control over Russia waned. Tamerlane (Timur the Lame), a ruthless warrior from Central Asia, further eroded Mongol power by destroying many of their largest cities and repeatedly defeating Tokhtamysh, the Mongol chieftain who had beaten Mamai for supremacy. Tamerlane's destructive campaign played a significant role in weakening the Golden Horde. By the middle of the 15th century, the once-powerful Mongol empire had been reduced to a smattering of small khanates along the lower Volga in Kazan, Astrakhan, and the Crimea.

Vasilii II (1425–1462) ruled Moscow during a period of constant civil strife and repeated Tatar incursions. Lithuania threatened Moscow from the west, while in the east, the fragmentation of the Golden Horde enabled Vasilii II to consolidate his power and eliminate virtually all of the surviving Russian appanages by 1456. His predecessor, Vasilii I (1389–1425), had taken advantage of Mongol disunity to annex Nizhnii Novgorod, several hundred miles east of Moscow. Vasilii II defeated his chief rival, Dmitrii Shemiaka, in ancient Novgorod, ensuring that city's subordination to Moscow's authority. In 1452, Moscow extended its rule over the Tatar khanate of Kasimov, and ceased paying tribute to the Golden Horde in the same year.

An event of equal significance for Muscovite Russia was the fall of Constantinople to the Ottoman Turks in 1453. As we have seen, Byzantium's cultural, political, economic, and religious influence on Russia was enormous. However, Russia's ties to Byzantium had been eroded by the Mongol conquest and the growth of the northern trade routes. Byzantine influence on Russia had peaked between the 11th and 14th centuries, and declined thereafter. Under threat from the Muslim Turks, at the 1439 Council of Florence, the Greek Orthodox Church recognized the supremacy of the Roman Pope, antagonizing Russia's Orthodox hierarchy. This betrayal by the Greek Church, and the subsequent punishment in the form of Turkish conquest, convinced many Russians that they were left as the sole defenders of true Christianity. In the 16th century, this conviction would find expression in the doctrine of Moscow as the third and final Rome. These developments enhanced Russia's sense of its uniqueness and its isolation from mainstream European culture, and contributed to Russian xenophobia.

Ivan III (The Great, 1462–1505) continued the process of gathering the Russian lands together, expanding and centralizing the Muscovite state and effectively ending the Appanage period. When Tver solidified an alliance with Lithuania in 1485, Ivan invaded the principality and incorporated it into Muscovy. Ivan attacked Tatar Kazan in the 1460s, incorporated Novgorod under Moscow's control in the 1470s, and invaded Tver in 1485.

Ivan III used the vast lands acquired through his conquests as rewards, forming a centralized, loyal contingent of army officers among the upper classes to whom he granted estates. He deported Novgorod landowners, redistributing their lands to his supporters on the condition that they serve in his military campaigns. This system, called *pomest'e,* assured the Grand Prince of a loyal and dependent cavalry, and curtailed the military resources that were available to the remaining Appanage princes.

Governing and defending an enlarged Russia required the creation of a small bureaucracy and more professional armed forces. Ivan III appointed governors and district chiefs to administer Russia's new territories, arranging for them to provide Moscow with revenue, most of which went to support the army, through a system of feeding (*kormlenie*). The feeding system both enhanced the independent authority of regional governors and, since they were allowed to keep the surplus of what they collected, also encouraged corruption. A national law code enacted in 1497, the first *Sudebnik,* standardized judicial authority, restrained administrative abuses, limited peasant mobility, and helped integrate an expansive Moscow.

Vasilii III (1505–1533) continued the process of consolidation, expansion, and centralization pursued by his father. Pskov was annexed in 1510 and its *veche* bell was taken down; Ryazan was incorporated into the Muscovite empire in 1517. The owners of large estates in these former appanages were deported, and their lands were redistributed to Vasilii's servitors. Vasilii III was a strong ruler, yet he consulted regularly with the boyars in the Duma.

Muscovite Russia developed an imperial and nationalist ideology, bolstered by Russian Orthodoxy, during the reigns of Ivan III and Vasilii III. Both rulers occasionally used the title *tsar* (or Caesar), implying sovereign authority and the rejection of subordination either to the Mongols or to Byzantium. With the fall of Constantinople, the seat of Greek Orthodox Christianity, to the Muslim Turks in 1453, Russians increasingly thought of Moscow as the last citadel of genuine Christianity. A letter from Abbot Filofei to Vasilii III in 1510 drew on biblical references to enunciate the doctrine of Moscow as the Third Rome: "Two Romes have fallen, the Third stands, and there shall be no Fourth." This doctrine legitimized Russia's imperial expansion and the divine right of Russian autocracy.

The concept of Russia's divine mission as the center of Christianity and the role of the tsar as God's direct representative on earth were further advanced during the long reign of Ivan IV (1533–1584), who is better known in the West as Ivan the Terrible. Ivan IV, who succeeded to the throne at age three, witnessed bitter factional fighting among the boyar families before he formally assumed the crown in 1547. Terrified by a massive fire that consumed much of Moscow later that year, and convinced God was punishing him for his transgressions, the young tsar formed a Chosen Council of nobles and church leaders to serve as an advisory body. In order to enhance public support, Ivan IV consulted openly with Moscow's elites, calling the first full *zemskii sobor* ("assembly of the land") in 1549. He issued a new law code (*Sudebnik*) in 1550 to ensure that the same laws were applied equally throughout the newly acquired territories and to protect the lower gentry's interests against abuses by regional governors. Ivan's *Sudebnik* reflected the growing division of Russian society, based on rank and position.

Ivan IV also created a series of central chanceries to run Moscow's growing bureaucracy and to provide a more efficient mobilization of resources for war. Finally, in 1551, Ivan and the priest Sylvester, author of the *Domostroi,* a manual for governing upper-class households, imposed a series of reforms on the Orthodox Church titled the *Stoglav* (Hundred Chapters). The *Stoglav* sought to control the Church's accumulation of wealth, criticized corrupt monastic practices, proscribed a number of pastimes as indecent (including chess, playing the trumpet, and enjoying pets), condemned shaving one's beard as a heretic Catholic practice, and prescribed certain modifications in church rituals. The *Stoglav* and *Domostroi* infused religious content into virtually all aspects of 16th-century Russian life by condemning secular pursuits as frivolous or sinful.

The central thrust of Ivan IV's rule was to consolidate and strengthen centralized rule, which meant weakening the influence of the top boyar families.

Ivan was extremely suspicious of the boyars, in part due to his experiences as a child and in part as a result of the unseemly political maneuvering that occurred during his grave illness in 1553. Angered by Ivan's capricious rule and dismayed by Russia's poor performance in the Livonian War of 1558–1582 (fought to expand Russia's territory westward and secure access to the Baltic Sea), a number of the boyars had defected to Lithuania, Livonia, or Poland. Among the disaffected boyars was Prince Andrei Kurbsky, a literate man whose vitriolic correspondence with the tsar has provided scholars with a record of the clash between Ivan IV and the upper classes.

Late in 1564, Ivan IV took a calculated risk designed to enhance his power. Taking a large retinue, he left Moscow for Aleksandrovskaya Sloboda, a small settlement in the northeast, from which he announced his intention to abdicate. Thrown into consternation, the tsar's followers begged him to return to Moscow and resume his office. Ivan IV agreed, but with certain conditions. Ivan demanded complete autonomy, including freedom from the moral strictures of the Church, to punish traitors as he saw fit.

To carry out his revenge against the treacherous boyars, Ivan divided Russia into two separate states. Within the *oprichnina,* which consisted of some two dozen cities, 18 districts, and part of Moscow, the tsar exercised total power. In the remainder of Russia, the *zemshchina,* direct rule would theoretically be exercised by the boyar Duma. However, Ivan created a loyal militia, the *oprichniki,* to wage a form of civil war against nobles and property owners in the *zemshchina.* The fearsome *oprichniki,* some 6,000 strong, dressed in black and carried a dog's head and broom on their horses to symbolize their mission of hunting down and sweeping away the tsar's enemies. Ivan used the *oprichniki* to arrest, torture, imprison, and execute any of the nobility, the clergy, their families, and supporters whom he imagined posed a threat to his rule.

For seven years, Ivan IV carried on a vendetta against his own people. Early in 1570, Ivan led his *oprichniki* against the city of Novgorod, whose inhabitants once had the temerity to call their town "Lord Novgorod the Great." Apparently infuriated by the city's refusal to abjectly submit to his authority, Ivan spent five weeks torturing, raping, and slaughtering his subjects. In all, he is estimated to have massacred more than 3000 people, many of whom were monks and city officials . After routing Novgorod, Ivan set out to destroy the city of Pskov. However, one of the so-called holy fools of Pskov, the monk Nicholas, threatened Ivan the Terrible with heavenly destruction should he harm the city. Frightened, Ivan withdrew to Moscow, and Pskov was spared. Two years later, he executed most of the leaders of the *oprichniki,* bringing an end to this bloody period of Russian history.

Although Ivan IV adhered to the rites of the Russian Orthodox Church and considered himself God's representative on earth, by the time of the *oprichnina,* he had rejected the Church's traditional role as the tsar's moral conscience.

Religious authorities who tried to remonstrate with the tsar—the Metropolitan Philip, for example—were tortured, banished, or killed. The clergy had acted as a restraining influence on the tsar during the early years of his reign; by the latter part of his rule, however, he had terrified the Church hierarchy into supporting his cruel tyranny. With the nobility and the clergy completely broken, there were no checks on Ivan's despotic rule. All Russians were the tsar's slaves.

From a modern Western perspective, it is difficult to imagine how a people would accept such a cruel, debauched ruler as Ivan the Terrible. At one point, he had a giant skillet constructed in Red Square in which his hapless enemies were roasted alive. Ivan also reveled in personally torturing prisoners, often after attending mass or before retiring to one of his wives or mistresses. Ivan frequently shared drunken orgies and torture sessions with his older son, Ivan, as a type of medieval male bonding. The two also enjoyed turning wild bears loose on unsuspecting Muscovite crowds and watching the ensuing chaos.

The Russian people were terrified of their tsar, but few contemplated conducting any sort of uprising against him. Some, like Prince Kurbsky, condemned him from afar. The few who were courageous enough to oppose his bloody methods and remain in Russia generally did not survive. One must recognize that a dominant strain in Russian Orthodoxy was the theme of achieving spiritual rewards through suffering. The tsar, the earthly king, was no less justified in visiting calamities on his people than God, the heavenly king. The decisions of both were likely a just punishment for their transgressions, and, in any case, they could not be questioned or even understood by most Russians.

The last years of Ivan's reign were characterized by foreign policy adventures and domestic failures. In the 1550s, Ivan's forces had subjugated the Tatars of the Kazan and Astrakhan khanates to the east and south, ending the raids that had periodically threatened Moscow. To celebrate his victory over the Kazan khanate, Ivan commissioned the construction of the famous St. Basil's Cathedral in Moscow's Red Square. Toward the end of Ivan's reign, the Cossack Ermak conquered the Kuchum khanate in western Siberia, the first step in an extended process of expansion eastward to the Pacific Ocean and eventually into North America.

Ivan the Terrible's successes in dealing with the Muslim Tatars in the east were more than offset by his failures in the wars with his Christian neighbors to the west. In 1558, Ivan, determined to expand Muscovy's frontiers to the Baltic Sea, and thereby enhance Russian commerce, launched a war against Livonia in what is now Latvia and Estonia. By 1560, the year his beloved first wife Anastasia died, Ivan's initial successes were reversed with the entry of Lithuania, Poland, and Sweden into the war against Russia. The Livonian War dragged on for 25 years, draining the Muscovite treasury, dividing the court, and feeding Ivan's paranoia and his obsession with traitors.

Ivan's cruelty and depravity reached their apogee when, in a fit of rage, he struck and killed his eldest son with the iron-tipped staff he always carried. This poignant moment, captured in a famous painting by the 19th-century artist Ilya Repin, signaled the close of Ivan's bloody regime. Following his death in 1584, his son Feodor ascended the throne. However, Feodor was weak and incompetent, and could not manage the legacy of war and internal division bequeathed to him by his father. Russia was soon immersed in the chaos of dynastic struggle and civil war referred to as the "Time of Troubles," which lasted until the establishment of the Romanov dynasty in 1613.

RELIGION AND CULTURE

Religion was by far the dominant influence in medieval Russian culture. The Orthodox Church mobilized Russia's national identity, legitimized political authority, molded social relations, dominated literature and architecture, and controlled a significant share of the economy. At the beginning of the 16th century, for example, the Church owned between one-quarter and one-third of Russia's arable land.

Russian church architecture had recovered by the late 15th and early 16th centuries. Vassilii II and Ivan III undertook huge construction programs, using Italian and later German and Dutch builders. The great Moscow Kremlin ("fortress") was reconstructed in the 15th century; most of the cathedrals housed within the Kremlin were built at this time. In 1552, Ivan IV had St. Basil's Cathedral constructed on the edge of what is now Red Square to commemorate his victory over the Tatar khanate in Kazan. Based on the pattern of Russian wooden churches, St. Basil's, the quintessential backdrop for television reporting from Moscow, is a colorful group of nine octagonal churches topped by golden cupolas and set on a single foundation.

In the 15th century, several sects and divisions appeared in Russian religious life. There were the Judaizers, who were not really Jews, but, rather, Russian Christians who rejected parts of the New Testament and certain teachings of the Orthodox Church. The *strigolniki* (shaved ones) also denied the authority of the Church, criticizing it as corrupt, and sought individual salvation through Buddhist-like contemplation. As in Europe at that time, such heretics were not easily tolerated by the dominant church, and were frequently burned at the stake.

A major schism of the late 15th century within the Orthodox Church was between the so-called possessors and the non-possessors. The non-possessors, led by Nil Sorskii, insisted that the Church should renounce worldly wealth, that monks should adhere to vows of poverty, and that church and state should be separate. However, a Church council of 1503 supported the possessors, led by Joseph of Volotsk, who advocated a rich, powerful Church glorified by the splendor of icons, extensive land-holdings, and impressive rituals. The possessors stressed the importance of a close, harmonic relationship between Church and ruler, which strengthened the concept of the divine right of the tsar.

Literature and art represented religious themes almost exclusively during this period, in contrast to the secular intellectual currents developing in Europe. Medieval Russian literature, according to historian Victor Terras, was a vehicle of religious devotion, ritual, and edification written by monks, for monks, about monks. Hagiographies, or saints' lives, were one of the most common forms of literature. The purpose of these stories was to glorify God and his loyal servants, not to present accurate biographies. Similarly, Russian chronicles, another prominent genre, mixed history with political propaganda and morality tales. Among the more significant of these chronicles were the *Life of St. Sergius of Radonezh* by Epiphanius, the story of the founder of the Holy Trinity–St. Sergius Monastery, and the *Tale of the White Cowl of Novgorod*, which promoted the concept of Moscow as the Third Rome.

Religion was an important influence in popular culture, although its influence was not enacted through literature. Few Russians, and virtually no members of the lower classes, knew how to read. Religious icons and oral traditions substituted for the written word. Even modest peasant huts (*izby*) reserved a corner for holy icons, which were believed to protect families from harm. However, peasants also preserved some old Slavic pagan beliefs and customs, including offerings to the house sprite (*domovoi*). They also retained certain marriage and funeral practices dating from pre-Christian times. Popular entertainment included Russian folk songs and folk tales, and the epic poems (*byliny*) that recounted the exploits of both ancient and contemporary heroes.

ECONOMICS AND SOCIETY

The Mongol invasion crushed the robust urban commercial life that had characterized Kievan society. Many towns simply ceased to exist, others lost much of their population, and Russians abandoned trade for a more insular, self-sufficient agricultural life. Landowning became the major basis of prosperity. Since landlords' wealth depended on peasant labor, the freedom of this class, which comprised some 70 to 80 percent of the population, to change their place of residence was gradually curtailed. By the end of the 15th century, peasants were tied to the estate, except for a two-week period around St. George's Day, November 26, when they could pack up and leave their masters. Ivan the Terrible further curtailed the peasants' freedom of movement. The institution of serfdom, tying peasants to the land permanently, evolved gradually through the medieval period and was fully legalized by the law code (*Ulozhenie*) of 1649 enacted under Tsar Alexis (1645–1676).

The social classes of medieval Russia were not much different from those of Kievan Rus. At the top remained the boyars, the handful of nobles who served as advisors to the Grand Prince. Just below the boyars were the junior boyars (or boyars' children—*boyarskie deti*) and the gentry. The higher clergy—the metropolitan, archbishops, and influential priests and monks—were also part of the upper classes. Next came the merchants, followed by skilled urban artisans, such as carpenters, bootmakers, masons, and silversmiths.

Most Westerners know about Russia's Cossacks, who first appeared during this period, but few have an accurate understanding of these colorful people. Cossacks were free peasants who emerged in various frontier regions of Russia and Ukraine, particularly Zaporozhe, Ryazan, and the Don region, during the mid-15th century. At first resistant to Moscow's authority, they gradually came to be loyal subjects of the tsar. Their lifestyle, based on a steppe existence, was quite different from that of the forest-dwelling Russians or Ukrainians. Cossacks lived by fishing, trapping, and plundering. Largely Slavic, they also accepted Germans, Swedes, Tatars, Greeks, and other adventurous types as long as they were tough fighters and nominally Christian. Although renowned for their horsemanship, the Cossacks were also great sailors and fearsome pirates who periodically threatened trade on the Volga River and the Black Sea.

Cossacks played a pivotal role in medieval Russia, as explorers and rebels. It was a Cossack, Ermak Timofeevich, who, under contract to the wealthy Stroganov family, ventured across the Ural Mountains and attacked Khan Kuchum at his capital of Sibir. By defeating the Siberian Tatars and the various Siberian tribes who were their allies, Ermak opened the huge Siberian territory to eastward Russian expansion. Although Ermak was eventually killed by the Tatars, other Cossacks followed the massive Siberian rivers, reaching the Pacific Ocean by the middle of the 17th century, in their search for sable furs and walrus tusks. These intrepid explorers apparently crossed the Bering Strait into Alaska sometime before the 18th century.

Peasants, as noted above, constituted the great majority of the population in medieval Russia. As a whole, the peasants were illiterate, superstitious, and poor. They were forced to work on the landlords' estates and were required to give their master a large proportion of their produce or, in certain cases, payments in cash. By Ivan IV's time, taxes on the peasantry, levied to pay for frequent military campaigns, had become increasingly burdensome, leading many to desert the estates and seek more favorable conditions in the south or east.

At the lowest rung of the social ladder were slaves, who comprised about 10 percent of the population. However, Russian slavery, which continued into the 18th century, was quite different from that of the United States. First, there was no ethnic or racial difference between slave and master. Second, slaves did not work in agriculture, but were employed primarily as household servants. Third, slavery was, as Richard Hellie has suggested, a form of social welfare for medieval Russia. Those free individuals who could not pay their debts or otherwise support themselves might become slaves. The slave owners then assumed legal obligations to clothe and feed their slaves and treat them humanely, and were prohibited from freeing them during famines to avoid their obligations. Finally, the male slaves who served as stewards for rich households acquired considerable authority and responsibility. These elite slaves ranked above their ordinary counterparts in the hierarchy of Muscovite society.

It is interesting to note that while medieval Muscovy was far from a tolerant society, the lines of division were based on class, gender, and religion, not race or ethnicity. For example, the grand princes would often recruit defeated Mongol princes for their court following a battle, provided they converted to Orthodox Christianity. Ivan the Terrible took a Circassian princess as his second wife, although she had to be baptized into the Orthodox faith prior to the wedding. Church law, however, strictly prohibited marrying across class lines; a free man who married a slave woman would lose his freedom.

Medieval Russian society, with its rigid hierarchy enforced by religious strictures, relegated women to subordinate positions politically, economically, and socially. The Russian Orthodox Church, like other Christian denominations, viewed women as inherently sinful and a temptation to men, based on biblical teachings. Accordingly, good women were quiet, submissive, and humble. Just as men were supposed to be obedient to the tsar, women had to obey their husbands in all matters. The *Domostroi*, a set of rules for keeping a well-ordered, upper-class household that was published in about 1556, instructs wives to consult their husbands on every matter and to fulfill all of their commands diligently. If they disobeyed, the wise husband would beat them judiciously. However, the *Domostroi* also elaborates on the many responsibilities of running a large household that resided with upper-class women, including supervising the servants and raising the children.

To protect their status within the patriarchal order, upper-class women in medieval Russia were secluded in specific living quarters and prohibited from socializing with men. They were also granted generous protections against any slights to their honor. Women from the artisan, slave, or peasant classes had far fewer restrictions on their social interactions. The economic demands on lower-class families forced women to work alongside men in a variety of occupations. Women were useful because they served important functions— they worked, produced and raised children, and managed the household— not because they were considered important in their own right. Nonetheless, even women of lower social status were protected against rape, abuse, or insult by Russian law.

RUSSIA'S TIME OF TROUBLES (1584–1613)

When Ivan the Terrible died in 1584, he left Muscovy with a mixed legacy. Russia was far larger and more powerful than at any time in the past; the Mongol yoke had been broken, the state centralized, and all restraints on the tsar's authority abolished. With the Turkish occupation of Constantinople, Moscow proclaimed itself the center of Orthodox Christianity, the Third Rome. Western influences in the form of traders and delegations from Germany, France, and Britain, though not always welcome, raised the level of technology in Russia, particularly in the military sphere.

However, the protracted Livonian War, excessive taxation, natural disasters, and Ivan's cruel exploitation of his own people strained Russia to the breaking point. The upper classes had suffered the loss of their estates, exile, or worse during the *oprichnina*; peasants had fled the central provinces to avoid heavy taxes and further restrictions on their freedom. After Ivan the Terrible died, Russia was once again consumed by dynastic struggles. The late tsar had killed his more able son and heir Ivan Ivanovich in a fit of rage in 1581; hence, it was the weak and incompetent Feodor who ascended to the throne in 1584. Within three years, however, Boris Godunov, an astute and capable boyar, emerged as the real power behind the throne. A younger son of Ivan IV, Dmitrii, died in 1591 under mysterious circumstances; unsubstantiated rumors suggested that Boris Godunov was responsible. Feodor died in 1598 without an heir, and the Riurikid dynasty finally came to an end.

In the chaos that followed, a *zemskii sobor* (assembly of the land) chose Boris Godunov to succeed Feodor as tsar of Russia. Using a combination of public works programs and state repression, Boris unsuccessfully sought to stem Church and boyar opposition, peasant flight from the estates, and Cossack rebellion. In the last years of Boris' reign, a pretender to the throne, a "false Dmitrii" claiming to be Ivan IV's son, organized an opposition force of Poles, Ukrainians, and Cossacks. When Boris Godunov died in 1605, the rebels took Moscow and installed the pretender as Dmitrii I.

Dmitrii's Polish connections, particularly his marriage to the Catholic Marina Mniszech and the presence of hundreds of Poles in Moscow, enraged Russians, and Dmitrii I was murdered within a year. Prince Vasilii Shuiskii was installed as Vasilii IV (1606–1610), but he could not put an end to the civil strife and foreign intervention that plagued Moscow. Ivan Bolotnikov, a Don Cossack, led a bloody uprising against the upper classes. Once this revolt had been crushed, a second False Dmitrii arose to challenge Vasilii IV, and for two years, Russia endured another civil war. After years of turmoil, a large *zemskii sobor* convened in Moscow in 1613 to choose a new tsar. The assembly selected Mikhail Romanov, a mere youth of 16, but a member of one of Moscow's most distinguished families, as their sovereign. With the selection of Tsar Mikhail, Russia's Time of Troubles drew to a close. The Romanov dynasty would rule Russia for the next three centuries, until its overthrow in the Revolution of 1917.

4

Russia under the Romanovs: Empire and Expansion, 1613–1855

Legislation, civil administration, diplomacy, military discipline, the navy, commerce and industry, the sciences and fine arts, everything has been brought to perfection as he intended, and, by an unprecedented and unique phenomenon, all his achievements have been perpetuated and all his undertakings perfected by four women who have succeeded him, one after the other, on the throne.

—Voltaire, *Russia under Peter the Great* (1763)

In the 112 years from the beginning of the Romanov dynasty in 1613 to the death of Peter the Great in 1725, an isolated, fragmented, and weak Russia evolved into a major European power with new industries, a standing army, and a new capital. In the late 17th century, Russia was a far cry from Peter's ideal of a modern, efficient industrial power, and he struggled incessantly with recalcitrant nobles, peasants, and townsfolk to Westernize Russian society. Peter's efforts to modernize medieval Russia injected contradictions and contrasting perspectives that would fuel social tensions and political disputes, which have persisted into the beginning of the 21st century.

Most of the Romanov tsars who preceded Peter were weak and ineffectual rulers; his father, Alexis, was probably the best of the lot. Mikhail Romanov, selected as tsar at age 16 in 1613, was not able to put an immediate end to Russia's difficulties. According to Nicholas Riasanovsky, Russia's most pressing problems in the early Romanov years were internal disorder, foreign invasion, and financial collapse. Mikhail's father, the Metropolitan Filaret, served as the real power behind the throne until his death in 1633. When Mikhail died, his son Alexis, a cultured but weak leader, ruled Russia from 1645 to 1676. Tsar Alexis frequently deferred to his boyar advisors, whose greed and corruption provoked peasant and Cossack rebellions in 1648, 1662, and 1670–1671. The last and most famous of these revolts was led by Stenka Razin, a Don Cossack and hero of the common people who was eventually captured and executed.

In the first few decades of the Romanov dynasty, the power vacuum at the center strengthened the *zemskii sobor* (assembly of the land), which advised Mikhail and Alexis, passed legislation in certain areas, and represented the gentry and merchants against the boyars. Unlike the English Parliament, however, the Russian *zemskii sobor* never accumulated enough power to challenge the tsar's authority; by the 1650s, its influence was waning. Peter the Great's strong centralized rule decisively ended any chance of a representative legislature emerging in Russia.

Much of the groundwork for Peter's strengthening of the Russian state was laid during the 17th century. State control over society was embodied in a 1649 law code (*Ulozhenie*). This legislation, premised on the idea that inequality and rank were central to a well-ordered society, formalized a rigid hierarchy of class relations, from boyars and the highest church ranks, through the upper and middle service classes, merchants, and townspeople, to peasants and slaves at the bottom of the ladder. The *Ulozhenie* spelled out in detail the duties and responsibilities of each social group—for example, their obligation to provide carts for the postal service, the payment due to an individual for injured honor, or the sum that would be paid to ransom someone from foreign captivity. These strict provisions tied the peasants more closely to the land, ended what remained of their limited freedom of movement, and largely eroded the distinction between serf and slave.

The 17th century was an age of great exploration eastward, following in the path of the Cossack Ermak. Cossack explorers reached the shores of the massive Lake Baikal, the largest body of fresh water in the world, in 1631. Fur and gold were the primary motivations for opening up this frigid and inhospitable region. By about 1650, Russia controlled much of Siberia, and by the time Peter I was crowned tsar in 1689 (his sister Sofia had governed as regent from 1682 to 1689, since Peter was only 10 years old when he became tsar), Russian territory extended to what is now the Bering Strait. It was Peter the Great who, in 1724, sent the German explorer Vitus Bering eastward to map the icy body of water dividing Russia from North America.

At that time, north and central Siberia was an area inhabited by small tribal peoples—the Yakuts, Buriats, Chukchis, and others—whom the Russians easily subdued. However, further south, Russia's explorers clashed with a powerful neighbor, China, whose Qing Dynasty rulers feared that Russian traders might strike an alliance with the fierce nomadic warriors on their northern borders. In 1689, the Russians and the Chinese, with the assistance of Jesuit missionaries acting as interpreters, signed the Treaty of Nerchinsk. This agreement granted Russia most of Siberia, while reserving the area around the eastern Amur River for China. The Treaty of Nerchinsk was a critical turning point in Russo-Chinese relations since it demarcated their border over the course of the next three centuries.

Since the fall of Kiev to the Mongols in 1240, Ukraine had been outside Moscow's domain. By the late 14th century, much of Ukraine (which means "the border") had been incorporated into Catholic Lithuania, and would later be supplanted by joint Polish-Lithuanian rule. Crimean Tatars controlled the southern part of what is now Ukraine. Ivan the Terrible had captured some of the eastern Ukrainian lands for Muscovy; however, Poland continued to threaten Moscow through the Time of Troubles. The Lublin Union of 1569, joining Poland and Lithuania, restrained Moscow's influence in the southwest. In 1596, the formation of a Uniate branch of the Russian Orthodox Church, which was Eastern Orthodox in rite but formally subordinate to Rome, exacerbated religious tensions in Ukraine.

In the early 17th century, Zaporozhe Cossacks, freebooters living along the southern reaches of the Dniepr River, fought the Poles in their role as protector of the Orthodox. Polish repressions in Ukraine sparked the revolt of 1648, led by the Cossack Bogdan Khmelnitsky. The Cossack leader and his followers captured Kiev but, under pressure from the Poles, turned to Moscow for protection. Ukraine suffered as a battleground between Russia and Poland for 13 years, from 1654, when Ukraine swore allegiance to Tsar Alexis, to 1667, when the Treaty of Andrusovo granted all of Ukraine east of the Dniepr River, together with Kiev, to Moscow.

While medieval Russia had developed into a physically imposing country by 1689, from the perspective of most Europeans, it remained a curious, rather primitive nation of fur-capped barbarians. Peter the Great both expanded Russian territory and sought to modernize his country by adopting European customs, manufacturing practices, and military technologies. Peter relied on brute force and the strength of his will to create a modern nation that would be internationally respected.

Peter's favorable orientation toward the West was acquired in childhood. Although he was formally proclaimed tsar at age 10, following the death of Tsar Feodor in 1682, Peter's half-sister, Sofia, assumed the regency. Court politics quickly degenerated into vicious intrigue. Neglected, Peter frequently entertained himself in the foreign quarter of the capital. The skills he learned from his Dutch and German friends were reinforced by a tour of the Continent in 1697. As a child, he assembled play regiments to conduct war games; these formations evolved into two elite guard regiments, the Preobrazhenskii and Semenovskii.

Peter was very intelligent, energetic, insatiably curious, and physically imposing at nearly seven feet tall. He was very much a hands-on ruler, insisting on learning some 20 different trades, such as carpentry, shipbuilding, and shoemaking, and in keeping with his commitment to meritorious advancement, he worked his way up through the ranks of the army. Peter also founded the Russian navy, starting with the Sea of Azov fleet, which he needed to defeat the Turks during the 1695–1696 campaign. Later, he constructed the Baltic fleet to pursue the Great Northern War with Sweden. Peter studied naval construction at Dutch and English shipyards, recruited European experts to advise Russians in the military sciences, and built a large ship entirely by himself.

Although committed to modernizing Russia militarily, economically, and socially, Peter rejected political liberalization as inappropriate for Russia. When the *streltsy* (royal musketeers) revolted in 1698 in an attempt to restore Sofia to the throne, Peter cut short his European tour, cruelly executed over a thousand of the conspirators, sent others into exile, and forced Sofia and his first wife, Evdokia, into a convent. Later, Peter would decentralize Russian government, enact civil service reforms (by establishing the Table of Ranks), and create a Senate to administer affairs of state while he was absent from the capital. While these reforms provided for more efficient administration of state affairs, the absolute power of the tsar was not eroded, as in Britain during the same period. Rather, Peter's reforms strengthened the power of the state and the tsar.

Much of Peter's reign was consumed by the Great Northern War against Sweden. Following the conclusion of a treaty with the Turks, Peter joined his Saxon and Danish allies in declaring war on Sweden. Russia was promptly defeated by a much smaller force of Swedes, led by the 18-year-old military genius King Charles XII at the Battle of Narva in November 1700. This major loss led Peter to rebuild his army, and the famous decision to melt down Russia's church bells to make cannonballs. Peter also introduced general military conscription, constructed a Baltic fleet, and laid the foundations for a new northern capital on the Gulf of Finland as part of his northern campaign. In July 1709, Russian forces destroyed the Swedish army at the battle of Poltava in Ukraine. Although the fighting with Sweden dragged on until 1721, when the Treaty of Nystadt finally brought an end to hostilities, the victory at Poltava stunned Europe and confirmed Russia's emergence as a major military power. Russia was now an established presence in the Baltic region, with Peter's new capital city, St. Petersburg, positioned as his window on the West.

Peter's constant military campaigns expanded Russia's boundaries, but at a considerable cost to the Russian people. In order to pay for the armies, ships, and armaments, the Russian government imposed heavy financial burdens on the population. Mills, beehives, bath houses, and coffins were all taxed to provide revenue for the army. In keeping with Peter's goal of discouraging traditional Russian practices, beards were also taxed (some stubborn court figures had their facial hair shaved off by the tsar himself!). Late in his reign, a head tax was imposed on all male peasants in place of the household and land taxes to make it more difficult for them to evade their assessments.

Russia's middle and upper classes were also expected to fulfill their obligations to the state. The nobility were registered and were required to serve either in the military ranks or the growing civil bureaucracy. Government officials were to be promoted based on merit. The Table of Ranks, established in 1722, essentially replaced the medieval system of state appointments corresponding to the importance of one's noble family (*mestnichestvo*), which had been abolished in 1682. The Table listed 14 ranks each in the military, civil, and judicial services. Since promotion was to be based on accomplishment, this system provided for limited upward social mobility. A member of the lower class who attained the fifth rank would be granted status in the gentry for life; reaching the ninth rank conferred gentry status on one's heirs.

New laws on provincial and municipal government were enacted in 1719 and 1721, respectively, in an attempt to separate judicial and administrative functions. Peter also sought to create a more activist state to provide social services, govern the economy, and create a respect for law and sense of communal responsibility. Yet there was no equivalent to the American concept of a law limiting government. As the British historian B. H. Sumner has pointed out, Peter relied heavily on his guards and officers to override ordinary government, rule Ukraine, and force officials to carry out his edicts. This practice of relying on a state above the state had been employed by Ivan the Terrible and his *oprichniki,* and would be used in later years by Russian tsars and Soviet dictators.

When Peter I died in 1725, he left a Russia transformed. His rule embodied both the technological and rationalistic spirit of the West and the autocratic and cruel properties of the East. He injected these conflicting values into Russian society, creating tensions that would endure for centuries. The upper classes had accepted many of the European customs he forced on them, while the great mass of the population remained culturally Russian. Over the next century, this cultural divide would widen even further, creating virtually two worlds having little in common. Only in the late 19th century were there any serious efforts to bridge the gap, not via reform, but through various populist and terrorist movements that would destabilize Russian society and prime it for revolution.

RELIGION AND CULTURE

The Russian Orthodox religion underwent a series of reforms in the mid-17th century, which pitted traditionalists against those who would modernize and revitalize Russian Orthodoxy, leading to a major schism in the Church. The proposed reforms also pitted church against state. Patriarch Nikon, who had assumed office in 1652, promoted a number of corrections to Orthodox religious texts and rituals to bring the Church more into line with prevailing Greek practice. An Orthodox Church council meeting in 1666–1667 deposed the ambitious Nikon, but enacted his proposed reforms. While outsiders might consider the changes to be rather trivial (for example, making the sign of the cross with three fingers rather than two), many of the faithful rejected these innovations.

These Russian protestants, the Old Believers, often fled east to the wilds of Siberia or to remote areas in the north. The more extreme congregations burned themselves to death in their churches, rather than give in to the ecclesiastical authorities. As cultural historian and Librarian of Congress James Billington has observed, through their self-imposed seclusion, the Old Believers relinquished Russian urban culture to foreigners and the Westernized service nobility. Old Believer communities preserved the mystical and anti-Enlightenment elements of Muscovite society into the early 20th century.

Russian culture became increasingly secularized in the decades after the Great Schism. Billington notes that theological education in Russia became more Latin than Greek in content—more inclined to rational discourse, and therefore more secular. The Orthodox Church had been opposed to music, sculpture, and portraiture; under Tsar Alexis and the regent Sofia European-style paintings, literature, poetry, and historical writing made inroads into Russian culture. During Peter's reign, though, there was not much progress in either philosophic or artistic culture.

Peter the Great was tolerant of different religious faiths. He frequently invoked Russian Orthodoxy when it suited his needs, but he was also notorious for organizing blasphemous drinking parties ridiculing the Church hierarchy. More importantly, Peter made the Orthodox Church subordinate to government authority as part of his broader efforts to strengthen the Russian state. In 1718, he established an Ecclesiastical College, or Holy Synod, a sort of governing board of clerics, to replace the independent patriarchate. The Ecclesiastical College was one of nine specialized administrative bodies patterned after the German model. He subsequently created the office of Chief Procurator of the Holy Synod (1722) to monitor and enforce state control over Church affairs.

With the abolition of the patriarchate and the creation of the Holy Synod and its head, the Chief Procurator, Peter brought an end to the symphonic relationship of Orthodox Church and Russian state. No longer the moral conscience of the nation, the Church was now pressed into state service. Clearly, Peter viewed the Church, with its conservative, bearded clerics, as a mainstay of old Russia. His son and heir Alexis, who was weak and unfit to rule, had allied himself with some of the more reactionary clergy in opposing his father's reforms. Lured back from his refuge in Austria in 1716, Alexis was tortured and imprisoned in the Peter and Paul fortress, where he died in 1718. This experience likely confirmed Peter's intention to subordinate the Church firmly under state control.

Education in Russia made major advances under Peter the Great, which were continued by his 18th-century successors. Peter's view of education, however, was narrow and highly functional. In his estimation, broad education was less useful than practical training in military science, construction, or languages, which he deemed vital to building a stronger Russian state. In keeping with Peter's determination to make Russia Europe's equal, the Russian Academy of Sciences was established in 1725. Although initially both instructors and students were German, the academy could soon boast of Russian luminaries, among them the poet, scientist, historian, and educator Mikhail Lomonosov (1711–1765).

Moscow University, Russia's first and most prestigious institution of higher education, was founded in 1755, with the assistance of Lomonosov. Lomonosov was Russia's first Renaissance man. He studied in Germany, at the University of Marburg, and upon his return to Russia, adapted Germanic practices to Russian higher education. Lomonosov was a pioneer in chemistry, experimented with electricity, and promoted scientific approaches to marine navigation. A Russian nationalist determined to place the Russian language on par with European tongues, his study of Russian grammar contributed significantly to the development of the country's language and national identity.

Elizabeth (1741–1762) and Catherine II (1762–1796) carried out vigorous building programs, making St. Petersburg into one of Europe's most beautiful cities. Under Elizabeth, the great Italian architect, Bartolomeo Rastrelli, designed some of Russia's most prominent landmarks, including the Catherine Palace at Tsarskoe Selo, Smolnyi Convent, and the fourth Winter Palace in St. Petersburg. The latter, the chief residence of later tsars and tsarinas, is now the great Hermitage Museum. Catherine sponsored architectural competitions and depleted Russia's already strained treasury to construct such monuments as the Merchants' Arcade (Gostinyi Dvor) in St. Petersburg, designed by Vallen de la Mothe, and Vasilii Bazhenov's great Kremlin Palace in Moscow.

Women made marginal advances during the late 17th and 18th centuries. The regent Sofia had freed herself and other noble women from the *terem*, which consigned them to household seclusion; Peter commanded them to appear in public to dance and converse with men in the European style. The examples of Elizabeth and Catherine the Great encouraged women to occupy more prominent roles in Russian society. For example, under Catherine II, a member of her royal court, Princess Dashkova, served as director of the Russian Academy and the Imperial Academy of Sciences.

Paul I, Catherine's son, erased much of the progress made by women in the 18th century with his edict of 1797. This measure mandated succession by primogeniture (through the eldest son), thus privileging all possible male heirs to the throne, ahead of women. Aleksandr I continued his father's policy of relegating women to marginal roles in Russian politics, as did his successor, the ultraconservative Nicholas I. However, Barbara Alpern Engel, in her study of 19th-century women (in Clements et al., *Russia's Women*), has noted that German Romanticism and French and British utopian socialism created a culture among the Russian intelligentsia that was more accepting of women's participation in political and social debates. By the late 19th and early 20th centuries, women had become key actors in the Russian revolutionary movement.

CATHERINE THE GREAT

Peter died before he had the chance to designate a successor. His wife, Catherine I, ruled for less than two years and was followed on the throne by Peter's grandson, Peter II (1727–1730). Peter II was only 11 years old when he was elevated to the throne, and he accomplished nothing. Two tsarinas followed: Anna I (1730–1740) and Anna II (1740–1741). The two Annas were distinguished mostly by their appetites for German culture and sexual adventures with court officials of either gender. Elizabeth I (1741–1762), Peter I's daughter, deposed Anna Leopoldovna, banished her to Germany, and imprisoned the only male Romanov successor, the infant Ivan VI, in the Peter and Paul fortress. Elizabeth realized that much of the popular opposition to Peter I's successors stemmed from their German nationality. For this reason, historian Bruce Lincoln argues, she consciously sought to restore Russian pride by promoting Russian culture, reducing the number of foreigners at the court, and, in contrast to her predecessors, taking only Russian lovers.

Peter III served for only a few months after the death of Elizabeth I. He adored military affairs, idolized Prussia's leader, Frederick the Great, and was so detested by the royal guards that they willingly deserted him in favor of his wife, a German-born princess from Anhalt-Zerbst named Sophie Auguste Frederike. Sophie was brought to Russia at age 14 as a bride for the weak and ineffectual Peter Ulrich, Duke of Holstein. She mastered Russian, converted to the Orthodox religion, and quickly learned the game of court intrigue. The young German princess learned to hunt and became an expert horsewoman. She adopted the name Catherine and, although she married Peter, the two were not close and did not produce any children. In the years to come, the ambitious and intelligent young woman took a series of lovers, one of whom, Count Grigorii Orlov, organized the coup that deposed her husband and crowned Catherine II Empress of all Russia in 1762.

Like Elizabeth, Catherine deliberately minimized her European connections, stressing her commitment to Russia to win the support of the nobility. However, Catherine continued the Westernization process begun by Peter the Great. While Peter's interest in the West had been practical, Catherine's was largely philosophical and cultural. Early in her reign, Catherine sought to embody the ideas of the French *philosophes* in a progressive law code, the Great Instruction, which combined enlightenment with Russian absolutism. This document embodied Catherine's ideas of herself as a rational, enlightened sovereign who served the Russian people. It also illustrates the didactic character of her personality. A commission of representatives of various social groups was assembled to codify the Great Instruction, but quarrels among the nobility ultimately undermined Catherine's efforts to implement a coherent program of reform.

Catherine read voraciously as a young woman, and as empress, selectively drew her political inspiration from Europe's greatest thinkers, including Voltaire, Diderot, and Montesquieu. She used Montesquieu's writings, for example, to justify exercising strong, centralized, and absolute authority in the extensive Russian empire. However, his concept of the separation of legislative, executive, and judicial powers, which was later adopted by the American revolutionaries, was deemed inappropriate for Russia.

Catherine the Great was determined to bring the great ideas of the Enlightenment to Russia. She was a great patron of the arts—theatrical productions, poetry, and painting all flourished under her rule. The publication of books and periodicals mushroomed in the early years of her rule, and most of these were secular. One satirical magazine Catherine sponsored, *Odds and Ends*, mocked the Russian nobility, who constituted the bulk of the reading public. In another, *Hell's Post*, Catherine published an article deriding Russian doctors as ignorant quacks who killed more patients than they cured.

Russia's adoption of European customs was largely superficial. The nobility learned French and German, practiced fencing and dancing, and read the latest European works. Russian military leaders often paid more attention to the spectacle of the parade ground than to the fighting ability of the troops. Although she prided herself on being an enlightened monarch, Catherine could not tolerate criticism of her rule or the general principles of Russian autocracy. When Alexander Radishchev published his biting critique of serfdom in *A Journey from St. Petersburg to Moscow* (1790), Catherine ordered copies of the book destroyed and exiled the author to Siberia. The French Revolution's terror against the aristocracy so alarmed her that she ordered all of the writings of the *philosophes* destroyed.

Catherine's success depended on her alliance with the Russian gentry, and she pursued policies that clearly favored the upper classes. In 1785, a Charter of the Nobility recognized the district and provincial gentry as legal bodies and granted them the right to petition the court directly. The status and treatment of Russia's peasants deteriorated as the nobility's privileges expanded. Serfdom was strengthened, and expanded through Ukraine and into the Don region of southern Russia. Serfs were completely subject to their masters; their mobility was strictly limited, and they could receive harsh punishment, even for submitting a petition to the tsarina.

The social grievances that had accumulated among the lower classes exploded late in 1773, when a Cossack, Emelian Pugachev, proclaimed himself to be Peter III and led an uprising in the Urals. Pugachev's promise of freedom from taxation, serfdom, and military service, and his threats against landlords and officials, won him a substantial following among Cossacks, Old Believers, serfs, metalworkers, Tatars, and other disaffected elements. For over a year, his ragtag troops terrorized the central Urals region, but his forces were ultimately defeated by the Russian army. Pugachev was sent to Moscow in chains, where he was brutally dismembered and his body burned as an example to other potential rebels.

While Catherine could be, and frequently was, cruel to the lower classes, she enhanced the privileges of the Russian gentry. She often took a personal interest in handsome young men, promoting their cultural and intellectual development while enjoying their company as lovers. Possessed of a strong pedagogical streak, the Empress founded the Smolnyi Institute for young noblewomen in 1764, and established a school for young women of non-noble birth the following year. She created a Free Economic Society to encourage agricultural experimentation, and in 1786, set up a system of elementary schools in provincial cities to provide basic education to the children of free urban classes. Catherine also established a network of confidential hospitals to treat venereal disease, and decreed the formation of Russia's first Medical Collegium in 1763.

Catherine commissioned a wave of construction by noted Italian, French, and Russian architects in St. Petersburg, Moscow, and Kiev. Giacomo Quarenghi designed the Smolnyi Institute in St. Petersburg, the State Bank, the Horse Guards Riding School, and the Academy of Sciences. At Catherine's request, Etienne Falconet created "The Bronze Horseman," an impressive monument to Peter the Great, mounted on a huge granite pedestal and placed not far from St. Isaac's Cathedral in the center of St. Petersburg. The construction of St. Isaac's, a beautiful circular cathedral reminiscent of St. Paul's in London, began in 1768, although it was not completed for another 90 years.

ECONOMICS AND SOCIETY

Under Peter the Great, Russia's textile, mining, and metallurgical industries expanded rapidly. As industry expanded, state peasants were often forced to work under inhuman conditions in the new factories. The government squeezed the peasantry for more revenue and ratcheted up the nobility's service obligations to the state. With the census of 1719, all male members of a household were subject to taxation. This eliminated the distinction between slaves and serfs, and marked the end of slavery as an institution in Russia. Slaves did not pay taxes, and the landowners frequently tried to avoid having to assume the tax burden for their serfs by declaring them slaves. Peter's census eliminated this tax loophole.

Peter sought to make Russia more self-sufficient by enacting mercantilist policies, protecting Russia's new industries from foreign competition, and using the state as an engine of economic development. The government encouraged the development of private industry, but with limited success. A few nobles and merchants established factories, often with state assistance, but the entrepreneurial mindset was very weak in Russia.

In the 18th century, about 90 percent of Russia's population consisted of peasants and 4 percent lived in towns, while the final 6 percent consisted of nobility, clergy, bureaucrats, and military personnel. Russia's lower classes—Cossacks, peasants, village priests, and laborers—were resentful of the heavy tax burdens, hostile toward the foreign influences that had come with Peter's reforms, and infuriated by the tsar's insulting behavior toward the Church.

This anger boiled over in occasional rebellions during the first decade of the 18th century. These and later rebellions by the lower classes were not directed against autocracy (they could scarcely conceive of an alternative system), but rather against those bureaucrats and officials whom they believed were frustrating the will of the tsar. Another common theme in peasant revolts was the search for the true tsar. Convinced that the figure on the throne was an imposter, the rebels often took up the cause of a charismatic pretender.

Conditions worsened for the peasants under Catherine the Great. Their tax burden increased substantially, serfdom was extended into Ukraine and the Don region, and the gap between the upper and lower classes widened. The nobility became increasingly privileged under Catherine; she released them from compulsory state service in 1762, and often distributed land and serfs to those who supported her politically. Lords were free to use serfs as they wished, short of executing them. They could beat them, sell them or their families, send them to the army or to work in the factories, win or lose them at cards. A Russian serf's life was not much different from that of an American slave in the Antebellum South.

FOREIGN AFFAIRS

Russia's expansion of empire continued under Catherine the Great. In the first Turkish War of her rule (1768–1774), Russian armies defeated Turkish forces in Bessarabia and the Balkans, and then captured the Crimea. The Treaty of Kuchuk Kainarji granted Russia strategic points along the Black Sea coast, although Moldavia and Wallachia in south-central Europe were returned to Turkey. However, Russia extracted promises from the Muslim Turks that they would protect Christian churches in these regions, and allow construction of an Orthodox church in the Turkish capital, Constantinople. In the second Turkish War of Catherine's reign (1787–1792), the great Russian general Aleksandr Suvorov captured the fortress of Ismail, threatened Constantinople, secured Russia's control over the Crimea and Black Sea region, and settled the Turkish threat.

Russian territory also expanded westward with the successive partitions of Poland in 1772, 1793, and 1795. By the 18th century, Poland had become weak and ripe for dismemberment. Polish kings were elected and had to share power with a fractious parliament, or *sejm*. The Polish nobility were extremely jealous of their prerogatives, including the *liberum veto*, the ability of any one deputy to stymie parliamentary business. In the three partitions, Russia, Prussia, and Austria incorporated the eastern, western, and southern parts of Poland, respectively, wiping the country off the map of Europe. Through the partitions, Russia gained White Russia (Belarus), western areas of present-day Ukraine, and Lithuania. Poland's great patriot Tadeusz Kosciuszko, who had aided the Americans in their fight for independence, led a futile uprising against the Russians in March 1794. Suvorov and the Russian army crushed the Poles, leaving a legacy of bitterness between the two peoples that would endure for over 200 years.

PRELUDE TO REFORM: ALEKSANDR I

When Catherine died in 1796, she was succeeded by her son, Paul I (1796–1801). Paul, who suffered from mental problems, deeply resented being excluded from state affairs by his mother for a decade and a half. Paul had coped with his frustration by conducting military exercises at Gatchina, his estate outside St. Petersburg, attending to every detail of the parade ground. Paul's obsession with rituals, his abuse of power, and his chaotic domestic and foreign policies left Russia weakened. Attacks on the nobility's privileges together with mismanagement earned him many enemies. In March 1801, a group of conspirators murdered him in his bedroom. Paul's eldest son, Aleksandr, was aware of the plan to depose his father, and reluctantly supported the plot, but was dismayed and wracked with guilt over his father's death.

This inauspicious beginning troubled Aleksandr I, who would rule from 1801 to 1825. The new Emperor surrounded himself with a circle of young, reform-minded friends, the Unofficial Committee, dedicated to promoting Russia's economic development and Westernization. The Russian Senate, comprised of leading noblemen, proposed measures that would have enhanced their powers and limited those of the tsar. Aleksandr initially compromised, permitting the Senate some supervisory powers over the government bureaucracy and the right of remonstrance, questioning tsarist decrees that violated law or past practice. However, Aleksandr soon rescinded even these limited concessions to power sharing.

Mikhail Speransky, the son of an Orthodox priest and a brilliant academic, worked his way up the civil service ranks and, by 1807, had become Aleksandr's chief political advisor. Speransky advocated reorganizing Russia's political system to introduce a form of separation of powers: an executive branch comprised of ministers; the Senate as the chief judicial body; and an indirectly elected State Duma serving as the legislature. These limited reforms, which embodied Speransky's notion of a state based on the rule of law, and which could have set Russia on the path to a constitutional monarchy, were rejected by the tsar. Aleksandr could not accept the idea of legal restrictions on his authority, and adopted only Speransky's proposal for a State Council, which was created in 1810.

Speransky also promoted the idea of merit and competence in state service through compulsory examinations, antagonizing many of Russia's inept and corrupt bureaucrats. In general, education made great progress during Aleksandr's reign. At the beginning of his reign, Russia had only one university, in Moscow. By 1825, five additional universities had been created, at St. Petersburg, Kazan, Vilnius, Kharkov, and Dorpat (the German university). Many of the nobility resented the egalitarian orientation of these developments and blamed the erosion of their privileges on Speransky. Under pressure, the tsar dismissed him in 1812.

Aleksandr's advisors agreed that serfdom was a backward institution and recognized the need for reform. In an attempt to reduce the nobles' privileges, Paul had reduced the serfs' *barshchina,* their labor obligation to the landlords, to three days per week from an intolerable high of five or even six. A law passed by Aleksandr in 1803 permitted landowners to free their serfs either individually or in groups, but only some 50,000 were freed as a result of this legislation.

International Affairs

Under Aleksandr I, Russia was becoming a nationalistic, militarily powerful European country. The expansion of the Russian presence into the Caucasus during the first decade of Aleksandr's reign led to the Russo-Persian War of

1804–1813, and the Russo-Turkish War of 1806–1812. Russia's victory in both conflicts resulted in the incorporation of Georgia, home to an ancient mountain people who, like the Russians, followed the Orthodox religion. Further to the north, war with Sweden (1808–1809) won the Russian Empire control of Finland.

The conflict with France, however, dominated Russian foreign policy in the early 19th century. Leo Tolstoy's monumental novel *War and Peace* commemorates the decade of struggle against the French and presents a fascinating portrait of Russian life during this period. In the first conflict, from 1805 to 1807, Russia and its allies, Austria, Britain, Sweden, and Prussia, could not defeat the French and were forced to sign the Treaty of Tilsit in July 1807. Aleksandr I and Napoleon met on a raft in the Niemen River in Poland to sign the treaty. Europe was effectively divided between France and Russia, and the latter agreed to enforce a continental blockade against Britain, a major trading partner, in an attempt to weaken its export-oriented economy.

Tensions between Russia and France mounted over the next five years. French attempts to establish influence in southeastern Europe and the eastern Mediterranean antagonized the Russians, while the blockade against Britain harmed the interests of Russia's landlord class. In June 1812, Napoleon led a force of over 400,000 troops in an invasion of Russia; eventually, this number increased to about 600,000. Roughly half of Napoleon's forces were French, while the other half were conscripts or volunteers from countries he had conquered. These included Poles determined to free their country from Russian rule, Germans, Spaniards, and other mercenaries. Russia could field only half as many troops. As Napoleon marched through Vilno, Vitebsk, and Smolensk toward Moscow, the Russian forces under the aged and obese Field Marshal Mikhail Kutuzov gradually fell back, rather than engage the numerically superior enemy directly.

Russian forces did challenge the French at the village of Borodino, just west of Moscow, on September 7. Although the Battle of Borodino lasted only one day, the two sides suffered a total of 100,000 casualties. Kutuzov withdrew to the southeast, and Napoleon entered Moscow a week later. Whether deliberately or by accident, scores of fires broke out in the ancient city, depriving the French of food and shelter. On October 19, Napoleon decided to withdraw his forces. Kutuzov's army denied the French a more southerly retreat, forcing them to retrace their steps along the devastated invasion route. Hunger, disease, cold, and constant harassment by Cossacks and peasant detachments reduced Napoleon's *Grande Armeé* to a mere 40,000 troops by the end of the year.

Kutuzov's forces pursued the French dictator into Europe and, with the aid of Austria, Prussia, and Britain, defeated France and occupied Paris in March 1814. At the Congress of Vienna in 1815, Aleksandr I and the allies presided over the redrawing of Europe's boundaries. Russia now posed as the defender of stability in Europe; through the remainder of Aleksandr's reign and that of his brother Nicholas I (1825–1855), Russia stood as a bulwark of monarchical order against the liberal and revolutionary movements of 19th-century Europe.

The Napoleonic wars strengthened Russia's sense of national identity and popular patriotism, while enhancing the nation's position as a world power. The invasion sparked widespread sacrifice for Mother Russia among all social classes. As British historian Geoffrey Hosking has noted, the Russian peasants were motivated by fear of the invaders destroying their homeland and by expectations that loyal service to the tsar would be rewarded with land and freedom. However, the nobility opposed all serious reform efforts, and Aleksandr's increasingly mystical religious leanings stifled the reformist impulse. In 1820, a member of Aleksandr's original Unofficial Committee, Nicholas Novosiltsev, proposed dividing Russia into 12 large, relatively autonomous provinces, but this reform, too, was never enacted.

In place of reform, reaction and obscurantism characterized the later years of Aleksandr's reign. One of his closest advisors, Count Alexis Arakcheev, convinced the tsar to sanction the creation of Prussian-style military colonies, which combined agricultural production with military training. Arakcheev, a cruel landowner, commanded all the women of his estates to produce one child every year. Designed to reduce the expenses of maintaining a large standing army, the colonies became repressive, mismanaged experiments that provoked popular resistance among the lower classes.

Another prominent official, Minister of Education Prince Aleksandr Golitsyn, believed that all useful knowledge was contained in the Bible and distrusted secular learning. Golitsyn imposed an intolerant religious doctrine on Russia's schools and universities, dismissed teachers who advocated liberal or free-thinking perspectives, and placed religious fundamentalists in charge of education. University students resented the military-style discipline, censorship, and compulsory attendance at religious services. Over time, the most disaffected elements of the intellectual class and the aristocracy began plotting against the government.

REVOLT AND REPRESSION: NICHOLAS I

Frustrated by Russia's inability to change, a number of young nobles formed secret political societies that advocated a variety of reform measures. From their experience in the Napoleonic wars, these former officers had become painfully aware of Russia's backwardness compared to Europe. When Aleksandr died in November 1825, the conspirators quickly decided to launch a revolt on December 14, the day Aleksandr's brother, Nicholas I, was to ascend the throne. Poorly planned and executed, the Decembrist Revolt was easily crushed when Nicholas ordered loyal troops to fire on the demonstrators, who had gathered in St. Petersburg's Senate Square. Five leaders of the revolt were sentenced to death, and over 100 were exiled. Among the pantheon of Russia's revolutionary heroes, the pampered aristocrats' wives who gave up comfortable lives to accompany their husbands to Siberia, provided an example of loyalty and sacrifice that inspired later generations.

Nicholas' 30-year reign (1825–1855) is generally described as conservative, militaristic, and repressive. His minister of education, Count Sergei Uvarov, expressed the ideology of the period in a policy of Official Nationality, consisting of three principles: Russian Orthodoxy, autocracy, and nationalism. Orthodoxy provided the religious values to unify society and the concept of divine right to legitimize the sovereign's absolute power. Defending autocracy meant rejecting any constraints on the tsar's authority, whether in the form of power sharing with other institutions or a greater role for popular participation in governance. Nationality privileged the Russian people as the dominant culture within the multinational empire; further, it implied that Russian civilization was superior to that of the much-emulated Western nations.

In his effort to exercise absolute control over Russia, Nicholas curtailed the authority of the Committee of Ministers, Senate, and State Council, preferring instead to operate outside the formal state machinery. Early in his reign, Nicholas established His Majesty's Own Chancery, consisting of several departments dealing with law and public order, education, charity, state peasants, and the Transcaucasus region. Mikhail Speransky, Aleksandr's reformist minister, was given responsibility within the Second Department to reform Russia's antiquated laws. By the early 1830s, a Complete Collection of the Laws of the Russian Empire was published, in 55 volumes, in an effort to reduce the arbitrary and tyrannical influence of Russia's administrators.

In the interests of preserving domestic political order, however, Nicholas readily adopted draconian measures. Officials of his Third Department, a predecessor of the Soviet KGB secret police, became notorious for their harsh and intrusive methods. Unrestrained by legal niceties, these secret police investigated every possible revolutionary plot or subversive act, monitored literature (including that of the great Russian poet Aleksandr Pushkin), and encouraged a network of informers.

One of the subversive groups monitored by the Third Department was the Petrashevsky Circle, a political discussion group of gentry. Members of the group, including a promising young writer named Fyodor Dostoyevsky, were arrested in 1849, sentenced to death and, at the moment of their execution, had their sentences commuted and were exiled to Siberia. This traumatic experience helps explain the dark psychological nature of Dostoyevsky's novels, including his masterpieces *Crime and Punishment* and *The Brothers Karamazov*.

Aleksandr Pushkin, the leading Romantic poet of the early 19th century, was treated much more leniently by the authorities. Pushkin, a Russian nobleman whose grandfather was an African courtier of Peter the Great, led a tempestuous life of drinking, seducing women, and dueling. Exiled to the Caucasus by Aleksandr I for his unrestrained verse, Pushkin wrote several poems influenced by this exotic locale, including *The Captive of the Caucasus* and *The Fountain of Bakhchissarai.* He returned to St. Petersburg in 1826, with Nicholas' approval, and was allowed to reside in the capital and continue his writing, but with the tsar himself as the great poet's censor. Killed in a duel over his wife's honor at age 38, Pushkin left a legacy of poetry, fiction, and literary criticism. *Ruslan and Lyudmila, Boris Godunov, Eugene Onegin,* and *The Bronze Horseman,* a rumination on St. Petersburg and its founder, are among his most famous works. Russians of all ages revere him as their country's greatest national poet.

Russian thought in the first half of the 19th century was strongly influenced by French and German Romanticism. Some Russian Romantics, particularly the Slavophiles, echoed the German philosopher Hegel's idea of the historical evolution of the human spirit. The infusion of these ideas, together with Russia's expanding imperial presence, stimulated a modern spirit of nationalism and the conviction that Russia possessed a unique mission. As Nikolai Gogol proudly remarks in the conclusion of his novel *Dead Souls,* "[A]rt thou not, my Russia, soaring along even like a spirited, never-to-be-outdistanced troika? The road actually smokes under thee, the bridges thunder. . .all things on earth fly past, and eyeing it askance, all the other peoples and nations stand aside and give it the right of way."

Russia's intellectuals, however, were divided on what that destiny should be. From this mix of intellectual fermentation and political repression, two broad currents of thought emerged—those of the Slavophiles and the Westernizers. One of the most prominent Westernizers was Peter Chaadaev (1793–1856), who was linked to the Decembrists and who, in a series of letters published in the journal *Telescope,* criticized Russian history for contributing nothing to modern civilization. The government accused Chaadaev of insanity, the same tactic the Soviet regime would later use against dissidents. However, other Westernizers, including T. N. Granovskii and Vissarion Belinskii, continued to criticize Russian Orthodoxy, advocated improving education and enacting a constitutional form of government, and stressed the importance of individual freedom, science, and rationalism.

The Slavophiles, led by K. Aksakov and A. Khomiakov, rejected much of the Western influence that Peter the Great had introduced to Russia. For the Slavophiles, the common Russian people, the *narod,* possessed a pure and simple spirituality far superior to the West's cold, scientific, materialistic worldview. For Russia, absolute monarchy, guided by the moral strictures of Russian

Orthodox Christianity, was the proper form of government. Constitutional democracy and individual freedom were concepts alien to the Russian experience and could only harm the nation. Russia would surmount its troubles when the tsar managed to break down the barriers between government and people that had been erected with the slavish adoption of Western practices over the last century.

Nicholas I, unwilling to tolerate criticism or independent thinking of any sort, harassed and repressed both the Slavophiles and the Westernizers. In the later years of his reign, Nicholas became increasingly reactionary. Education was restricted in order to discourage hopes of rising above one's position in the social order. Nicholas was determined to defend the old order of monarchy and hierarchy, and to resist the gathering pressures for reform and republicanism within his own country and throughout Europe.

THE CRIMEAN WAR

The Crimean War, fought in the final years of Nicholas I's reign, shattered Russia's confidence in its military and diplomatic capabilities, and underscored the need for social reform after three decades of reactionary government. The causes of the war were complex. A dispute between Orthodox Christians and Catholics over access to sites in the Holy Land led Nicholas to demand that Turkey, which controlled the region, guarantee the rights of Orthodox believers. Negotiations collapsed, and war between the two powers began in October 1853. Great Britain, France, and Sardinia joined Turkey in the conflict on the peninsula, while Austria, formerly Russia's ally, threatened in Moldavia and Wallachia.

Much of the fighting centered around the Russian naval base of Sevastopol on the west coast of the peninsula, which was besieged by allied forces. The British poet Alfred Lord Tennyson conveyed much of the senselessness of the fighting in his poem "Charge of the Light Brigade." Nicholas died in March 1855, and was succeeded by his son, Aleksandr II. After nearly a year of bombardment, Russian forces abandoned Sevastopol in September. In March of the following year, the Treaty of Paris was signed. The terms were not especially onerous. Russia ceded part of Bessarabia and the mouth of the Danube to Turkey, agreed that the Black Sea would be a neutral body of water, and gave up claims of serving as protector of the Orthodox in the Ottoman empire. Russia's role as the defender of monarchy and reaction in Europe, so resolutely cultivated by Nicholas I, had suffered a major setback. Fundamental reform, which Nicholas had resolutely opposed for three decades, was now judged to be critical for Russia's future.

5

Reform, Reaction, and Revolution, 1855–1921

We are at least two hundred years behind the times, we have as yet absolutely nothing, we have no definite attitude toward the past, we only philosophize, complain of our sadness or drink vodka.
—Anton Chekhov, *The Cherry Orchard*

REFORM

Russia's victory over the French in 1812, and the revolutionary upheavals of 1830 and 1848 in Europe, with their demands for an end to empire and repressive monarchy, had confirmed the correctness of resisting change for Russian conservatives. However, the Crimean War destroyed this complacency and convinced many sectors of the population that fundamental reform was vitally important. Russia's army was equipped with antiquated weapons and poorly supplied, and the peasant recruits did not constitute the most effective fighting forces. Many had volunteered to fight out of the mistaken belief that their service to the tsar would be rewarded with freedom.

Although he was conservative and committed to maintaining autocracy in Russia, Alexsandr II, who ruled from 1855 to 1881, understood the stultifying

effects of serfdom on his country. In economic terms, forced peasant labor was highly inefficient. Many of the landed estates operated at a loss, and members of the gentry were often mired in debt. Serfdom was increasingly viewed as morally repugnant by Russia's intellectuals. Ivan Turgenev's *Hunting Sketches,* with its charming portrayal of rural life, had humanized the peasantry for the reading public. This collection of stories, published in 1852, the same year as Harriet Beecher Stowe's classic antislavery novel, *Uncle Tom's Cabin,* presented the upper classes with their first authentic glimpse of peasant life.

Contrary to the romanticized notions of peasant life held by the upper classes, rural life in 19th-century Russia was extremely primitive. The extended family lived in one large room, which was heated by a huge stove in one corner, on which a privileged family member slept during cold winter nights. Another corner was reserved for the family icons: religious paintings of the holy family or favorite saints on wood. Most peasants subsisted on a paltry diet of bread and cabbage soup, only occasionally enjoying meat. Diseases such as typhus, tuberculosis, diphtheria, and smallpox were common. Many infants did not survive their first year, and few peasants lived beyond 50 years.

Peasant life was extremely patriarchal, with clear divisions of responsibility between men and women. Women took care of the children, worked in the gardens, sewed clothes, prepared food, and took care of the house. Men governed the home, controlled the land, and dominated household finances. Women were treated as property. As one 19th-century peasant explained, "We need a wife and horse equally. A muzhik cannot survive long without both. If the housewife dies, you must find another. If the horse croaks, you must get another. To live on the land the muzhik must have a horse and a wife." Historian Rose Glickman (in Clements et al.'s *Russia's Women*), who discovered the latter quote from a peasant interviewed in 1880, remarks on the tremendous imbalance between Russian peasant women's contributions to the home and their meager rewards. The one area in which peasant women had any power, Glickman notes, was in their role as respected folk healers.

During the first half of the 19th century, hundreds of peasant revolts indicated a deep sense of dissatisfaction with rural conditions and the oppression of serfdom. Poor, largely illiterate, and bound to the estates, Russia's serfs lived in conditions akin to slavery. Although none of the peasant revolts reached the scope or size of the 18th-century rebellions, they caused great alarm in the government. Upon the enactment of the Treaty of Paris, which ended the Crimean War in March 1856, Aleksandr II warned the Moscow nobility, "It is better to destroy serfdom from above than to await the time when it begins to destroy itself from below."

While there was a general consensus among the Russian upper classes that reform was long overdue, the landowning gentry wanted to ensure that emancipation would not prove too costly. Aleksandr appointed advisory committees in the various provinces to study the problem in 1858, and his State Council also considered proposals for emancipation. The Emancipation Act of February 18, 1861 (going by the Old Style calendar, which was 12 days behind the Western Gregorian calendar in the 19th century) granted freedom to some 52 million Russian serfs, who comprised about 45 percent of the population. Two years later, Abraham Lincoln would free 4 million American slaves with his Emancipation Proclamation. In both countries, these emancipated peoples would face a long struggle for equality.

Many Russian peasants were understandably dissatisfied with the terms of their emancipation. First, they were obligated to continue to work for their landlords for a two-year transitional period. Second, only serfs directly engaged in farming were to receive land; household serfs did not. Third, the state compensated the gentry for the lands they lost (usually, land was divided fifty-fifty between the peasants and their former masters), and the peasants then had to make redemption payments to the state over 49 years. These payments were frequently well in excess of the value of the land, and were greatly resented. The peasants were now to be taxed, with revenues collected through the village commune, or *mir*. Peasants were tied to the village through their obligations to the *mir*; land plots were allocated through the *mir*, and the peasants' mobility was restricted by village authorities.

As historian Gregory Freeze notes, the number of peasant revolts mushroomed immediately after Alexander's decree, from 126 in 1860, to 1,889 in 1861. The nobility were also unhappy since they lost much of their land and few had the capital or know-how to modernize their estates. While a handful of the nobility were quite rich, owning huge estates where thousands of souls dwelled, others had no more than a few servants and lived in virtual poverty. Many of the lesser gentry became further impoverished in the latter half of the 19th century.

The emancipation of the serfs was only one, albeit certainly the most important, of a series of official acts called the Great Reforms. In January 1864, a local government reform was implemented to create new authorities in the villages to fill the vacuum left by the collapse of the landlords' power. *Zemstvo* assemblies and boards were created at the provincial and district levels to address local needs, including education, medical and veterinary services, insurance, roads, and bridges. The *zemstvos*, which were, in effect, county councils, were also something of a democratic experiment; they were elected by townspeople, peasant communes, and individual landlords. Those not owning property could not vote, and, in any case, the central government retained control over the police and other important functions. But the *zemstvo* reform did introduce the concept of self-governance, in a very limited sense, to Russia's peasantry. This system of local government lasted until the Revolution of 1917.

Other major reforms enacted under Aleksandr II included the modernization of the legal system (1864) and the military (1874). Russia's judicial system in the early 19th century was inefficient and corrupt, and based on class privilege. Drawing largely upon the French model of code law and inquisitorial process, the new system separated the judiciary from administration, provided for open trials and equal treatment before the law, created a legal profession, and allowed certain cases to be decided by juries. But peasants, who comprised 80 percent of the population, were excluded from these judicial reforms.

Military reform, however, did have a major impact on the peasantry. From early in Catherine's reign, the nobility had been granted the right to opt out of military duties, whereas the 1874 statute mandated service for all classes. Military service for the lower classes was previously onerous, and draftees were obligated to serve for 25 years! Since young men were not likely to return from the army, villages would often hold funerals when they were conscripted. After 1874, the length of service was shortened to six years, military law was reformed, and elementary education was provided to all draftees.

Progress in education was an important part of the Great Reforms. In 1864, Russia's Ministry of Education adopted a Public School Statute to design a national system of primary schools. This resulted in the rapid expansion of elementary schools in the countryside to educate the newly freed but largely illiterate serf population. The university population also expanded rapidly, from 4,125 in 1865, to 16,294 at the end of the century, according to British historian Geoffrey Hosking, creating a larger and more active intellectual class. The bulk of these students was drawn from two classes—the nobility and the clergy.

The reform process heightened expectations and spawned social turmoil in the Russian empire. In 1863, the Polish minority rebelled and was decisively crushed. A new generation of university students, highly critical of the regime and its reforms and dedicated to scientific and rational thinking, became alienated from the old order. Influenced by the empiricism of Auguste Comte and the discoveries of Charles Darwin, they rejected the Romantic perspective of earlier decades.

Literature reflected changing attitudes in Russian society. A novel appearing the year after Turgenev's classic *Fathers and Sons* (1862) was Nicholai Chernyshevsky's *What Is to Be Done?*, written while the author was imprisoned in the Peter and Paul Fortress. A mediocre writer at best, Chernyshevsky depicted a socialist utopia where men and women were equals and all nationalist and religious prejudices were abandoned. One of his main characters, the disciplined revolutionary Rakhmetov, dedicates his life to the people. Chernyshevsky's novel inspired many of Russia's idealistic youth; Vladimir Lenin would later write that he pored over the novel for weeks, and clearly, his ascetic and single-minded devotion to revolution echoed Rakhmetov's example.

Political liberalization of an authoritarian regime virtually always guarantees a growing chorus of demands for more change, and a subsequent reaction by those who wish to halt the reform process. As the Italian political philosopher Niccolo Machiavelli observed in *The Prince,* "There is nothing more difficult to carry out, nor more doubtful of success, nor more dangerous to handle, than to initiate a new order of things." Machiavelli argued persuasively that reformers were bound to alienate the supporters of the old order, but could garner only lukewarm backing for the new order. This was precisely the case in Aleksandr II's Russia. The Great Reforms spawned diverse opposition movements in the second half of his reign, including populism, pan-Slavism, socialism, terrorism, and conservative reaction.

The populists, or *narodniki,* were intellectuals who placed their faith in the Russian people—the peasants. Influenced by the ideas of the French and British utopian socialists, Russian populists led a movement to the people in the mid-1870s. Committed activists left the comfort of the cities to work as teachers, doctors, agronomists, or artisans in the villages. The populists believed the peasant *mir* could serve as a uniquely Russian form of local governance; the intellectuals' duty was to raise the economic and cultural status of the peasantry. Fundamentally transforming rural life, however, proved beyond the capabilities of a few hundred dedicated individuals. Peasants and local officials resented their unsolicited advice, and many were turned over to the police and sent into exile.

Having failed in their peaceful efforts, some of the populists turned to revolutionary violence. One of the more prominent populist organizations, Zemlia i Volia (Land and Will), evolved into a terrorist group dedicated to assassinating the tsar. Members of the People's Will (Narodnaia Volia) reasoned that eliminating the supreme autocrat would cause the entire edifice of the Russian state to collapse. From 1879 to 1881, they undertook various attempts on Aleksandr's life, all of which were unsuccessful. One member of the group infiltrated the staff of the Winter Palace, smuggled in dynamite, and succeeded in blowing up the tsar's dining room without causing any harm to the sovereign himself. Spurred on by the dedication of the female students, who were the backbone of the People's Will, the collaborators then attacked Aleksandr II as his carriage traveled along the Catherine Canal in St. Petersburg. This time, they succeeded. Ignacy Hryniewski, who threw the homemade bomb at the tsar's feet when he left the carriage, was killed in the attack. Five others were hanged for their role in the assassination, including Sofia Perovskaia, the brains and driving force behind the conspiracy.

REACTION

While Aleksandr II is known as the Tsar Liberator, his son, Aleksandr III (1881–1894), was an extreme reactionary. His tutor and later, his chief advisor, Konstantin Pobedonostsev, constantly warned against the dangers of constitutional government and representative democracy. What Russia needed, argued this former liberal jurist, was a powerful tsar who would maintain order and stability. Pobedonostsev, an ardent Russian nationalist and Director General of the Holy Synod, resurrected Nicholas I's policy of Official Nationality and promoted intolerance toward Russia's Jewish, Catholic, and Muslim believers. Pobedonostsev opposed virtually all forms of industrial progress and social or political development. The country's turn toward political repression and ardent nationalism under Aleksandr III yielded short-term stability at the cost of more enduring social tensions.

By the late 1880s, populism had been discredited, and terrorism quashed. However, in the final years of the century, Marxist socialism began to gain adherents among those hoping for change. The socialist Georgii Plekhanov, who was originally associated with the Russian populist movement, abandoned it in favor of Karl Marx's so-called scientific theories. Marx, a German Jewish political economist, had argued that history developed according to certain immutable laws. According to Marxist theory, the economic engine that drove the capitalist economies of industrial Europe created deep class divisions between the workers (proletariat) and the factory owners (bourgeoisie) that could only be overcome through revolution. When the working class became completely conscious of its exploitation by the bourgeoisie, realizing that the fruits of their labor were going to the capitalists and not to the workers themselves, they would rise up and overthrow the bourgeoisie (who also controlled the state). Once all the privately owned means of production—factories, land, tools—had become social property, production would be carried out for the benefit of the great mass of people, not the rich few. This was communism as envisioned by Marx.

One of Russia's young revolutionaries who turned to Marxism was Vladimir Ulianov, from the Simbirsk province in central Russia, who became a dedicated enemy of the tsarist regime when his older brother Aleksandr was executed for trying to assassinate Aleksandr III in 1887. Banished to Siberian exile for his activities, he adopted the name Lenin, probably after the huge Lena River near Shushenskoe, his place of exile. As most of his biographers note, Lenin became a revolutionary several years before he discovered Marx. A fiery ideologue, he was consistently willing to jettison principles in the interest of subverting the Russian state. Lenin and his Bolshevik Party succeeded with the November coup of 1917.

The socialist movement in Russia, like all groupings of intellectuals, was riven by factionalism and heated disputes. Lenin, Plekhanov, Vera Zasulich (acquitted for her attempt on the life of St. Petersburg's Governor General), and Paul Akselrod, all leading figures of Russian socialism, missed the founding meeting of the Russian Social Democratic Labor Party, which took place in a small house in Minsk, Belarus, in 1898. But most attended the party's second congress five years later, held in Brussels and London, where disagreements caused the party to split into two wings. One, favoring a more inclusive membership and a more passive role for the party, was dubbed the Mensheviks ("those of the minority"). A Jewish socialist, Pavel Martov, led this faction. Lenin claimed that his party faction, which preferred a more restrictive membership and a more active revolutionary posture, represented the *majoritarians* (Bolsheviks). In his book *What Is to Be Done?* (1902; the title is copied from Chernyshevsky's novel), Lenin had argued that the surest way to bring about a socialist revolution in Russia was through a dedicated band of revolutionaries who would be the vanguard or leader of the working class.

Turn-of-the-century Russia, however, did not have much of a working class to lead. Far behind Britain, the United States, or Germany in the economic sense, Russia had just begun to industrialize in the 1890s. A key factor in Russia's development was the decision in 1891 to build the Trans-Siberian Railroad. Although most of the country's population was concentrated west of the Ural Mountains (and still is), there was vast natural wealth in Siberia, an area larger than the entire United States. Siberia had very few roads, and virtually none that were paved, and the main transportation arteries, the great Ob, Irtysh, Lena, and Yenesei Rivers, ran north and south. Well aware that its empire in the east was over-extended, Russia had withdrawn from its North American colonies, selling Alaska to the United States in 1867 for $7.2 million. The TransSiberian line, the longest stretch of rail in the world at 5,000 miles, would more closely link these distant territories to European Russia. The project would take 12 years to complete and would ultimately bring Russia into armed conflict with its eastern neighbors.

Russia was consolidating its eastern territories just as Japan embarked on the industrialization and imperial expansion of the Meiji Restoration (1868–1945). Both countries sought control of land in Manchuria, a province of northern China. Russia had concluded a secret agreement with China permitting construction of the Chinese Eastern Railroad to link the Trans-Siberian east of Lake Baikal through Chinese Harbin, and on to Vladivostok on the Pacific coast.

Certain Russian leaders also had designs on Korea. Japan, which had confronted China on the Korean peninsula in 1894–1895, was seeking access to coal and iron ore in Manchuria and on the island of Sakhalin. In the Russo-Japanese War of 1904–1905, much to the surprise of racist Europeans, Japan destroyed the Russian fleet and defeated their army in the Far East. President Theodore Roosevelt negotiated a peace treaty at Portsmouth, New Hampshire, which granted Japan control over Korea, the Liaotung Peninsula, southern Sakhalin, and the Kuril Islands north to Kamchatka.

Ironically, Russia's reactionary Minister of Interior Viacheslav von Plehve had suggested that the country needed a "small victorious war" to rebuild national unity in the wake of the strikes and pogroms of 1903. The Russo-

Japanese War had precisely the opposite effect of stimulating discontent and revolution.

RUSSIA'S FIRST REVOLUTION: 1905

Under the iron hand of Aleksandr III, Russia had been at peace internationally and calm internally. When he died unexpectedly in 1894, his son, Nicholas II, became the last Russian tsar. Nicholas was weak, not terribly bright, and completely unprepared to assume the duties of governing Russia. Like his father, he was greatly influenced by the reactionary Pobedonostsev. But while Nicholas opposed any infringement on the tsar's power as autocrat, circumstances would force him to make concessions to the demands of an increasingly restive population.

In the 1870s and 1880s, Russia slowly began to enter the industrial age. Aleksandr III's finance minister, Ivan Vyshnegradsky (1887–1892), was determined to strengthen Russia's economy through massive grain exports, heavier taxes on the peasantry, putting the country on the gold standard, and encouraging foreign investment in industry, particularly the railroads. Initially successful, these measures depleted the countryside's food reserves, resulting in a massive famine in 1891–1892, in which some 400,000 peasants died. Sergei Witte, who succeeded Vyshnegradsky, continued his policies of forcing peasants to market grain at reduced prices to provide revenue for Russia's industrialization. The result was resentment, peasant flight to the cities, and a more fertile environment for revolutionary agitators.

Russia's industrial development created new social forces—an emerging middle and professional class, a new bourgeoisie, and a small working class concentrated in a few large cities. The early phase of Russia's industrial revolution, like that in Britain a century earlier, created miserable conditions for much of the population and heightened social tensions. Long working hours, the exploitation of children and women, unhygienic working conditions, and prohibitions against organizing prompted opposition. Major strikes occurred in St. Petersburg in 1896–1897 and in the southern towns of Rostov-on-Don and Odessa.

Loathe to permit independent union organizing, the government did allow police officials and Orthodox priests to try to co-opt labor through officially approved unions. This strategy was the brainchild of Sergei Zubatov, a former double agent who became chief of the Moscow Okhrana (secret police) in 1896. Zubatov's unions were supposed to convert Russia's literate socialist workers into supporters of the monarchy.

The success of this experiment was mixed at best. In December 1904, one such organization, an Assembly of Russian Factory Workers led by Father Georgii Gapon, planned a general strike in the capital and a peaceful march to the Winter Palace to present a petition for help to the tsar. Nicholas did not meet with them and, in an act of colossal stupidity, on January 22, 1905 (New Style) Cossacks and government troops cut down the unarmed petitioners bearing icons and portraits of the tsar. The death of more than 100 protesters, including women and children, inflamed public opinion and, for much of the Russian public, destroyed the ancient myth that the tsar was sympathetic to the plight of his people and would help them once he was made aware of their condition.

The events of Bloody Sunday, as the massacre was called, sparked the Revolution of 1905. Student demonstrations, labor strikes, and peasant unrest mounted throughout the summer. Sailors on the battleship *Potemkin* mutinied in the Black Sea; their story was later dramatized in Sergei Eisenstein's classic (but historically inaccurate) movie. Peasant radicalism was encouraged by the Socialist Revolutionaries (SRs), a radical party established by disaffected intellectuals in 1901. The SRs, who blended Russian populist and terrorist traditions, encouraged peasant rebellions during 1902–1904 and throughout 1905.

Worker opposition was central to the revolution. Early in 1905, a group of liberals led by historian Paul Miliukov formed the Constitutional Democratic (or Kadet) Party, which supported worker demands. The Kadets were quite moderate, however. A more radical strike committee formed in the capital and framed itself as a workers' council, or *soviet*. A firebrand socialist, Leon Trotsky, who would establish Russia's communist government with Lenin in 1917, was elected chairman. Both the Bolsheviks and the Mensheviks were active in the St. Petersburg Soviet, as were the Socialist Revolutionaries. An executive committee was formed, and similar councils sprang up across the country. The St. Petersburg Soviet would serve as the model for revolutionary government organizations that took power after the collapse of tsarist autocracy in 1917.

With his room to maneuver sharply limited by the war with Japan, Nicholas signed the October Manifesto, granting civil liberties and conceding the formation of a parliament, or Duma. This lower house would be elected by the public; the State Council was transformed into an appointive upper chamber. Yet another political party was formed; this one, the Octobrists, was comprised of moderates who supported the provisions of the October Manifesto. When the first two elections returned large numbers of representatives from the more radical parties, the President of the Council of Ministers, Peter Stolypin, rewrote the electoral law to ensure a more compliant assembly. The third Duma reflected an overrepresentation of the landowners and more conservative groups; Octobrists and nationalist forces dominated, and the tsar was easily able to overrule or ignore parliament. This third Duma completed a full five-year term (1907–1912), and the fourth Duma (1912–1917) served nearly a full term.

Nicholas made these concessions toward a constitutional monarchy not out of conviction, but because he was forced to. As the tumult of 1905 subsided, the government tried to withdraw some of these concessions. Measures were implemented to promote social stability. Stolypin, who, in effect, served as Prime Minister from 1906 to 1911, supervised a plan to create a conservative, landowning class of small prosperous farmers, similar to the stolid farmers of middle America. Russia had endured another famine in 1906–1907, and Stolypin was concerned about the potential for peasant unrest. His program aimed to abolish the *mir* and make it possible for individual peasants to buy and consolidate strips of land from the communes, and to augment their holdings by purchasing additional land from the state.

To a certain extent, Stolypin succeeded. The number of well-to-do private farmers (kulaks) grew, but slowly. A 1910 law supposedly dissolved the *mir*, but on the eve of the Revolution of 1917, most peasants still lived in communes. Stolypin's agrarian reforms lagged after his assassination in 1911, and came to a halt with the outbreak of World War I in August 1914. Lenin, who had been concerned that agrarian reform was creating a conservative class of small landowners less inclined to overthrow the monarchy, favored keeping the misery quotient high. To the extent that Stolypin's reliance on the strong and sober made the population more affluent and more contented, that same population would be less prone to use violence against the government.

Culture and Society

Nineteenth-century Russia produced some of the world's greatest literature, music, and art. The cultural heritage of this period is so rich that only a few of the most outstanding contributors can be discussed here.

Ivan Turgenev (1818–1883) was the first Russian novelist to be read widely in the West. Turgenev was part of the realist school in Russian literature: he is far more accessible than Dostoyevsky or Tolstoy, but less of a romanticist than the writers of the 1830s and 1840s. His novel *Fathers and Sons* (1862) brilliantly captured the generational divide of the 1860s. One of the central characters, Bazarov, disdained all traditions, sentiments, and emotions in favor of rational scientific calculation. Bazarov was a nihilist—he rejected everything and believed in nothing. For many readers of the time, he represented the rational, pragmatic side of Western influence in Russia, which they saw as fundamentally opposed to core Russian values.

The Romanticism of the 1830s and 1840s was replaced by a darker realism in the 1860s and 1870s. Fyodor Dostoyevsky's writings blended religious, political, and social themes. His masterpiece *Crime and Punishment* explored the psychological impulses that drove the protagonist, Raskolnikov, to murder an old pawnbroker for her money. Raskolnikov, whose name derives from the Russian word for schism, suffered from a split personality. He believed that as a superior man, he was entitled to exercise life-and-death power over the old woman; as a human being with some remnants of Christian morality, he was obsessed by the enormity of his crime and eventually confessed to the authorities.

Dostoyevsky's writing was shaped by powerful forces—his mock execution for membership in the Petrashevsky literary circle and subsequent exile, his addiction to gambling and the huge debts he accumulated at the roulette tables, his rejection of Western secular rational society, and his powerful religious beliefs. Dostoyevsky was appalled by the amorality of Turgenev's generation of nihilists, and treated them far more bleakly. In *The Possessed*, Dostoyevsky equates Russia's nihilistic revolutionaries with devils. *The Brothers Karamazov*, his last major work, deals with religious faith, the struggle against nonbelief, and divine justice. Three warring aspects of Dostoyevsky's personality are embodied in the three Karamazov brothers, one of whom is charged with the murder of his middle-aged father. In one famous chapter of the book, "The Grand Inquisitor," Dostoyevsky attacks the arrogance of the established Church, whose officials cynically manipulate the mass of believers. Although Dostoyevsky made an example of the Catholic Church during the 16th-century Spanish Inquisition, his blistering critique could apply to any state church, including the Russian Orthodox.

Count Leo Tolstoy (1828–1910) is revered for his great historical epic novel *War and Peace*, which recounts the lives of Russia's nobility, a social group he was quite familiar with, during the Napoleonic wars of 1805 to 1815. Tolstoy also knew war from his experience as a subaltern in the Crimean conflict. Like Dostoyevsky, Tolstoy was very much a philosopher and a Russophile. In *War and Peace*, history and life are a series of accidents and events beyond conscious human manipulation; even the greatest figures—Napoleon, Aleksandr I, General Kutuzov—are merely acting according to a divine script over which they have no control. Tolstoy's *Anna Karenina* is a morality tale and a critique of modernism. The protagonist, a married woman who does not love her husband and cannot resist the advances of the dashing Count Vronsky, abandons social respectability for passion. Anna's sins destroy more than her reputation; in despair, she throws herself beneath a train, a symbol of Russia's industrialization.

Preoccupied with sin and morality, later in his life, Tolstoy adopted an ascetic philosophy and lifestyle of sexual denial, pacifism, and simple peasant labor, to the dismay of his long-suffering wife. He criticized the monarchy and the Orthodox Church for ignoring the plight of Russia's poor and the will of God, earning enemies in the government. From Yasnaya Polyana, his estate south of Moscow, Tolstoy condemned the Russian government for the repressions that followed the Revolution of 1905. His last novel, *Resurrection* (1899), did not deal with Russia's aristocrats, as his earlier works did, but, rather, chronicled the sufferings of the lowest classes—Siberian prisoners, peasants, and criminals. By the time he died, Tolstoy had an international following, and his pacifist ideas would influence Mohandas Gandhi and Martin Luther King.

The period from Aleksandr II's assassination to the Revolution of 1917 is often called the Silver Age of Russian literature. Poetry was revived in the form of the Symbolists, a turn-of-the-century group of writers influenced by French Symbolism, who reflected the sense of doom that pervaded Russia at that time. A diverse movement, Russian Symbolism was mystical, sometimes religious, and inclined toward sexual decadence. Major Symbolist figures included Aleksandr Blok, Vyacheslav Ivanov, and Andrei Bely. Russia's major dramatist of the era was Anton Chekhov (1860–1904). Chekhov's *Cherry Orchard*, written in the year before his death and still popular in American theaters, illustrates the decline of the traditional gentry, who became impoverished and unable to cope with post-emancipation life.

Russia's great musical composers of this era are also deservedly famous. Surprisingly, few of the Russian classical composers had much formal musical training. What they did have was a commitment to producing truly Russian music, not simply imitations of European operas, ballets, and symphonies. Modest Mussorgsky, a lieutenant in the Preobrazhensky Guards, would write the great opera *Boris Godunov*, set in Russia's Time of Troubles. Aleksandr Borodin, who was a medical doctor before turning composer, penned *Prince Igor*. Nikolai Rimsky-Korsakov derived his music from Russian folklore and the stories of Pushkin and Gogol; his best-known works are *The Snow Maiden* and *Scheherazade*.

Peter Tchaikovsky (1841–1893) produced a huge body of work, of which the *1812 Overture* is probably his best known. An inspiring and very emotional work that reflects the composer's ardent Russian patriotism and celebrates Napoleon's defeat, the *1812 Overture* starts as a sedate pastorale and then builds to a thunderous climax, with bells ringing and cannons firing in celebration of the French troops' flight from Russian soil.

Like Rimsky-Korsakov, Tchaikovsky delighted in the magical and fantastic. His ballet, the *Nutcracker Suite*, has become a Christmas standard around the world. Other masterpieces included *Swan Lake, Romeo and Juliet, Eugene Onegin*, and *Sleeping Beauty*. Tchaikovsky's great works, and those of his fellow composers, were performed at the Imperial Mariinsky Theater in St. Petersburg and the Bolshoi Theater in Moscow, which remain great centers of Russian culture to this day.

Less famous than literature or music, Russian painting of the late 19th century is no less deserving of attention. One major school of painters, the Itinerants, displayed their portraits of Russian life and historical themes in exhibits that traveled around the major Russian cities. Stifled by the conservative canon of the St. Petersburg Imperial Academy of the Arts, which insisted on depicting only classical subjects, a group of 14 talented students resigned from the Academy in 1863. Ivan Kramskoi was the first leader of the movement, while Ilya Repin (1844–1930) was the most widely known artist. Repin, like his fellow Itinerants, painted unvarnished, realist scenes. His *Ivan the Terrible and the Death of His Son* portrays the moment after the brutal tsar, in a fit of anger, fatally struck his son with his staff. Repin's *Religious Procession in Kursk Province* (1880–1883) illustrates the priests, beggars, police officials, and common folk of the Russian provinces. Another Itinerant painting, Vasily Surikov's *The Boyarina Morozova,* shows a proud and defiant boyar lady, an Old Believer, bundled into a sleigh and forced into exile for her beliefs. Vasily Vereshchagin's painting *The Apotheosis of War,* showing a huge mound of skulls situated in the center of an arid plain, depicts the horrors of war; Vereshchagin had witnessed such scenes during his service in the Russo-Turkish conflict of 1877–1878.

Many of the Itinerants' works are now housed in the Tretyakov Gallery in Moscow. Renovated and reopened in 1995, this huge collection of native Russian art was collected by Pavel Tretiakov, a wealthy Moscow merchant who spent nearly three decades and a million rubles purchasing the works of Repin, Vereshchagin, Kramskoi, Nikolai Ge, and other Itinerants, together with ancient religious icons. When he died in 1898, Tretiakov bequeathed a trove of masterpieces to Russia.

As the Romanov dynasty neared its end, several unique schools of art, influenced by European Cubism and Post-Impressionism, and radically different from the realist depictions of the Itinerants, emerged in Russia. These Russian painters in turn had a major impact on modern art in Europe. One such painter, Kasimir Malevich (1878–1935), produced a modernist art of abstract collages and geometric shapes called CuboFuturism. Malevich was also responsible for the Suprematist movement, a mystical approach he defined as the supremacy of feeling over form in art. A talented young artist from Vitebsk, Marc Chagall (1887–1985), painted colorful and whimsical works inspired by the Jewish shtetl, or village, in which he was born. Vassily Kandinsky (1866–1944), a Russian artist who became a major figure in the German Blue Rider school, is generally acknowledged as the founder of abstract painting.

Several women were prominent members of the Russian modern art movement, although their contributions are often overlooked. One major figure was Natalia Goncharova (1881–1962), a talented member of the Primitivist movement who drew on icons and traditional Russian themes to produce a nativist art form. Vladimir Tatlin (1885–1953) and Aleksandr Rodchenko (1891–1956) were leading figures in the Constructivist school, which reflected their revolutionary dedication to building a new society. Tatlin is best known for designing a monument to commemorate the founding of the Third International Communist Movement (the Comintern) in 1919. Rodchenko started with abstraction, but bowed to the Communist Party's demands to paint socialist realism during the Soviet period.

WAR AND REVOLUTION

Throughout much of the 19th century Russia allied itself with Europe's authoritarian states, particularly Germany and Austria. However, Russia perceived the unification of Germany in 1871, its rapid industrialization, and the formation of alliances with Austria and Italy as a potential threat to its security, particularly after 1890, when Germany abandoned a treaty relationship with Russia. Russian public opinion urged the government to protect the Serbs and other South Slavic peoples in the Balkans, where the Turkish Empire was crumbling, and on which Austria had imperial designs. To strengthen its position vis-à-vis Germany and Austria, Russia concluded an alliance with France in 1894 and an entente with Britain in 1907. After its defeat by Japan, Russia's foreign policy priorities were to preserve access to the Mediterranean through the Straits and to exercise influence in the Balkans by posing as the defender of the Slavs.

When Serbian terrorists, incensed by Austria's domination of Bosnia-Herzegovina, assassinated the Archduke Franz Ferdinand on June 28, 1914, they set in motion a chain of events that culminated in World War I. Austria declared war on Serbia, prompting Russia to mobilize its army to defend the Serbs. Kaiser Wilhelm II of Germany unconditionally supported Austria. When fighting between Russia and Germany broke out in August, prominent figures across Russia's political spectrum rallied behind the tsar. Only Vladimir Lenin, hiding in neutral Switzerland, condemned what he termed the "bourgeois" war and urged Russian workers not to fight.

Popular support for the war soon ebbed. Russia's armed forces were ill prepared for a conflict with modern Germany. There were not enough rifles or artillery, and Russian railways were insufficient to deliver necessary supplies to the front. Russia's military leaders were incompetent and the budget was inadequate. At times, recruits would be thrown into battle unarmed, with instructions to scavenge weapons from their dead and wounded comrades. Certainly, there was no shortage of casualties—nearly 3 million Russian soldiers were killed, wounded, or taken prisoner in the first year. Disgusted by inept leadership, and propagandized by radicals, many soldiers deserted the front during the latter stages of the war. They would comprise an important element of the revolutionary movement in 1917.

The extraordinarily inept leadership of Nicholas II also helps to explain the collapse of the Romanov dynasty. The government's insensitive Russification policy—forcing the Russian language and Orthodox religion on non-Russians—had alienated the Empire's national minorities, particularly the

Finns, Jews, and Ukrainians (the Poles had never been very loyal). For nearly 10 years, the Court was under the influence of the mystical Siberian monk Gregorii Rasputin, whom the Tsarina Aleksandra believed could cure her son's hemophilia. Rasputin seduced many ladies of Russian high society, secured lucrative positions for his cronies, and in general exercised a pernicious influence over the nation's politics. His life and spectacular death (he was poisoned, stabbed, shot, and left in a Petrograd canal to drown by a group of nobles in 1916) have provided material for a number of books and movies.

Nicholas also did not help matters by taking direct command of Russian forces at the front. In late 1916 and early 1917, the country was suffering from food and fuel shortages, desertions, strikes and demonstrations, and outbreaks of such infectious diseases as cholera and typhus. A large demonstration of women in the capital in February 1917 protesting high bread prices sparked a general strike, and within a week, Nicholas II had abdicated in favor of his brother, who refused the throne. The Royal family was placed under house arrest immediately after the Revolution to preclude a counterrevolutionary movement from being organized abroad. In July 1918, they were executed by their Bolshevik guards.

The Romanov dynasty was replaced by a Provisional Government of moderate and liberal former ministers, most of whom were members of the Constitutional Democratic (Kadet) Party. The Provisional Government planned to exercise authority until a constituent assembly could be held to create a new, constitutional government. However, a second, more radical political organization, the Petrograd Soviet, formed, patterned after the short-lived soviet of the 1905 Revolution. Workers, soldiers, and radical intelligentsia were represented in the Petrograd Soviet. Mensheviks and Socialist Revolutionaries were the largest factions; the Bolsheviks were initially much smaller. The socialists who made up the Soviet's Executive Committee believed that Russia was not ripe for a socialist revolution; instead, the country would need to mature through a bourgeois phase, under the Provisional Government, before socialism could succeed.

Thus, an uneasy situation of dual power existed throughout most of 1917. The Provisional Government quickly guaranteed civil rights, including freedom of speech, the press, assembly, and religion; enacted a series of reforms in education, labor, and local government; and promised to move Russia toward democracy and the rule of law. The Petrograd Soviet issued more radical decrees, including the democratization of the army. Russia was in chaos. Peasants were seizing land from the nobility, workers continued to strike, and thousands of armed soldiers had simply walked away from the front. The Provisional Government was warmly welcomed by the French and British Allies, who quickly granted it diplomatic recognition as Russia's legitimate government. But the Provisional Government could not restore order to a country wracked by massive problems of inflation, the collapse of food production, disease, transportation bottlenecks, and general social disorder.

In hindsight, the greatest failing of the Provisional Government was its continuation of the war. The British, French, and Americans (the latter entered the conflict in April 1917) needed Russia to stay engaged so that the Germans would be forced to fight on two fronts. But the war was immensely unpopular in Russia. When Lenin arrived at Petrograd's Finland Station by train from Switzerland in April 1917, he immediately called for an end to the war and condemned the Petrograd Soviet's reticence in taking action against the Provisional Government. Lenin's "April Theses," which set out a more radical program for Russia than virtually any other socialist had proposed, was summarized in his slogan "Bread, Peace and Land," designed to appeal to the peasants, workers, and soldiers.

Condemning the Provisional Government, Lenin called for "all power to the soviets." He urged the workers and peasants to seize control of factories and land. Rejecting the war cause, Lenin urged the international proletariat to begin a civil war across Europe, with the goal of bringing about other socialist revolutions. According to Marxist theory, the workers' revolution should be international in scope. Backward Russia would need the more advanced industrial countries—Germany, Britain, France, and the United States—to become socialist in order to support socialism in Russia.

Public opinion was becoming more radicalized during the summer of 1917, and in July, the Bolsheviks, urged on by radical elements, tried to take power in an abortive coup. Fearful of growing leftism, conservative forces among the gentry, merchants, and military encouraged General Lavr Kornilov to march on the capital the following month. Kornilov's motley force of Cossacks and troops from the Caucasus melted away before reaching Petrograd, and the General was arrested. But Alexsandr Kerensky, a former Socialist Revolutionary who had headed the Provisional Government since July, could not stem the collapse of society and the slide toward extremism.

Over the course of the summer of 1917, the more militant Bolshevik Party expanded dramatically, and its influence in the Petrograd Soviet grew. Lenin continued to agitate for an armed uprising from his hiding place in Finland, where he had fled in June to avoid arrest based on charges of being a German agent. He returned to Russia in July, but continued to operate sporadically out of Finland until October. By then, the Petrograd and Moscow soviets had enough popular support to usurp the Provisional Government. In October, Lenin convinced the Bolshevik Central Committee to vote 10–2 to take action against the government. Leon Trotsky, who had returned from New York in May and become chairman of the Petrograd Soviet, strongly supported Lenin's plan to assume power. Trotsky was put in charge of the Bolshevik Party's military forces, the Red Guards. He secured control of the capital's military garrison, arranged the surrender of forces at the Peter and Paul Fortress, and led the assault on the Winter Palace, from which Kerensky's government had been operating. This almost bloodless coup, which took place on the night of November 7 (or October 25, going by the Old Style Russian calendar), was later glorified as the October Revolution by Soviet propagandists.

Control of Petrograd did not give the Bolsheviks control of the entire country. Within a week, the Moscow Soviet had seized power, and its control was quickly extended to central Russia. But Russia would suffer through three years of bloody civil war and a major famine before the communists consolidated their hold over the entire country. Even then, substantial territory around the periphery would be lost: Finland, the Baltic states (Latvia, Lithuania, and Estonia), eastern Poland, and Bessarabia (to Romania).

The new Bolshevik government immediately enacted a series of decrees allowing workers to take control of the factories. The Land Decree dispossessed all but the peasants of their land. The government nationalized banks, railroads, and some of the largest factories, and established a monopoly on foreign trade. Additional decrees outlawed inheritance, expropriated urban property for the state, and repudiated all state debts (much to the outrage of the French, who had invested heavily in the Russian economy). These radical socialist measures, backed by military force, characterized the period of war communism (1918–1921).

In the early months of the Revolution, Lenin was willing to align his party with the radical Socialist Revolutionaries, who were popular among the peasantry. For the most part, though, he was unwilling to compromise with other political forces and sought to crush his opponents. Russia's government under the Bolsheviks would not be democratic, but a dictatorship of the proletariat. Lenin claimed that the proletariat, the great majority of the people, were justified in repressing the exploitative elements—landowners, capitalists, priests, and other defenders of the old order. As the vanguard of the working class, the Party was entitled to make and carry out decisions in the name of the people.

The communists rejected liberal democratic ideas about the rule of law and constitutional protections as bourgeois. The Bolsheviks did permit elections to be held for a Constituent Assembly early in 1918. To their surprise, they received only 25 percent of the votes that were cast, compared with 58 percent for the Socialist Revolutionaries and 13 percent for center-right parties. The Constituent Assembly met once; this session was disrupted by uncooperative guards loyal to the Bolsheviks, and then ordered dissolved as an instrument of the "enemies of the people." Clearly, Lenin and the Bolsheviks had little respect for democratic procedures.

The major governing authority set up by the Bolsheviks was the Council of People's Commissars, or Sovnarkom. The Sovnarkom embodied a principle that distinguished the entire period of Soviet rule: the fusion of state and party. Of course, the Bolshevik Party, which would become the Communist

Party of the Soviet Union (CPSU), did not resemble democratic political parties. In democracies, parties by definition compete for power, and exercise power only if the voters choose them. The communists quickly established a monopoly of political power in Russia, controlling or destroying all competing organizations. Political parties, trade unions, local government committees, and army units were all subordinated to the Party.

As a pragmatic revolutionary leader, Lenin realized how important it was to bring an end to the war with Germany. Diplomacy was a new concept for the revolutionaries; if the major countries of Europe went communist, they reasoned, relations among the states should change fundamentally. War, imperialism, nationalism, trade disputes were all supposed by Marxists to be unique to the bourgeois world order, and few of Russia's new rulers really believed that the country could survive very long as a communist state surrounded by hostile capitalist countries. When the international revolution did not take place, Soviet leaders had to accommodate themselves to the existing order. In March 1918, this meant signing a draconian agreement with Germany, the Treaty of Brest-Litovsk, to halt the German advance and buy time to deal with their pressing domestic problems. Negotiated by Leon Trotsky, acting as Commissar of Foreign Relations, this treaty ceded huge areas of western Russia and Ukraine to Germany, much of which would be recovered after the armistice of November 1918.

Within a month of the communist takeover, Lenin sanctioned the formation of an Extraordinary Commission, or secret police organization, to suppress counter revolution. Headed by Felix Dzerzhinsky, a ruthless Polish revolutionary, the Cheka, as it was called, arrested, shot, and exiled opponents of the Revolution, frequently without the benefit of a trial. Lenin clearly approved of using terror to preserve Bolshevik rule. In July 1918, when it appeared that Nicholas and his family might be freed by a detachment of Czechoslovak troops en route to Vladivostok, Lenin ordered them to be shot in an Ekaterinburg cellar and their remains burned and scattered.

By the summer of 1918, a loose coalition of monarchist and conservative forces, termed the Whites, had begun a civil war against the Red, or communist, forces. Trotsky, appointed Commissar of War, was charged with mobilizing the Soviet Red Army to defend the Revolution. The White forces were especially strong in Ukraine, which existed as an independent country for nearly three years, and in remote Siberia and the Russian Far East. Encouraged by the prospect of communism's overthrow, the Allies deployed modest numbers of troops in the northeast (who were mostly British and French) and along the Amur River in the Far East (Japanese and American). These forces were insufficient to gain a victory for the Whites; the intervention did, however, provide grist for Bolshevik propaganda about capitalism's threat to the infant Soviet state.

While the Bolsheviks preached worker solidarity, they quickly discovered that national identity was a more important source of motivation for many of the non-Russian peoples of the Empire. Initially committed to a centralized, unitary state, the Bolsheviks soon realized their mistake. In July 1918, the Sovnarkom proclaimed the Soviet state to be a dictatorship of the proletariat, the workers, and peasants—the Russian Soviet Federated Socialist Republic (RSFSR). Russia's first constitution granted representation to industrial workers and peasants, but did not allow "exploiters" to vote. However, the real responsibility for governing was not entrusted to the working masses. Power was to be exercised through the supreme organs of Soviet government, while local and regional authorities might exercise only limited control over local affairs. As historian Richard Pipes notes, the first revolutionary constitution was short and confused; in any case, the Party leadership would retain ultimate power in Russia. This and all subsequent constitutions did not subordinate officials to the rule of law, nor did they protect the civil rights and liberties of the people. This pattern of arbitrary governance would persist throughout the Soviet period.

Lenin's promise to share power with Russia's minorities in a type of ethnic federalism was not nearly as attractive to these minorities as was complete independence. By the summer of 1918, Ukraine had established a national government, and it would exist as an independent country for nearly three years. Neighboring Belarus was self-governing for about a year; Georgia, Armenia, and Azerbaijan existed outside Soviet control during much of the Civil War. A Far Eastern Republic was proclaimed, with its capital at Vladivostok, under Japanese sponsorship; it lasted for four years, from 1918 to 1922. In Central Asia, sporadic resistance to Soviet rule continued as late as 1928.

Over the course of the Civil War (1918–1921), the Bolsheviks learned the effectiveness of harsh methods of repression and the uses of terror. Lenin and his fellow revolutionaries resisted sharing power with other political forces. The left-wing Socialist Revolutionaries, the only party radical enough for the Bolsheviks to cooperate with, withdrew from the governing coalition in March 1918. Soon, even competing ideas within the Bolshevik Party were suppressed. In March 1921, at the Tenth Party Congress, Lenin crushed the Workers' Opposition, a small group of populists who favored greater workers' self-government, and convinced the Party to adopt a ban on factionalism within its ranks. Dissension in the Party, he reasoned, would weaken it and provide opportunities for communism's enemies.

Russia's population suffered greatly during the Civil War. As with most civil wars, the fighting was brutal and atrocities were common. Millions were displaced, and an estimated 3 million eventually fled Russia. The latter included former tsarist bureaucrats and army officers, members of the noble and business classes, priests, and Old Believer communities. Russia also fought a brief war with Poland in 1920, as the Poles availed themselves of Russia's weakness and Germany's defeat to reestablish their independence.

The impact of nearly eight years of continuous war and revolution on Russia's economy was devastating. Industrial production collapsed; by 1921, it was only one-fifth that of 1913, the year before the war began. Food supplies dwindled as peasants were uprooted and armies roamed across the countryside fighting and looting. The Bolsheviks resorted to forcible grain requisitioning to ensure food supplies for the cities, but this only led peasants to hoard food. Resentful peasants were often forced to surrender their grain to workers' detachments at gunpoint. Boris Pasternak's lyrical novel, *Dr. Zhivago,* conveys much of the chaos and brutality of this period.

Toward the end of the Civil War, Russia was in a virtual state of collapse, a period of anarchy much like the Time of Troubles. Scholars estimate that as many as 20 million people had died in Russia from 1914 to 1921, from war, hunger, disease, and executions. By early 1921, peasants, outraged over forcible requisitions and the Bolsheviks' attempts to foment class warfare in the countryside, revolted. The economy was in ruins. Most Russians had turned to bartering to obtain what few goods were available. Russia faced famine in the winter of 1920–1921; relief efforts organized by the U.S. Secretary of Commerce, Herbert Hoover, saved thousands of lives. Conditions were so bad that in March, some of the Bolsheviks' most loyal supporters, sailors at the Kronstadt naval base in the Gulf of Finland near Petrograd, revolted. The sailors demanded an end to the harsh measures of War Communism, namely the Soviet government's policies of abolishing private enterprise, nationalizing land, forcibly requisitioning grain from the peasants, and forcing industrial workers into labor brigades. The Kronstadt sailors urged greater democracy in elections and called for the formation of a constituent assembly. Trotsky led a detachment of soldiers across the ice and crushed the uprising. Kronstadt, however, convinced the Bolshevik leadership that repression was becoming counterproductive.

At the tumultuous Tenth Party Congress that same month, Lenin persuaded the Party to adopt the New Economic Policy (NEP), which would last until 1928. NEP was to be a breathing spell for the new Soviet state, a period of relaxation now that the Civil War was over. Private enterprise would be allowed in farming and small businesses to restore production. The government would retain control of the commanding heights of the economy—heavy industry, railways, banking, and foreign trade. Grain requisitioning was abandoned, the summary justice of War Communism tempered, and the country entered a period of moderation and experimentation in education and culture. Limited capitalism under NEP restored a measure of prosperity and stability to Russia. This tactical retreat, however, was only temporary. By the end of the decade, Joseph Stalin would renew the communist offensive, bringing more chaos and bloodshed to the Soviet people.

6

Building Communism, 1921–1953

Communism alone is capable of giving really complete democracy.
—Vladimir Lenin, *The State and Revolution*

In order to overthrow capitalism it was necessary not only to remove the bourgeoisie from power, not only to expropriate the capitalists, but also to smash entirely the bourgeois state machine, its old army, its bureaucratic officialdom and its police force, and to substitute for it a new, proletarian form of state, a new socialist state. And that, as we know, is exactly what the Bolsheviks did.
—Joseph Stalin, "Report to the Eighteenth Congress" (1939)

Stalin is the personification of the bureaucracy.
—Leon Trotsky, *The Revolution Betrayed*

The years of war, revolution, intervention, civil war, and famine left Russia exhausted, but established that the Bolsheviks were firmly in control of the country. The expected world communist revolution had not materialized, so

Russia's new communist rulers turned their efforts toward building "socialism in one country," as Stalin termed it. Aside from the loss of a few territories on the periphery, Soviet Russia retained most of the domains of the tsarist empire. Ethnic Russians constituted only three fifths of the population of this multinational state; over 100 separate ethnic groups made up the remainder. The Soviet government's proclaimed commitment to equality for all nations led to the formation of a unique structure of state authority that was national in form, but socialist in content.

Although the Bolshevik leadership was ideologically committed to centralized control, Lenin urged the creation of a system of national republics, equal in status, to allow limited autonomy for different ethnic groups. Stalin, who was Commissar of Nationalities, favored subordination of the minority groups within Russia, but he lost to Lenin on this issue. Russia's second constitution, adopted in 1924, created the Union of Soviet Socialist Republics (USSR). In a concession to the national minorities, the USSR was to be organized as a federal system providing for limited autonomy—education and publishing in national languages, some cultural freedom, and local control over minor matters. But this was sham federalism. The republics had no sovereign authority; that is, powers which were legally guaranteed. Moscow could override any actions that were deemed incompatible with the interests of socialism, as defined by the Communist Party.

The Party itself was to remain highly centralized, and, of course, Party decisions were final. Theoretically, the Party was a democratic institution organized on the principle of democratic centralism: ideas and suggestions would be put forward and voting would occur at each level of the Party, starting from the lowest cell and eventually reaching the Politburo, the highest decision-making body. Once decisions were reached at the center, they would be carried out loyally, without question, by lower Party organizations. In reality, the process was never very democratic, and provided an ideal vehicle for the concentration of power. Stalin, who was appointed General Secretary of the Party in 1922, used this position to build a loyal cadre of supporters within the Party bureaucracy. Stalin's organizational talents and his strategic position in the Party would enable him to outmaneuver Leon Trotsky, Nikolai Bukharin, Gregorii Zinoviev, Lev Kamenev, and the other more visible, gifted leaders of the October Revolution, and establish an absolute personal dictatorship by the early 1930s.

Although Lenin never possessed the power that Stalin later accumulated, he was clearly the dominant figure of the Revolution. But Lenin had been in poor health since 1919, when he was wounded in an assassination attempt. In 1922, Lenin had his first stroke; a second followed in 1923, and the "old man" (he was not yet 54) died in January 1924. Absent any institutionalized means of succession, the top Party leaders engaged in the behind-the-scenes jockeying for power that was typical of authoritarian political systems. Lenin had left a political testament assessing the characteristics of his potential successors, which Joseph Stalin later suppressed. Trotsky, Lenin wrote, was clearly the most intellectual and capable of the Bolshevik leaders, but too self-confident. The Georgian Stalin had concentrated boundless power in his hands through his control of the Party Secretariat, and might not use it wisely, according to Lenin. In any case, Stalin was rude—he had clashed with Nadezhda Krupskaya, Lenin's wife—and the dying leader recommended that his comrades find a way of easing Stalin from power. But Stalin used Lenin's funeral as an occasion to enhance his own legitimacy, employing pseudo-religious imagery to create a cult worshipping the dead revolutionary. Busts and statues of Lenin became ubiquitous; a mausoleum was built on Red Square to house his remains; and the former capital was renamed Leningrad in his honor.

Stalin was born Josef Vissarionovich Djugashvili, the son of a drunken Georgian bootmaker from Gori, in 1879. He studied for five years at an Orthodox theological seminary in Tiflis. He joined a Georgian socialist movement in 1898, the year of the founding congress of the Russian Social Democratic Labor Party. He joined Lenin's Bolshevik faction shortly before the outbreak of the Revolution of 1905. Arrested several times in his revolutionary career, Stalin (the name means "man of steel") spent close to seven years in tsarist prisons or Siberian exile. Stalin, or Koba, as he liked to be called, helped fund the Bolshevik Party by organizing robberies in his native Caucasus. Never a towering intellect or a great orator (he spoke Russian with a thick Georgian accent until the end of his life), Stalin was an adroit political infighter and a master manipulator. Once he had consolidated power, he seldom ventured outside the Kremlin, and had virtually no contact with the Soviet people.

Communist Party politics in the 1920s were characterized by factionalism, as various coalitions formed and reformed in the Party hierarchy, based on their participants' positions on the New Economic Policy (NEP). Since the Revolution, political power had been concentrated in the Central Committee, especially the smaller Political Bureau (Politburo) of the Communist Party. Government cabinets had been renamed "commissariats" (which was deemed to be a more revolutionary term than "ministries"), and the cabinet was called the Council of People's Commissars (*Sovnarkom*). The general governing pattern was that government existed to carry out the Party's orders, and that the Party leadership was responsible to no one but itself. The fundamental democratic principle of holding rulers accountable to the public through elections had been rejected by Lenin and his successors as sham bourgeois democracy.

In the early post-Lenin power struggle, Stalin first aligned himself with Zinoviev and Kamenev against Trotsky. Stalin's chief theoretical contribution of the time—the idea of building socialism in one country—was presented as an alternative to Trotsky's insistence on pursuing world revolution. Soviet communists had established the Third Communist International, or Comintern, in 1919, with the express purpose of spreading communism around the world.

By the time of Lenin's death, however, the prospects that other industrial nations might go communist seemed dim, and the Comintern became essentially an instrument of Soviet foreign policy, forming and guiding communist parties in the colonial regions of China, India, and Africa. Stalin used his assertion that the Soviet Union could build socialism by itself, together with his influential position in the Party, to discredit Trotsky and secure his dismissal as head of the Red Army in 1925.

In the latter half of the 1920s, Stalin deserted Zinoviev and Kamenev, and allied with Nikolai Bukharin, the Party's chief theoretician. Stalin and Bukharin promoted their moderate positions on NEP, critiquing the more radical, leftist positions of Trotsky, Zinoviev, and Kamenev. By 1928, Stalin had forced all three out of the Communist Party. Zinoviev and Kamenev admitted their mistakes and had their Party membership reinstated. Trotsky refused to recant, was exiled briefly to Alma Ata, the capital of Soviet Kazakhstan in Central Asia, and, in the following year, was deported from the Soviet Union. After brief stays in Europe and the United States, he settled in Mexico City, where, in 1940, an agent of Stalin's secret police gained his confidence and subsequently murdered him with an ice pick. Ironically, Trotsky was finishing a biography of his nemesis at the time of his assassination.

Under NEP, the economy recovered quickly, although agriculture outpaced industry. A grain surplus in 1923 drove down prices for farmers, while the prices of manufactured goods, still in short supply, were increasing. This "scissors crisis" led peasants to withhold their products in the hope of obtaining higher prices in the future. For many Bolshevik leaders, this market behavior threatened their plans for industrialization and reinforced their suspicion of the peasants' political reliability.

During NEP, most villages had reverted to traditional practices—rotating land strips, governing through the *mir*—in short, to rural Russian life much as it had been before the Revolution. One difference was the existence of a network of private traders, or Nepmen, some of whom became quite wealthy. Nepmen were frequently resented for their prosperity, as were the kulaks, or prosperous peasants. By 1927–1928, NEP had succeeded in restoring agriculture and industry to prewar levels. NEP's limited capitalism, however, had also increased social differentiation. The privileges and wealth of some private entrepreneurs and officials provoked jealousy and conflicted with the egalitarian goals of the Revolution. In 1928–1929, Stalin used this simmering resentment to convince the Politburo to embark on a massive program of rapid industrialization.

CULTURE

The early revolutionary era was a time of great expectations and cultural experimentation. Lured by a radically new vision of society, the avant-garde flocked to Petrograd and Moscow. Anna Akhmatova, Aleksandr Blok, and Boris Pasternak read their poems to rapt audiences in smoky cafes. Directors Vsevolod Meyerhold and Evgenii Vakhtangov staged political plays for the masses. Constructivist artist Vladimir Tatlin designed his model for a huge monument to the Comintern, consisting of three geometric shapes. The top level of this 400-meter (1,300 foot) tower would rotate once a day, the middle level once a month, and the base once each year. The project was never begun; the model, however, can be seen today in Moscow's Pushkin Museum.

Few Bolsheviks were enthusiastic about these new art forms. They believed that art should be accessible to the masses, promote communist values, and not be too complicated—in other words, art should serve political purposes. This was the reasoning behind socialist realism, the guiding principle of art that emerged in the 1920s and exerted a stifling influence on creativity. Early on, democratically minded intellectuals had resisted the authoritarian impulse of the Bolsheviks. Evgenii Zamyatin, a freethinking member of the Party since 1905, published a powerful dystopian novel in 1920, *We,* about a society in which individualism was crushed by the collective, and numbers replaced names. Reviled by the authorities, Zamyatin left Russia in 1922, as did the painters Marc Chagall (after briefly serving as Commissar of Culture for his native Vitebsk province) and Vassily Kandinsky. The poet Sergei Yesenin killed himself in a Leningrad hotel in 1925; Vladimir Mayakovsky shot himself in 1930. Those who stayed in Russia, and stayed alive, were forced to work within the constraints of socialism. The alternative was to write for the drawer, hiding politically unacceptable manuscripts from the authorities. Merely possessing such material was grounds for a stiff sentence in the labor camps.

Socialist realist artists produced novels, paintings, and music that advanced the cause of building socialism. Soviet literature created idealized worlds where individuals sacrificed themselves for the common good, whether fighting the Whites in the Civil War or completing massive construction projects against great odds. Painters portrayed hard-working peasants, heroic Lenins and Stalins inspecting the progress of socialism, and dedicated factory workers or Red Army soldiers. Vera Mukhina's massive statue of a worker and a *kolkhoz* (collective farm) woman, located just outside the Exposition of the Achievements of the National Economy (now called the All-Russian Exhibition Center) in north Moscow, is stereotypical socialist realism. Young, strong, and made of steel, the two stand side by side, emblematic hammer and sickle raised skyward, pointing toward the future.

Some examples of socialist realism rank as solid artistic achievements. In film, for example, Sergei Eisenstein's *Battleship Potemkin* (about the sailors' revolt during the 1905 Revolution), and *October* (the 1917 Revolution), both released in 1925, are superb examples of early cinema. His 1938 movie, *Aleksandr Nevskii,* recounts the famous battle on the ice of Lake Peipus, when the Novgorod leader defeated the Teutonic Knights. Released shortly before Hitler launched World War II, *Aleksandr Nevskii* was a patriotic call to arms for Russians, as well as superb cinema. Mikhail Sholokov's *And Quiet Flows the Don* (published between 1928 and 1940 in serial form), a novel about the Revolution and Civil War, won its author a Nobel Prize for literature in 1965. Unfortunately, many other great novels, stories, plays, and films could not elude Soviet censorship until the glasnost era under Mikhail Gorbachev.

CREATING THE NEW SOVIET MAN

Soviet communists deliberately sought to transform society, breaking down the inegalitarian class structures of the tsarist era. For Karl Marx and Friedrich Engels, the bourgeois family was based on property relations; women were enslaved to their husbands in a form of legal prostitution. Proclaiming the full equality of men and women, the new Soviet regime enacted legislation weakening the family unit. Property inheritance was abolished, divorce procedures were simplified, common law marriages were recognized, abortion was granted on demand, and women were given equal legal status with men. Prominent feminist revolutionary Aleksandra Kollontai argued that the family was an outmoded institution that was repressive to women. Women, she insisted, had the right to full sexual freedom, and family burdens such as child rearing could be accomplished more effectively by the collective.

The task of achieving Revolutionary equality for women was assigned to the Women's Department (*Zhenotdel*), created in 1919. However, the idea of true equality met with strong resistance from Russia's male-dominated culture. Claiming that equality between the sexes had been achieved, the government abolished the *Zhenotdel* in 1930. With the increasing regimentation of Soviet society in the 1930s, laws strengthening the family were enacted. Abortion was made illegal in 1936, and divorce became more difficult. Soviet art and propaganda glorified women's contributions in building socialism, but much of the emphasis was on their traditional familial roles.

Young people were a special target of the regime since the attitudes of youth are more malleable. The Communist Party created a youth wing in 1918, the All-Lenin Communist League of Youth, or Komsomol, with membership open to those between the ages of 15 and 27. The Komsomol organization paralleled that of the Communist Party: the chain of command was hierarchical, with units in high schools, universities, workplaces, and military units. Furthermore, the Komsomol functioned as the Communist Party's primary source of new members. Political lectures, sports contests, chess clubs, nature hikes, and auxiliary labor brigades (for example, to bring in the potato harvest) were organized through the Komsomol. All of these activities were infused with a strong dose of communist propaganda designed to socialize the participants to Marxist-Leninist values. Younger children were taught obedience and loyalty through the Young Pioneers in middle school and by the Octobrists at the elementary-school level.

Religion, like the family, was viewed by the Bolsheviks as a mainstay of the old order and an ideological competitor. Marxist theory held that religion, like the state and other parts of the superstructure, would eventually wither away after the transition to socialism. Many leading communists, however, preferred a more active program to exterminate religion. Thousands of Russian Orthodox priests, monks, and nuns, who generally supported the White forces, were arrested or shot during the Revolution and Civil War. Churches were razed or converted into warehouses, and church property was nationalized. Patriarch Tikhon, the leader of the Russian Orthodox Church, was arrested and forced to recant his earlier condemnation of the Soviet government.

While religion was sporadically persecuted in the 1920s, agricultural collectivization in the following decade was accompanied by a comprehensive attack on all forms of religion. In Russia, religion was strongest in the rural areas, where 80 percent of the population lived. Priests were equated with rich peasants (kulaks) as reactionary elements. A League of the Militant Godless, aided by the Komsomol, organized atheist lectures, satirized religious holidays, published anti-religious posters and pamphlets, and confiscated church bells and icons. Schools required coursework in scientific atheism, and the newspapers attacked religion as the enemy of socialism. Of the more than 54,000 Orthodox churches that were active before the Revolution, only a handful still functioned in 1939, and those were heavily taxed. Jewish temples, Muslim mosques, and Protestant congregations suffered the same fate. Believers were excluded from Communist Party membership, denied access to prominent positions, and actively harassed in schools and by Soviet youth groups.

Religious persecution eased during World War II, when Stalin discovered that the Church could be useful in mobilizing public sentiment against fascism. The Russian Orthodox Church under Metropolitan Sergei readily lent its support to the struggle against the German invaders. In turn, Stalin permitted churches to reopen, religious literature to be disseminated, and the Patriarchate to be restored. Restrictions were relaxed on other major denominations. However, it was the reinvigoration of Russian Orthodoxy, combined with patriotic Russian nationalism, that strengthened the will to resist Nazism. Marxism-Leninism could not command the same allegiance.

INDUSTRIALIZATION AND COLLECTIVIZATION

Lenin and the other Bolshevik leaders had intended NEP to be only a temporary retreat. The country had recovered to prewar levels of industrial and agricultural production by the late 1920s, but the accompanying social and economic inequalities and the growth of bureaucracy troubled many communists. There was a consensus that the Soviet Union was vulnerable to capitalist remnants internally, as well as to hostile nations in Europe and Asia, and that the country needed to industrialize rapidly.

The leadership, however, was divided over the pace of renewed industrialization. Party theoretician Nikolai Bukharin led the Right Opposition, those who wanted to prolong NEP and allow some limited market forces to operate in Soviet Russia. In contrast, Stalin advocated rapid development, essentially adopting Trotsky's position, which he had previously criticized. In 1928, Stalin got his way, and the Communist Party released the first Five-Year Plan, which based industrial production on mandated quotas and shifted the economy toward a command structure. The basic mechanism of supply and demand was ignored. The emphasis was on rapid expansion of heavy industry; approximately 84 percent of investment went into coal, steel, cement, electric power, machine tools, and tractors, rather than consumer goods. Soviet workers were to postpone improvements in their standard of living to build the country's industrial base. Furthermore, the rapid development of heavy industry was deemed vital to Soviet national security. In a 1931 speech, Stalin observed, "The history of old Russia consisted, among other things, in her being beaten continually for her backwardness." The Mongols, the Swedes, the Poles, the Japanese, the Turks, and the Anglo-French capitalists had defeated and exploited Russia in the past, Stalin continued; transforming the Soviet Union into an industrial power would make it militarily invincible.

The idea behind the centrally planned economy was the following: the Party Politburo would set general production targets of major sectors of the economy, dictating the minimal growth rates that must be achieved. The State Planning Committee (*Gosplan*) would coordinate production among the different government ministries that were tasked with actually carrying out production. Each ministry would have a complex of factories and enterprises to supervise, and just as each ministry was responsible for fulfilling its quota, each enterprise would have a production quota it was required to meet. Quotas were based on the Five-Year Plan, broken down into annual and monthly quotas, and were based on quantitative indicators.

It mattered little to the planners in Moscow whether a factory produced poor-quality products, as long as it produced the required amount. The reward system was geared toward fulfilling (and overfulfilling) one's quota; a factory manager who failed could lose bonuses or might even lose his position. In any case, Soviet consumers had no competing products from which to choose. Production was standardized, so that consumers found the same generic products at the same prices on shelves from Vladivostok to Vitebsk.

The central planning system encouraged deception at all levels of the economy. Government officials responsible for fulfilling Party directives were afraid to point out to their superiors that their quotas were impossibly high. They in turn passed along impossible demands to the factories, where records were routinely falsified to make it appear that the quotas had been fulfilled when, in reality, they had not. "Family circles" of local Party officials and factory managers, acting out of a perfectly rational sense of self-preservation, assured their superiors that the plans were being fulfilled. This cycle of impossible demands from the top down and falsification from the bottom up built misinformation and inaccuracies into the Soviet economy. Officials and economists, as well as outside observers, found it extremely difficult to gauge the real performance of the Soviet economy.

Capitalist incentives, such as pay, differentials were rejected in favor of moral exhortations. Party propaganda and agitation organs promoted campaigns to motivate workers to accomplish great feats, such as the one achieved by coal miner Alexei Stakhanov, who overfulfilled his norm by 800 percent. The intent was to create a climate of heroism, urgency, self-sacrifice, and emulation of model workers who were glorified by the state. Since exhorting workers grew old after a while, Soviet planners eventually turned to a system of bonuses to encourage higher production. They also encouraged factory teams to engage in socialist competition to try and outdo one another in overfulfilling their quotas. Since this competition took place within a socialist system, it was perceived as being superior to capitalist competition.

Stalin was convinced that the resources for a successful industrialization program would have to come from the peasantry in the form of extracting enough food from the countryside to feed the new armies of labor and exporting the surplus to pay for foreign machinery and technology. To do this, the Soviet government undertook a program of collectivization—appropriating private land from the peasants to form large socialist farms. The collectivization of agriculture was not initially part of the first Five-Year Plan. When faced with the prospect of grain shortages in 1929, Stalin approved the use of force to requisition grain from the peasants. Under pressure from Moscow, young industrial workers sent from the cities and Party officials began fomenting class warfare in the countryside, pitting poor and middle peasants against the affluent kulaks. The Marxist terminology of class struggle meant nothing to the peasants, who were either confused by it or saw an opportunity to dispossess their richer neighbors of their property or settle scores with personal enemies. The result was chaos in the countryside.

On the eve of collectivization, only about 3–4 percent of holdings had been converted to collective farms during the eight years of NEP. Of the different models that had evolved, the most acceptable was the *artel*, in which land, barns, and most livestock were socialized, while peasant families were allowed to retain their homes and a small private plot of land about an acre in size. In these collective farms, or *kolkhozy*, workers were paid a share of the total farm income for the year. Theoretically, if the entire *kolkhoz* did well, so would the individual peasants. Of course, if blight or drought ruined the crops, the peasants would suffer commensurately. Because of this, many peasants in the post-Stalin period preferred to live on state farms (*sovkhozy*), where they were paid a set wage regardless of output.

One central aspect of agricultural collectivization was the goal of establishing complete Communist Party control over the rural villages, where four-fifths of the population lived. The formation of the collective farms was supervised by the Party, and, eventually, each *kolkhoz* and *sovkhoz* would have a Party cell headed by a secretary to monitor its operation. Large machinery was owned by the state; tractors, combines, and other implements were rationed out to the collective farms through machine-tractor stations, adding another element of political control.

The alleged enemies of Soviet power, kulaks, were to be liquidated as a class. What this meant was that over a million families, or 5 to 7 million of the most productive peasants, had their farms and belongings confiscated. Often, the kulaks were not much better off than their neighbors—they might have a cow and a few extra chickens. These supposed class distinctions were artificial, but necessary from Stalin's perspective in order to implement his goal of subjugating the Russian peasantry. Most of the households that were dekulakized were deported to bleak regions in central Siberia, Kazakhstan, or northern Russia and forced to start over with nothing. Those who were especially suspect, or who resisted (about 100,000), were shot. Rather than have their land, homes, and animals confiscated, many peasants chose to burn their farms and slaughter their livestock. Occasionally, they formed armed bands of resistance.

The process of collectivizing agriculture was brutal and inflicted tremendous damage on Soviet agriculture. Peasants could be arrested or shot for withholding grain for next season's planting or merely to survive through the winter. In 1932–1933, the Party had extracted so much grain from the countryside that it created a massive famine in Ukraine, southern Russia, and Kazakhstan. In Ukraine, the breadbasket of the USSR, an estimated 5 million peasants died of starvation. Collectivization in Kazakhstan consisted of changing an entire way of life—destroying the nomadic existence of this Turkic Muslim people by forcing them into a sedentary lifestyle, appropriating their livestock, and forcing them to plant grain on land unsuitable for cultivation. In his 1986 book *The Harvest of Sorrow*, Robert Conquest estimates that well over a million Kazakhs died in the repressions of collectivization and the 1932–1933 famine; thousands more fled into neighboring China.

The Soviet government succeeded in obscuring the depth of this tragedy. Many Western observers were already favorably inclined toward the Bolshevik experiment and refused to believe the stories of mass repression. Walter

Duranty, a correspondent for the *New York Times,* toured the famine areas, but his readers learned nothing of the starvation and cannibalism taking place in the countryside. President Herbert Hoover, defeated in 1932 by the Democrat Franklin Roosevelt, once again organized relief supplies for the famine victims. The horrors of collectivization did little to dissuade left-wing idealists in the West. Entranced by the massive Soviet effort to transform society and nature, adventurers came from Europe, the United States, and Australia to be a part of this utopian experiment. Compared to the poverty and unemployment of the Great Depression, Soviet Russia may have seemed the wave of the future. In reality, Stalin was leading the country on a "journey into the whirlwind," as writer Evgeniia Ginzburg termed it in her book of the same title.

THE PURGES

Stalin inherited the secret police and concentration camps that Lenin had created; he greatly expanded the powers of the former and the scope of the latter. In order to complete the social and economic transformations of the 1930s, Stalin turned toward the massive and indiscriminate use of terror. Show trials were often utilized to make an example of enemies of the state. In the first one, the 1928 Shakhty coal miners' trial, 53 engineers, technical specialists from the tsarist era, were charged with being part of a foreign conspiracy to sabotage the coal industry. There was no evidence of guilt, but after days of sleep deprivation, threats, and torture, the accused confessed. Most of the defendants were convicted; five were executed. The Shakhty trial established a pattern of fabricating charges against innocent individuals, coercing confessions from them, threatening retaliation against families to encourage the accused to implicate others, and then staging a trial to demonstrate the government's vigilance against spies and wreckers.

Terror was used against all social and occupational groups—no one was spared. Terror directed against the kulaks, who were only marginally better off than their fellow villagers, served to intimidate the rest of the peasantry. Arresting and executing those engineers and specialists who resisted the imposition of unrealistic production targets frightened the remainder into working at breakneck speeds to overfulfill the plan. Used against loyal Party members, terror combined with iron discipline to produce abject displays of public abasement and humiliation in the show trials of the 1930s.

The assassination of Sergei Kirov, popular Secretary of the Leningrad Party organization, by a disgruntled Party member in December of 1934 touched off a wave of arrests. Although the evidence is not clear, the assassin may have been encouraged by the NKVD (secret police) to kill Kirov; he was twice arrested with a loaded pistol and maps of Kirov's routes, and was released with his weapon each time. Stalin affected dismay at the incident; in fact, it was a golden opportunity to initiate a purge of those deemed disloyal. Kirov's assassination touched off a wave of arrests in 1935, including those of the Old Bolsheviks Zinoviev and Kamenev. In his book *Stalin in Power*, Robert C. Tucker refers to this period as the "quiet terror," the prelude to a full-blown assault on the population.

The Terror, or Purges (the Russian term is *chistka*, or "cleaning"), reached its height from 1936 to 1938, and was directed largely against officials in the upper levels of the Communist Party and government, members of the Comintern, leading cultural figures, officers in the Red Army, scientists, and others in prominent positions. Partly driven by Stalin's paranoia, the Purges had the effect of eliminating all possible opposition to him. The Old Bolsheviks—those who took part in the Revolution—submitted to the Party out of a strong sense of discipline, but Stalin was determined to ensure that no trace of possible resistance remained.

Zinoviev and Kamenev, two leading figures of the Revolution, were accused of plotting with Trotsky to murder Stalin, of having planned the attack on Kirov, and of being German agents. Pressured to admit their fictitious crimes at a staged trial in 1936, they were convicted and executed. The state prosecutor, Andrei Vyshinsky, railed against the defendants, declaring that for justice to be served, "the mad dogs must be shot." They were. Other prominent Bolshevik leaders came to a nasty end during this period. Mikhail Tomsky, head of the trade unions, committed suicide following an argument with Stalin. Minister of Heavy Industry Sergo Ordzhonikidze also killed himself. The Czech communist Karl Radek was sentenced to prison, where he was killed by inmates. In the last major purge trial, Alexei Rykov, Nikolai Bukharin, and 19 others were accused of heading an anti-Soviet bloc of Rightists and Trotskyists; they were executed in 1938.

Marxist theory had predicted that with the triumph of communism, the state, which had only served as a repressive mechanism to maintain the ruling classes in power, would begin to wither away. In Stalinist Russia, the reverse happened—the state grew and became extraordinarily powerful. The new Soviet Constitution of 1936 proclaimed that the gains of the Five-Year Plans had established socialism in the USSR. However, Stalin argued that progress toward the final goal of full communism would intensify resistance by counterrevolutionary forces, and so increased oppression would be necessary to crush the opposition.

THE FIRST TOTALITARIAN SYSTEM?

The political system that evolved in the Soviet Union has often been called totalitarian. As the name implies, a totalitarian system seeks to exercise total control over the thoughts and behavior of the population. Political power is highly centralized in a single party headed by a dictator; all other political parties, interest groups, and social and cultural organizations are either banned or thoroughly dominated by the ruling party. The economy is tightly controlled by the government; business and agriculture are either owned outright by the state or run by government bureaucrats. Virtually all aspects of life, including those usually reserved for the private sphere, are politicized. Education and the mass media are controlled by the state, censorship is exercised, and the public is subject to government propaganda and attempts at behavior modification. Government actions are justified through a single ideology, and ideological competitors, such as religion and other philosophies, are harassed or destroyed. State-sponsored terror is employed to ensure complete obedience.

Stalin may be said to have established the first totalitarian regime. Other totalitarian systems patterned after the Soviet model included China under Mao Zedong (1949–1976), North Korea under Kim Il-sung (1946–1995), and Cambodia under Pol Pot (1975–1978). Although none of the communist countries succeeded in exercising absolute control over their people, they did create dictatorships that were far more repressive than most authoritarian systems. The peculiar nature of totalitarianism is captured in several excellent novels: Arthur Koestler's *Darkness at Noon,* George Orwell's *1984* and *Animal Farm,* and Ray Bradbury's *Fahrenheit 451.* Each of these books depicts the horrors of life in a society where individual desires are completely subordinated to the goals of the state.

In Stalin's Soviet Union, real political power was concentrated in the upper levels of the Communist Party—the Central Committee and the smaller Politburo—and the government ministries. Major decisions on foreign and domestic policies were made in the Politburo, with Stalin having the decisive voice. Government ministers were charged with devising plans and carrying out Party directives; they had very little chance to exercise initiative. Appointments to positions of responsibility—Party secretaries, government officials, military officers, heads of schools and universities, newspaper editors—were controlled through a list of names, the Nomenklatura, coordinated through the Party Secretariat in Moscow. The Nomenklatura was similar to a security background check; it ensured that candidates for a position were politically reliable. Those with questionable class backgrounds, religious believers, criminals, and those who were not wholeheartedly committed to the Soviet cause were screened out.

Was the Soviet Union under Stalin really totalitarian? Scholars disagree. Certainly, the state exercised greater control over its subjects than any of the world's other great dictatorships had, including Hitler's. But the Smolensk archives, captured by the Germans during World War II and then retrieved by the Americans, demonstrate that local Party and government officials often colluded to frustrate Moscow's, and Stalin's, orders. Constant pressures from the center to achieve unrealistic goals fueled a culture of deception, where the localities inflated production figures and assured Moscow that the assigned plans were always fulfilled (or, even better, overfulfilled). Deception was a very rational course of behavior in the Soviet Union, and it pervaded public life. This inherent logic of lies and deception poisoned social relations. When Soviet communism finally collapsed, Russian society lacked the trust necessary to build a truly democratic political culture.

FOREIGN AFFAIRS AND THE GREAT FATHERLAND WAR

The question of the Soviet Union's role in world affairs was problematic from the very beginning. First, the course of history did not unfold according to Marx's or Lenin's predictions since no other industrialized nations experienced a socialist revolution. Second, the Bolsheviks' vitriolic condemnation of capitalist states, their repudiation of all foreign debts, and their avowed goal of fomenting world revolution ensured their international isolation. Third, the hostile approach of the Bolsheviks to capitalist Europe and America—their bitter propaganda campaigns, for example—in turn generated hostility from the West. The Treaty of Brest-Litovsk of 1918, in which the new Bolshevik government readily gave up huge territories in exchange for peace with Germany, demonstrated the Soviets' ability to deal pragmatically with their enemies in order to preserve the nascent Soviet state, while continuing to promote the goal of revolution abroad.

Spurned by France, Britain, and the United States, Soviet Russia turned to the other pariah nation of post-World War I Europe, Germany. During a 1922 economic conference in Italy, the two countries signed the Rapallo Treaty, in which Russia obtained formal diplomatic recognition from Germany, as well as expanded trade relations. More importantly, a secret agreement allowed Germany to construct arms factories and to train troops within the Soviet Union. This arrangement provided the Soviet Red Army with valuable technology and experience in joint military exercises, while allowing Germany to circumvent the provisions of the Treaty of Versailles (1919) against rearming. This punitive treaty, with its reparations payments and other humiliating conditions, had been forced on Germany by the victorious allies and was greatly resented by Germans.

In the 1920s, Soviet foreign policy evolved into a curious blend of revolutionary expansion and routine diplomacy. By the time Lenin died in 1924, the Soviet Union was no longer threatened by imminent attack. There were, however, potential threats to Soviet security from Britain and France in the West, and Japan in the East. Japan had withdrawn from the Soviet Far East in late 1922, but clearly had plans to expand onto the Asian mainland in its imperial quest. At that time, China was extremely weak and fragmented, presenting an ideal opportunity for foreign intervention. Concern about Japan led Soviet leaders, through the Comintern, to help establish the Chinese Communist Party in 1921. Mikhail Borodin, a Comintern official, reorganized the Chinese Nationalist Party (Kuomintang) along Leninist lines and sponsored a coalition of the Kuomintang and Chinese Communists in 1924. Moscow reasoned that a strong, unified China could more easily withstand Japanese penetration. When Chiang Kai-shek, head of the Nationalists, turned on his communist allies and massacred some 10,000 of them in 1927, Soviet influence in China was severely curtailed. Japan invaded Manchuria in northern China in 1931, and threatened the Soviet border throughout the 1930s.

The United States refused to grant formal diplomatic recognition to the USSR until 1933, but there were substantial economic contacts between the two countries during the 1920s. Ford Motor Company sold tractors, General Electric provided electrical equipment, Standard Oil and Sinclair signed contracts to develop Soviet energy reserves, and American cotton was exported to Soviet textile mills. Armand Hammer, the American entrepreneur, philanthropist, and art collector, laid the foundations for his massive fortune by setting up factories to manufacture pencils. An astute businessman, Hammer realized that the revolutionary state would soon become heavily bureaucratic, and pencils would be in great demand. Although he was one of the world's richest capitalists, Armand Hammer had close ties with every Soviet leader from Lenin to Brezhnev.

Stalin was initially slow to perceive the threat presented by Hitler's rise in Germany. From 1927 to 1934, he was convinced that the Social Democrats (SPD), the moderate, Western-oriented left wing of German politics, were a greater enemy of communism than the growing National Socialist Party. Stalin chose to overlook Hitler's tirades against communism, preferring to view the fascist movement as a manifestation of capitalism that might result in war within Europe, but which would leave the Soviet Union untouched. Through the Comintern, Stalin instructed the German Communist Party (KPD) to shun any form of cooperation with the SPD. By refusing to work with the German socialists, the communists helped destroy the Weimar democracy and facilitated Hitler's rise to chancellor in 1933.

By 1934, Hitler had destroyed the KPD and dissolved the military cooperation agreement signed at Rapallo. Stalin realized that Nazi Germany presented a real threat to the Soviet Union. In place of his earlier policy of semi-isolation, Stalin now initiated a collective security policy intended to link Soviet security to that of Europe. Maksim Litvinov, Commissar of Foreign Affairs, vigorously courted the former capitalist, aggressor nations to contain Nazi expansion. The Soviet Union joined the League of Nations and, in 1935, finalized mutual defense pacts with France and Czechoslovakia. Above all, Soviet diplomacy sought to prevent the USSR from being dragged into a war before military and economic preparations had been completed.

By 1938, it was clear that the policy of collective security was seriously flawed. The West was unwilling to stand up to Hitler's aggressive actions—his move into the Rhineland (1936), his assistance to General Franco's fascist forces during the Spanish Civil War (1936–1939), the annexation of Austria (1938), and the move into Czech Sudetenland and the eventual occupation of all of Czechoslovakia (1938–1939) had drawn no more than muted protests. In May 1939, Stalin replaced the Jewish Litvinov with his close confidant, Viacheslav Molotov, and in August of that year, the German-Soviet Non-Aggression Pact (also known as the Molotov-Ribbentrop Pact) was concluded. In addition to pledges not to attack the other party, the pact also included a secret protocol dividing up the territories that lay between the two countries. The Soviet Union would acquire the eastern third of Poland, the Baltic states, and Bessarabia (present-day Moldova); Germany could invade and occupy western Poland without fear of Soviet retaliation. The German attack on Poland one week later launched World War II.

The Non-Aggression Pact was signed to buy time for the Soviet Union, as was a neutrality treaty signed with Japan in April 1941. The first and second Five-Year Plans had laid the foundations for an industrial economy, but collectivization and the Purges had greatly weakened Soviet capabilities. Stalin's Terror had decimated the top officers of the Red Army, leaving it unprepared to deal with a German invasion. Robert C. Tucker notes that of the 101 members of the Soviet high command, 91 were arrested and more than 80 were shot. Some 3,000 naval commanders and 140 of 186 division commanders were executed during the Purges. After the Non-Aggression Pact was signed, Stalin ordered the western military fortifications in Belorussia dismantled, possibly to convince Hitler that the Soviet Union posed no threat to Germany, but also to build fortifications further westward in the newly acquired territories.

The suspicious Soviet leader was so determined to avoid provoking the Germans that he consistently ignored warnings by his own and Western intelligence services that Hitler was planning to attack the USSR. It is very likely that Stalin hoped Germany would be exhausted from a protracted war with Britain and France. He did not envision Germany's rapid victories in Europe, nor could he believe Hitler would be so rash as to fight on two fronts simultaneously. When 3 million German troops invaded Soviet territory on June 22, 1941, the Red Army was completely unprepared. Stalin was so shocked he went into seclusion for nearly two weeks. Britain and France quickly joined the USSR as allies, and America entered the war after the bombing of Pearl Harbor in December 1941.

The Great Fatherland War, as it patriotically came to be known, caused immense destruction. German forces quickly overran the western part of the

USSR, including Ukraine and Belorussia, and advanced through Russia along a front stretching from Leningrad in the north, past Moscow, to Stalingrad and the Caucasus in the south. They eventually occupied some 400,000 square miles of Soviet territory with 65 million people, controlled much of the best agricultural land, and approached the outskirts of Moscow. Leningrad was cut off and besieged for nearly three years; some 900,000 inhabitants of the city died, mostly from cold and starvation. Altogether, about 20 million people perished from various causes, 80 times the number of Americans killed.

Most Soviet people fought fiercely in defense of their homeland. Military historian William Fuller (in Gregory Freeze, ed., *Russia: A History*) claims that the Soviet Union was fairly even with Germany in both weapons and men at the start of the war; Germany's initial successes were due in large part to failures of leadership in the Soviet regime and to the vast destruction visited on Soviet society in the 1930s. It is a telling comment on Stalin's cruelties that in many parts of Ukraine, Belorussia, and the Baltics, the Germans were welcomed as potential liberators. Peasants often met the advancing German troops with the traditional Slavic welcome of bread and salt. It is also estimated that about 1 million defected and served the Axis war machine in various capacities. However, the barbaric treatment of Slavs, classified as subhumans fit only for slave labor by Hitler's racial scheme, quickly turned the population against the invaders. Jews and Communist Party officials fared the worst—they were shot, while others were herded into concentration camps. Nazi atrocities encouraged the Soviet people to fight doggedly, either in the regular forces or in partisan detachments, and this determined resistance contributed to the eventual defeat of the Germans.

The magnitude of Soviet losses in World War II is difficult for Americans to comprehend. Virtually everyone lost at least one relative, and many lost entire families. Millions were uprooted, suffered from hunger and privation, and saw their homes destroyed. The country's national wealth had been reduced by approximately 30 percent. The war reinforced Soviet patriotism, magnified Stalin's personality cult, and strengthened his hold on power. It also reinforced the perception of vulnerability to outside aggression, making it easier for Soviet leaders to demand continued sacrifices in the interest of state security. Finally, Soviet victory in World War II added new territory to the USSR—the Baltic states of Latvia, Lithuania and Estonia, Moldavia, and new areas in the west of the Belorussian and Ukrainian republics—and secured Eastern Europe as a communist buffer zone.

THE COLD WAR

World War II led to the formation of a new international order in which there were two dominant superpowers: the United States and the USSR. The Soviet

Union was virtually exhausted by 1945; agricultural production had declined by two-thirds, industrial production was skewed toward military needs, and housing was in such short supply that 25 million people were homeless or living in makeshift shelters. On the plus side, the USSR had incorporated parts of the Russian Empire that were lost after the Revolution—the Baltic states and Moldavia—and annexed East Prussia and new territory in Transcarpathia. The Soviet Union was now the second-most powerful nation in the world, even after demobilizing the bulk of its 11-million-man army.

There was no one reason why relations between the former allies deteriorated into the Cold War, a period of tension and competition between the Soviet-led Eastern Bloc and the American-led West. However, Stalin's renewed repression and isolation within the USSR, and the expansion of communism externally, reinforced the conviction in the West that the communists were indeed intent on world revolution. Over the next five years, communist governments came to power in Eastern Europe, North Korea, and China. A strong communist movement threatened to take power in Greece, and large communist parties existed in France and Italy. Soviet forces occupied northern Iran until May 1946, and stayed in Austria until Nikita Khrushchev withdrew them in 1955. No longer an isolated pariah state, the Soviet Union was now the acknowledged leader and role model for a dozen communist countries. Marxist predictions that communism would replace capitalism finally seemed to be coming true, although the victories were secured by armed force, or by revolutions in poor agricultural societies, rather than developed industrial ones.

Of immediate significance to Stalin was the creation of a buffer zone of friendly communist states in Europe, which was, in reality, a Soviet Empire. As the Red Army had pushed the Germans back through Eastern Europe, it had occupied Poland, Romania, Hungary, Bulgaria, and Czechoslovakia. Since Stalin had promised to support democracy in Eastern Europe after the war, he directed communist parties to form coalitions, or National Fronts, with parties of the democratic left and center in each of these countries. Over the next three years, the communist parties, with Soviet support, gradually discredited or destroyed their coalition partners and established communist dictatorships. Even in those countries where support for communism was strong, as in Czechoslovakia and Yugoslavia, Stalin insisted on replicating the Soviet model and complete subordination to Moscow.

Thorough control was difficult to achieve, however, in countries where communist forces had attained power without direct Soviet assistance, such as in Yugoslavia, Albania, and China. In Yugoslavia, under the leadership of Josip Broz Tito, communist partisans fought the Germans, and by war's end, had secured a dominant position in their country and in neighboring Albania. At first, the Yugoslav communists adamantly proclaimed their loyalty to Moscow. Soviet attempts to bind Yugoslavia into a web of controls through the Communist Information Bureau (Cominform, the successor to the Comintern) and the Soviet secret police backfired. In 1948, Tito announced that Yugoslavia would quit the Cominform and pursue its own path toward socialism, infuriating Stalin, who correctly perceived it as a challenge to Soviet leadership of world communism.

Following the conquest of Berlin and the division of Germany into four occupation zones by the Allies, Soviet-occupied East Berlin and East Germany were taken over by the German Communist Party, renamed the SED (Socialist Unity Party of Germany). Stalin was keen to keep Germany divided and weak. When, in 1948, the United States introduced a currency reform in the western sectors without consulting the USSR, Stalin ordered Berlin, located over 100 miles inside the eastern sector, blockaded. The United States and Britain responded with an 11-month airlift of supplies to the beleaguered city. Stalin finally lifted the blockade in May 1949, but the crisis resulted in the formation of separate East and West German states, solidifying the postwar division indefinitely. The Western allies also created the North Atlantic Treaty Organization (NATO) in 1949, as a means of containing Soviet aggression in Europe.

Stalin's actions at the wartime conferences in Teheran, Potsdam, and Yalta were directed toward the complete destruction of Germany and the creation of a protective buffer zone between the Soviet Union and Western Europe. A Communist Eastern Europe where Soviet troops were deployed, where the communist parties and security forces were thoroughly penetrated by and responsible to Soviet Party and secret police organs, and where Western Europe and the United States were denied any influence constituted just such a zone. In his 1946 speech at Westminster College in Fulton, Missouri, Winston Churchill aptly described this dividing line between communist East and democratic West: "From Stettin in the Baltic to Trieste in the Adriatic, an iron curtain has descended across the Continent."

Certainly, one factor contributing to the tension between the Soviet Union and the United States was the refusal of the latter to share the secrets of the atomic bomb. Both countries had been working on this superweapon throughout the war, but America's technological edge proved superior. When President Truman approved the August 1945 bombing of Hiroshima and Nagasaki, he apparently hoped that this destructive weapon would encourage Stalin to act more cautiously. However, Stalin could not tolerate an American nuclear monopoly, and ordered his scientists (and spies) to build a Soviet weapon with all dispatch. The first Soviet atomic (fission) bomb was successfully tested in 1949; a thermonuclear device was exploded in 1953.

In the Far East, Stalin's goals included regaining territory lost to Japan in the Russo-Japanese War (southern Sakhalin and the Kuril Islands), establishing a presence in northern China and on the Korean peninsula, and limiting the American presence in the region. Soviet forces had not fought Japan during the war, but did move very quickly into northern China and the northern part of the Korean peninsula in the few weeks before Japan's surrender in August 1945. While the United States willingly divided Korea into two zones of occupation along the 38th parallel, Stalin's attempt to secure a foothold in Japan was successfully resisted by General Douglas MacArthur and President Harry Truman. However, Soviet troops did manage to regain control of southern Sakhalin, and occupied the entire chain of the Kuril Islands, including the four southernmost islands, which had never been under Russian control. Continued occupation of these Northern Territories, as the Japanese call them, poisoned relations with Japan throughout the remainder of the Soviet period. Russia and Japan had still not reached a territorial settlement as late as 2009, and so had not signed a peace treaty formally ending the state of war between them.

As in Eastern Europe, Soviet occupying forces backed a pliant communist, Kim Il-sung, and helped his political faction consolidate power in the North. In June of 1950, Kim convinced a reluctant Stalin to support his invasion of U.S.-backed South Korea. Kim also managed to gain support from Mao Zedong and the new communist government established in the People's Republic of China in 1949. In June of 1950, then, North Korean forces struck southward across the 38th parallel, thus launching the Korean War (1950–1953). Stalin cautiously supported North Korea with supplies, pilots, and military advisors. It was not until his death that the stalemate on the Korean peninsula was broken and a peace agreement was negotiated.

Moscow did not seem very confident of a communist victory in China in the immediate postwar period, and signed a treaty of friendship and alliance with Chiang Kai-shek's Kuomintang government in August 1945. By 1947, the Chinese communists under Mao were scoring major successes against the Nationalists; Chiang's forces were driven off the mainland and onto the island of Taiwan, and the People's Republic of China was proclaimed on October 1, 1949. Although they had provided only minimal support to the Chinese communists during the civil war, the Soviets extended warm wishes to Mao and invited him to Moscow for a two-month conference in 1950, during which a mutual assistance treaty was signed. But personal relations between Stalin and Mao were not cordial, and the interests of these two large communist nations were incompatible. Communism was not a monolithic bloc as so many in the West thought, and the communist world would soon fracture along the Sino-Soviet axis.

STALIN'S FINAL YEARS

After the war, Soviet priorities included rebuilding the industrial base and restoring strict controls over society. After years of sacrifice, many were hoping for some easing of the repressions of the 1930s, some reward for their loyal defense of the motherland. But they would be disappointed. True, political terror was sporadic rather than pervasive, and the material well-being of the population was restored to prewar levels within a few years. However, private agricultural production, which was tolerated as a necessity during the war, came under renewed attack as resources were drained from the countryside to finance industry. Tens of thousands of collective farms had disintegrated under the German onslaught; now, the Soviet state set about rebuilding the *kolkhozes* and forcing peasants to deliver grain to the cities. Renewed pressure on the countryside led once again to famine. The young and able left the countryside for the cities, further aggravating the poverty of Russia's rural areas.

Stalin was determined to punish all those suspected of not being totally loyal to the motherland. Those who had collaborated with the Germans either fled to the West or were shot. Prisoners captured by the Germans were automatically suspected of disloyalty. If they survived the German concentration camps, then they must have been collaborators since the Germans treated POWs so cruelly. By the same twisted reasoning, escapees must have been working with their captors, given German efficiency. Sadly, many soldiers were repatriated from German POW camps to Soviet concentration camps.

Stalin also suspected the loyalty of national minorities within the former occupied territories. In 1937, concerned that they might cooperate with the Japanese, he ordered hundreds of thousands of Koreans living in the Soviet Far East rounded up and deported to Central Asia. During and after the war, many of the small nations of southern Russia and the Caucasus were brutally resettled in the vast expanses of Siberia or Kazakhstan. These deported peoples included Chechens, Crimean Tatars, and the Volga Germans, for example, as well as nationalists from the newly annexed Latvia, Lithuania, and Estonia. In his memoirs, General Secretary Nikita Khrushchev claims that Stalin contemplated deporting the entire Ukrainian nation of 40 million, but the logistics of moving so many people were simply unmanageable!

As the Cold War heated up, paranoia and isolationism reached new heights in the USSR. One of Stalin's top lieutenants, Andrei Zhdanov, the party boss of Leningrad and a cultural watchdog, initiated a campaign against all forms of cosmopolitanism in 1947. Cosmopolitanism was a code word for cultural influences that were not purely Russian, particularly those that were Jewish. Zhdanov publicly attacked the poet Anna Akhmatova and satirist Mikhail Zoshchenko for not publishing idealized, moral works in the vein of socialist realism. The *zhdanovshchina*, as it was called, exercised a stifling influence over the arts, the social sciences, and even the natural sciences. In biology, for example, Western genetics was rejected in favor of the quack theories of Trofim Lysenko, who claimed that characteristics acquired from the environment could then be transmitted to succeeding generations. Lysenko used his high-level connections to ruin his critics and to establish himself as dean of the scientific Soviet establishment. His ideas exercised a pernicious influence on Soviet science and agriculture well into the Khrushchev era.

During Stalin's final years, Soviet culture suffered greatly from the repressive atmosphere of the *zhdanovshchina*. Many of the best writers and artists had already fled to the West years before; the painter Marc Chagall and novelist Vladimir Nabokov are two notable examples. The late Stalin era was even more stultifying than the prewar USSR. Socialist realism sacrificed creativity for ideology, as painters churned out scenes of construction sites, idyllic collective farm life, heroic military battles, and, of course, scores of Lenins and Stalins. In music, talented composers such as Sergei Prokofiev, who had written the delightful children's score *Peter and the Wolf* in 1936, were accused of creating disharmonious music that was not appreciated by the working masses. The brilliant poet and novelist Boris Pasternak published mostly translations during the Stalin period; his masterpiece *Dr. Zhivago,* described by the author as "a spiritual history of the Russian revolution," was not published until 1957, and even then, it was available only to readers in the West.

Stalin's cult of personality rose to new heights during this period. The victory over Germany had confirmed his absolute power. Portraits, statues, and busts of the supreme leader adorned town squares, schools, offices, and many homes. Soviet newspapers such as *Pravda* and *Izvestiia* declared him "Friend and Teacher of All Toilers," the "Greatest Genius in History," and other absurdities; they carried stories glorifying Stalin for his political leadership, philosophical contributions, literary talents, and even his (nonexistent) expertise in linguistics, agronomy, and art. Academic writings would cite Stalin's works as the ultimate authority on every topic. The once-minor Bolshevik functionary who, as the Russian General Dmitrii Volkogonov explains in his biography, "had no skills or profession, unless being a half-baked priest can be considered a profession" became a godlike omnipotent figure in the last years of his life.

Constant public adulation did little to assuage Stalin's paranoia. The great dictator secluded himself in the Kremlin or various palatial retreats, surrounded by loyal retainers and under tight security. He seldom appeared in public, and in later years, traveled abroad only for the wartime conferences in Teheran (1943) and Potsdam (1945). Stalin worked late into the night, often summoning officials or experts for late-night Kremlin conversations. All of the suggestions conveyed at such meetings were understood to be orders and were carried out without question.

Soviet life in the late Stalin era was dreary, poor, and insulated from the rest of the world. Those few foreigners who were allowed entry were closely watched by the secret police. Even accidental contact with foreigners was cause for suspicion; marrying one was strictly forbidden. Soviet propaganda depicted life in the United States and other capitalist countries as wretched, while exalting Russian and Soviet accomplishments as the greatest in history. As Isaac Deutscher expressed it in his biography of Stalin, "Megalomania and xenophobia were to cure the people of their sense of inferiority, render them immune to those attractions of the western culture by which generations of the intelligentsia had been spellbound, protect them against the demoralizing impact of American wealth, and harden them for the trials of the Cold War and, if need be, for armed conflict."

Political control at this time was exercised through the Ministry of Internal Affairs (MVD), headed by Lavrentii Beria, a Georgian and close friend of Stalin. Beria, who had succeeded Nicholai Yezhov as head of the NKVD in 1938, was a complete moral degenerate. In Moscow, as in Tbilisi, where he had served as head of the Transcaucasian secret police, Beria used his unlimited power to abduct young girls off the streets and rape them. Fearful that Beria would use the MVD's vast power to assume the top position, his colleagues quickly engineered his arrest and execution immediately after Stalin's death.

Toward the end of Stalin's life, there were indications that he was laying the groundwork for a new purge. At the Nineteenth Party Congress in October 1952, a new, greatly enlarged Central Committee was elected; in addition, the Politburo was renamed the Presidium and was doubled in size. Stalin was very possibly getting ready to dismiss those Party veterans who, in the 1930s, had vaulted into the top ranks over the bodies of the Old Bolsheviks. In another ominous development, in January 1953, nine high-level Kremlin doctors were accused of plotting to use medicine to assassinate Soviet military leaders. This fabrication, termed the "Doctors' Plot," reflected a growing anti-Semitism since many of the doctors had Jewish surnames. Mercifully, the "Father of the Peoples" died before the next round of bloodletting got under way.

Stalin's death on March 5, 1953, at age 73 shocked a nation that had perhaps come to believe the propaganda that its god-leader was truly omnipotent. He suffered two strokes within a week, and his daughter, Svetlana Alliluyeva, recalled that leeches were used in the final hours to treat his illness. Beria clearly expected to succeed the great dictator, but the fear he inspired in other Presidium members led to his arrest and execution. A massive public funeral was held for Stalin, with 30-gun salutes and thousands of mourners filing past the bier. Afterward, Stalin's body was preserved and his remains were interred next to those of Lenin in the mausoleum on Red Square.

With Stalin and Beria gone, the most repressive aspects of Soviet rule abated. Those accused in the Doctors' Plot were released. Senior Party leaders—Nikita Khrushchev, Georgii Malenkov, Nikolai Bulganin, Anastas Mikoyan, Kliment Voroshilov, and Lazar Kaganovich—now spared a second purge, reduced the Presidium from 25 to 10 and agreed to rule the Soviet Union collectively. None of Stalin's successors held the absolute power he had acquired; they did not resort to terror as he had, nor did they seek to remake society. But for the next three decades, they preserved the essentials of the Stalinist system—the single-party monopoly of political power, socialized industry and collective agriculture, censorship, and indoctrination. The camps would eventually disgorge many of their political prisoners, but they were not closed down. Stalinism proved much more durable than Stalin himself.

7

De-Stalinization and Developed Socialism, 1953–1985

[W]e still have a lot to learn from the capitalists. There are many things we still don't do as well as they do. It's been more than fifty years since the working class of the Soviet Union carried out its Revolution under the leadership of the Great Lenin, yet, to my great disappointment and irritation, we still haven't been able to catch up with the capitalists.
—Nikita Khrushchev, *Khrushchev Remembers: The Last Testament*

In the wake of Joseph Stalin's death, the Soviet Union confronted the problem of succession, just as it had after Lenin's death in 1924. Stalin left no testament designating a successor; more significantly, it was not even clear what position conferred final executive authority. Stalin's power had evolved from his position as General Secretary of the Communist Party's Central Committee, which gave him control over personnel and administrative matters. By the end of his rule, Stalin's offices and titles mattered little—he had amassed virtually unlimited personal power. None of Stalin's heirs approached his stature, nor were the Presidium members willing to grant any one of their peers the arbitrary power Stalin had possessed.

The solution was to divide the top posts among themselves in a form of collective leadership. After Beria's arrest and execution, the Ministry of Internal

Affairs (MVD) was divided into two organizations: a criminal policing agency that retained the MVD title; and a separate secret police, the Committee for State Security (KGB), which would be subordinate to the Council of Ministers. Georgii Malenkov became Prime Minister, heading the government's Council of Ministers, and, for a time, appeared to be the most powerful of the top Soviet leaders. Nikita Khrushchev assumed the position of General Secretary (renamed First Secretary) of the Communist Party Central Committee. Khrushchev, a former Party Secretary from Ukraine, used his new position to appoint supporters to important republic and regional levels of the Party organization. Viacheslav Molotov, Stalin's confidant, who had signed the Nazi-Soviet Pact of 1939, became the Minister of Foreign Affairs. Once they had disposed of Soviet secret police chief Lavrentii Beria, the main threat, each began maneuvering against the others to consolidate and expand his power.

The Soviet leadership, aside from Molotov and Lazar Kaganovich, agreed on the need for reform, in particular to address the needs of Soviet consumers who had been asked to make heroic sacrifices during the Stalin period. Domestically, there was some dispute over whether to continue Stalin's focus on heavy industrial and military production or to emphasize agricultural production and consumer goods to satisfy pent-up demands. Malenkov argued for lower prices on food and industrial goods to curry favor with consumers, while reducing *kolkhoz* taxes. Costs would be covered through reductions in the military and heavy industry budgets. Khrushchev criticized Malenkov's plans to enact deep cuts in heavy industry and the military, countering with a low-cost scheme to bring millions of acres of new land in northern Kazakhstan, Siberia, and southern Russia under cultivation. This Virgin Lands project initially succeeded in boosting the grain harvest, but the arid land was soon depleted, and massive dust storms eroded much of the once-fertile topsoil. Moreover, the project enticed tens of thousands of Russians and Ukrainians to settle in Turkic Kazakhstan, laying the groundwork for ethnic tensions in the post-communist era.

In the absence of open political debate and competition among political parties, as occurs in democracies, political infighting in communist systems took the form of policy discussions couched in esoteric language. When a particular policy line was discredited, it also ensured the political decline of that policy's proponents. Malenkov's reform program was vulnerable because it broke radically with Stalinist tradition, threatened the interests of the Soviet military-industrial complex, and would likely fuel inflation. Khrushchev was able to exploit these opportunities and maneuvered Malenkov out of the premiership by the end of 1954, replacing him with his own appointee, Nikolai Bulganin.

New approaches were also needed in foreign policy. Confrontation in Europe had united the Western allies under NATO's military umbrella (the

North Atlantic Treaty Organization was established in 1949), while in the east, the stalemated Korean War led to an American military buildup in Japan and the western Pacific. The Soviet leadership moved quickly to end the impasse in Korea; an armistice was signed in July of 1953. Khrushchev also mended fences with Yugoslav leader Josip Tito, whom Stalin had excommunicated from the socialist camp. A high-level delegation of the Presidium visited Belgrade in May 1955, pledged not to interfere in Yugoslavia's domestic affairs, and acknowledged that different roads to socialism were acceptable. Harmony was restored in the communist world, as was Moscow's leading position, but both would soon be challenged.

In a conciliatory move to the West, Soviet troops were withdrawn from Austria in 1955, in exchange for that country's declaration of neutrality. But the Cold War, and the arms race it spawned, continued. The United States exploded its first thermonuclear (fusion) device in 1952; the Soviets tested their own hydrogen bomb the following year. Anti-communist paranoia had peaked in the United States during the McCarthy era (1950–1953), but hysteria over the possibility of a surprise nuclear attack continued to dominate American culture throughout the 1950s, and well into the 1960s.

Joseph Stalin's death unleashed demands for change that had been ruthlessly suppressed for years. The relatives of those arrested and thrown in the camps by the MVD used the regime's admission that Beria was a criminal to argue for the release of their loved ones. Camp prisoners (*zeks*) began demanding better treatment, and major camp uprisings were reported in Siberia and Kazakhstan. In Eastern Europe, workers went out on strike in East Berlin and Czechoslovakia. The Soviet Party leadership had to come to terms with the Stalin repressions, and a commission was appointed to study the question.

First Secretary Khrushchev delivered the results of this investigation at the Twentieth Party Congress in 1956. Party congresses had once been important expanded meetings of Party faithful, but had lost much of their significance and were rarely held under Stalin. Khrushchev restored the congress as a major forum for announcing new directions in Party policy. In a closed session held after the congress had completed its scheduled work, Khrushchev delivered his Secret Speech criticizing Stalin's cult of personality and detailing his crimes against loyal Party officials. Khrushchev was selective in his criticism—Stalin's forced industrialization program, the early repressions, and the horrors of collectivization were accepted as positive contributions toward building socialism. Likewise, critics of the Stalinist bureaucratic socialist system, most notably Leon Trotsky and Nikolai Bukharin, were not rehabilitated.

Nikita Sergeevich Khrushchev was very different from his predecessor, Stalin. While Stalin was slim, with a dark mustache and piercing eyes, Khrushchev was bald, stocky, and ebullient. Khrushchev was born in the village of

Kalinovka near Kursk in 1894. He worked as a shepherd and a locksmith, and was drafted to fight in World War I. Khrushchev joined the Communist Party in 1918, and fought with the Red Army in the Civil War. Later, he studied in Party schools and quickly worked his way up the ranks of the Party bureaucracy. During World War II, he served as Communist Party First Secretary for Ukraine when that republic was under German occupation. After the war, he helped reorganize Soviet agriculture, and always considered himself an expert on farming. Khrushchev did not share his predecessor's paranoia, and he was quite comfortable touring the countryside, joking with peasants or observing workers in the factories. In many respects, he was a populist leader—coarse, genial, and down to earth. However, his lack of culture and boorish manners, particularly when traveling abroad, embarrassed many Russians.

By embarking on his de-Stalinization program, Khrushchev planned to disassociate himself from Stalin's terror, and sought to reassure Communist Party officials that the arbitrary abuses they had suffered in the past would not be repeated. Soviet politics, he promised, would return to the Leninist practices of collective leadership. The principles of socialist legality would be observed, as would Communist Party regulations and the Soviet constitution. Tens of thousands of camp inmates, both political prisoners and criminals, were released after the Twentieth Party Congress speech; millions more were rehabilitated posthumously.

Khrushchev's de-Stalinization campaign clearly tried to preserve the legitimacy of the political, social, and economic system Stalin had created, while renouncing the more threatening aspects of Stalinism. Although the speech was supposedly available only to leading Party officials, the contents soon became readily available both within the USSR and abroad. It had a dramatic impact. Many older communists who had dedicated their lives to the cause became disillusioned. Members of the optimistic younger generation interpreted the attack on Stalin as a sign of impending political liberalization, raising their expectations for significant reform.

Khrushchev's revelations reverberated through the communist world. In Eastern Europe, intellectuals, workers, and students took to the streets demanding political reforms and the dismissal of their Stalinist leaders. Eastern Europeans naturally resented Soviet control over their foreign and defense policies, and the mandatory eight-year study of the Russian language required in schools. In Poland, where Soviet imperialism and the imposition of communism were bitterly resisted, the Party leadership ended Poland's collectivization drive and allowed some 80 percent of the farms to revert to private ownership. The Catholic Church, a repository of Polish national identity, was allowed a greater degree of independence. Poland's leaders also dumped the Stalinist Party Secretary Boleslaw Bierut and appointed Wladyslaw Gomulka, a Polish nationalist, in his place. Khrushchev and the Soviet leadership were furious that they had not been consulted on the matter, but Gomulka maintained stability and, after several rounds of high-level shuttle diplomacy, the Soviets acquiesced to the Poles' decision.

Hungary was a different matter. Replacing the Stalinist Matyas Rakosi only encouraged popular demands for greater democracy. In the fall of 1956, strike committees and independent workers' councils were formed, censorship was relaxed, and political parties began to form. Mobs attacked the secret police headquarters. American broadcasts through Radio Free Europe hinted that the West would support Hungary's bid for independence from the communist bloc. When the Hungarians announced their intention to withdraw from the Soviet-led defense pact, the Warsaw Treaty Organization (or Warsaw Pact), Soviet troops were sent into Budapest to crush the nascent revolution.

Soviet ties to the Eastern European empire were formalized through two institutions: the Council for Mutual Economic Assistance, or CMEA, established in 1949; and the Warsaw Treaty Organization (WTO), formed in 1955. The CMEA was designed as the communist equivalent of Western Europe's Coal and Steel Community to facilitate economic cooperation among member nations. Under Stalin, it was used mainly as a vehicle to funnel resources from Eastern Europe into the USSR. His successors promoted a more equitable division of labor, with the USSR supplying oil, natural gas, electricity, and other natural resources; the more developed East European states (Czechoslovakia and East Germany) provided manufactured goods, and the less developed (Bulgaria and Romania) contributed agricultural products. CMEA never achieved a high degree of integration, however, and most of its members (including the Soviet Union) believed that they were contributing more than they received in benefits.

The Warsaw Pact, a military defense alliance, was created at the same time that Soviet forces left Austria and West Germany was admitted into NATO. A Soviet general invariably commanded the WTO, and Soviet troops constituted the bulk of WTO forces. Though allegedly a bulwark against aggression from Western Europe and the United States, the Warsaw Pact was not an alliance of equals, and it is questionable how well Polish, Hungarian, or Czech troops would have carried out Soviet orders in the event of a conflict with the West. Nicolai Ceausescu, Romania's dictator from 1965 to 1989, refused to even allow armed WTO forces to be stationed on Romanian territory. The WTO's main function was to preserve the Soviet Empire in Eastern Europe. Warsaw Pact troops guaranteed Moscow's political control over Eastern Europe, but exercised direct military force on just two occasions: the invasion of Hungary in November 1956, and the invasion of Czechoslovakia in August 1968. As Poles liked to joke, when Soviet tourists visited Eastern Europe, they drove tanks instead of cars.

Challenges to communist rule in Eastern Europe and scattered instances of domestic protest within the USSR led some in the Soviet hierarchy to question the wisdom of de-Stalinization. Khrushchev's administrative reforms also sparked considerable opposition from Soviet officials. He had strongly condemned bureaucratic sclerosis at the Twentieth Party Congress, and advocated greater participation by workers and farmers in Soviet management. Oversight of industrial production was shifted from the center to the republics or regions. In 1957, Khrushchev sought to dismantle much of the central bureaucracy by creating 105 regional economic councils (*sovnarkhozy*) to manage economic development. The *sovnarkhozy* reforms shifted power from the central ministries in Moscow to the regions, and were opposed by Party and government elites in the Presidium and the Council of Ministers, who recognized them as a challenge to their authority.

Resistance to Khrushchev's experiments culminated in a move by several members of the Presidium to oust him from his position as General Secretary in June 1957. Claiming that the larger CPSU Central Committee had elected him, Khrushchev insisted that the Presidium's action must be ratified by this body. With the help of war hero Marshal Georgii Zhukov, Central Committee members were flown in from the provincial capitals at short notice. Since many owed their position to Khrushchev's patronage, the wily leader managed to prevail over his rivals, whom he later dubbed the Anti-Party Group.

This incident reveals much about the changed conditions in post-Stalin USSR. First, open opposition to Khrushchev's reforms indicated a more relaxed political climate. No single leader could exercise the absolute control over the Party and the government formerly wielded by Stalin. Second, Khrushchev triumphed by relying on formal Party procedures—the Presidium voted against him (eight to four), while a majority of the Central Committee voted to keep him in power. Arbitrary rule was being supplanted by more routinized and predictable ways of conducting politics. Third, the consequences of losing in Soviet politics were far less severe than they were under Stalin. Khrushchev's opponents resigned from the Presidium and were given less prestigious positions—Viacheslav Molotov became ambassador to Mongolia, Georgii Malenkov director of a power station in Kazakhstan, Lazar Kaganovich director of a cement plant in the Urals—but they kept their pensions, many of their privileges, and, most importantly, their lives.

After dismissing his opponents, Khrushchev appointed his supporters to the Presidium and further consolidated his power. In March of 1958, he eased Nikolai Bulganin out as Premier and assumed the top government office himself. Khrushchev then pursued a new round of reforms. Providing more meat, milk, and butter for the spartan Soviet diet was one of his top priorities. This was to be accomplished, though, without any fundamental changes in the collective farm system. Like many communist leaders, Khrushchev believed that campaigns and exhortations were preferable to material incentives in motivating people. In 1957, he had promised to overtake the United States in meat production within four years; enthusiastic local officials, tempted by the opportunity to boost their careers, achieved impressive short-term results that, over the long term, did more harm than good. Khrushchev also developed a fixation with corn, reinforced by a visit to Iowa in 1959, and ordered its planting throughout the USSR. Millions of rubles were then wasted on a crop unsuited to Soviet soil and climatic conditions, and by the early 1960s, the USSR was forced to import grain on the world market. In private, Russians ridiculed the First Secretary, calling him the "corn guy" (*kukuruznik*).

Great progress was made during Khrushchev's tenure in terms of providing housing for the Soviet consumer. A large portion of Soviet housing had been destroyed by the Germans during World War II, and Stalin had been slow to undertake reconstruction. Many families lived in *kommunalki*, small communal apartments where they shared a kitchen and bathroom with several other families. The truly poor lived in *barraki* (barracks), long two-story buildings that were very similar to college dormitories. A family of four might spend years in a 12' x 12'-foot room, cooking on a hot plate, and sharing toilet facilities with a dozen other families. Khrushchev ordered the construction of thousands of high-rise apartments to deal with the housing shortage. While the Khrushcheviki apartments were of poor quality and the elevators often broke down, the average family now had at least two or three rooms with a kitchen and bath they could call their own.

THE THAW

The decade after Stalin died was characterized by a relaxation of political controls in the cultural sphere and the revival of literature and the arts. Writers began to challenge the canon of socialist realism, which had reached a repressive zenith under culture tsar Andrei Zhdanov. Ilya Ehrenburg's novel *The Thaw* (1954), a critical look at life in a factory town, marked the beginning of this period and provided a label for it. In 1956, Vladimir Dudintsev's *Not by Bread Alone* portrayed an individualist inventor, Lopatkin, who struggles heroically against the stifling bureaucratism of his collective. Lopatkin eventually convinces his skeptical bosses to adopt his innovations, but only after being harassed and incarcerated in a labor camp. Although Dudintsev's book was published as one component of Khrushchev's campaign against bureaucratism, the Soviet writers' union and Khrushchev himself condemned Dudintsev's novel as unduly critical of life under socialism. Dudintsev's second major novel, *Robed in White*, a critique of hack biologist Trofim Lysenko, was not published until 1987, under Gorbachev.

Khrushchev's attack on Stalin at the Twentieth Party Congress encouraged even bolder efforts. The most explosive work of the post-Stalin period was that of Aleksandr Solzhenitsyn. An artillery officer arrested late in World War II for making derogatory comments about Stalin in his correspondence home, Solzhenitsyn was sentenced to eight years in the camps and another three in internal exile. His first novel was published in 1962 in the literary thick journal, *Novyi Mir* (New World). Titled *One Day in the Life of Ivan Denisovich*, it details an ordinary day through the eyes of a concentration camp prisoner incarcerated simply for surrendering to the Germans. Ivan Denisovich's life revolves around the meager rations, bitter cold, and brutal guards of a strict regime camp. Later, in his novels *First Circle* and *Cancer Ward,* Solzhenitsyn depicted conditions in the elite camps (for specialists and intellectuals who were engaged in scientific work) and in exile, both of which he had experienced directly. By the late 1960s, however, the Thaw was reversed. *First Circle, Cancer Ward,* and Solzhenitsyn's three-volume encyclopedia of the labor camp system, *The Gulag Archipelago,* were all rejected by Soviet publishers, and copies of *Ivan Denisovich* were quietly removed from public library shelves. Solzhenitsyn's powerful writing, however, did much to discredit communism in intellectual European circles.

Poetry was another popular vehicle of expression. Yevgeny Yevtushenko was the most popular young poet of the times; fans filled soccer stadiums to hear his readings. His poem "Stalin's Heirs" appeared in the Communist Party newspaper *Pravda* in 1957; in it, Yevtushenko warned against Stalin's followers, who were biding their time in the hope of returning to power. "Babi Yar" (1960) commemorated the massacre of Jews by Nazi troops in Ukraine during World War II. Acknowledging that the Jews had been singled out for extermination was sensitive in the Soviet Union; the regime preferred to assert that all Soviet peoples had suffered equally. Yevtushenko's poetry was tolerated because he praised socialism, but his was a humanist, tolerant, international socialism that had little in common with Stalinism.

The Thaw clearly had its limits. Censorship had not been abolished, and artists were still expected to follow the general principles of socialist realism. Boris Pasternak's novel about the Revolution and Civil War, *Dr. Zhivago,* was condemned as a reactionary work glorifying the enemies of socialism, and *Novyi Mir* refused to publish it. In his memoirs, Khrushchev insists that he favored releasing the novel in the USSR. Presumably, he could have easily ordered the manuscript published. When it was released in the West, Soviet authorities were infuriated at the praise heaped on the book. Pasternak was pressured into refusing the Nobel Prize for literature, which was bestowed on him by the Swedish Academy in 1958.

Artistic experiments were permitted during the Thaw, and works by Picasso and Matisse reappeared in the galleries of Moscow and Leningrad. But modern art encountered great resistance from the authorities, most notably Khrushchev himself. At the 1962 Manezh Exhibition in Moscow, Khrushchev personally viewed the modernist abstract works. After he crudely belittled some of the paintings, calling them "dog shit," Khrushchev peremptorily declared that artists would have to paint differently or leave the Soviet Union. Not one kopek of state money would go to support such work, he asserted. The exhibit was closed, and the Party launched a campaign to restore ideological purity and eliminate bourgeois influences in Soviet art.

INTERNATIONAL RELATIONS

Soviet foreign policy in the Khrushchev era was marked by several major setbacks, the biggest of which was the break with the People's Republic of China. The Chinese Communist Party claimed that Khrushchev's revelations at the Twentieth Party Congress undermined communism's international prestige. China's preeminent leader, Mao Zedong, personally resented de-Stalinization; he was determined to wield unlimited power and to build his own personality cult. Mao also bitterly opposed Khrushchev's promise at the Twentieth Party Congress to pursue peaceful coexistence with the West. Khrushchev's new doctrine rejected the Stalinist assertion that war between the socialist and capitalist camps was inevitable. Nuclear weapons could destroy civilization; in the atomic age, peaceful competition, premised on the Marxist notion that socialism would eventually triumph, was the only logical means of struggle between the two systems. This victory of socialism through peaceful competition is what Khrushchev meant when he startled the West by declaring, "We will bury you."

By contrast, Mao was perfectly willing to start a war; he wanted Soviet support to regain Taiwan, which was then militarily defended by U.S. troops. In 1958, he proposed to Andrei Gromyko (Soviet Minister of Foreign Affairs from 1957 to 1985) that in the event of a conflict between the United States and China, China's strategy would be to draw American forces deep into the interior, where they could be annihilated by Soviet nuclear weapons. With its huge population, Mao reasoned, China could absorb 300 million casualties and socialism would still triumph. In his *Memoirs*, Gromyko writes, "I was flabbergasted." He assured Mao that this proposal would never be approved by his fellow leaders in the Kremlin.

Convinced the Chinese communists might draw the Soviet Union into war, the Presidium terminated the Soviet-Chinese nuclear cooperation program late in the 1950s. In addition, Soviet technical advisors who were helping with some 330 Chinese industrial projects were recalled. The Soviet leaders were appalled by Mao's bizarre economic experiment, the Great Leap Forward (1958–1960), which was supposed to transform China into a major industrial power, but instead resulted in a massive famine. For their part, the Chinese strongly resented the Test Ban Treaty negotiated by the United States, the Soviet Union, and Great Britain in 1963 to limit the yield and venues of nuclear testing. The two largest communist powers also began competing for allies among the newly independent Third World nations. These factors, aggravated by the personal animosity between Khrushchev and Mao, led to open estrangement by the beginning of the 1960s.

Relations with the United States and Western Europe improved somewhat from the late Stalin years, but the Cold War continued to fester. When the Soviet Union launched the first spacecraft, *Sputnik*, in 1957, Americans were both surprised and intimidated by this accomplishment. Massive U.S. resources were poured into scientific and technical education, military hardware, and Soviet area studies. The downing of U.S. Captain Francis Gary Powers' U-2 spy plane deep inside Soviet territory in 1960 resulted in the cancellation of a summit meeting scheduled to be held in Paris. John F. Kennedy's 1960 presidential campaign included promises to overcome a missile gap; later evidence that the missile gap was nonexistent, and that U.S. nuclear forces were superior to those in the USSR, did little to stem the nuclear arms race.

The former German capital, Berlin, was a recurring source of tension. The exodus of nearly 2 million East Germans into West Berlin, the sector controlled by the French, British, and Americans, constituted a brain drain from communist East Germany. In 1961, the Soviets and East Germans stemmed the flow by constructing a wall around the perimeter of West Berlin. The Berlin Wall remained as a testament to oppression, and a major source of dispute between the United States and the USSR, until it was torn down in 1989, as communism collapsed throughout Eastern Europe.

A major forum for East-West confrontation was the struggle for allies and influence in the newly independent Third World nations of Asia, Africa, and the Middle East. Many of the former colonies rejected capitalism as being inextricably linked to colonialism. The socialist model offered an attractive alternative—impressive Soviet economic and scientific achievements provided convincing evidence that central planning and socialist ownership were more effective in promoting development than the free market. Under Khrushchev, the Soviet Union established close ties with Indonesia, India, Afghanistan, Burma, Egypt, and Iran, supplying generous loans, technical advisors, and military equipment. In addition, students from developing nations were invited to study free of charge at the best Soviet universities and institutes. Patrice Lumumba University in Moscow, named after the socialist leader of the Congo, catered exclusively to a Third World clientele.

However, few of these countries became puppets of the Soviet Union, although many foreign policy analysts in the United States believed this to be the case. Powerful nationalist forces limited Soviet influence, as did frequent regime changes, which deposed leaders who were friendly to the USSR. For example, links to Indonesia were severed in 1965, when President Sukarno was overthrown by General Suharto amid a massacre of thousands of Indonesian Communist Party members. Substantial investments in Egypt came to naught when President Gamal Abdel Nasser died and his successor, Anwar Sadat, expelled all Soviet advisors in 1972. The United States developed close relations with both of these nations once the Soviets had departed.

The most critical point by far in East-West relations during the Khrushchev era was the Cuban Missile Crisis of October 1962. After defeating Cuba's corrupt dictator Fulgencio Batista, and taking power in 1959, Fidel Castro declared Cuba socialist and aligned his country with the Soviet Union. In August of 1962, U.S. spy planes flying over Cuban territory discovered medium-range Soviet nuclear missile complexes in Cuba, 90 miles from Florida, that were capable of hitting most cities in the eastern United States, together with surface-to-air missile sites to protect the installations from air attack. After contemplating various options, President Kennedy ordered a naval quarantine, or blockade, of Cuba, which was technically an act of war, and demanded that the USSR withdraw the missiles. After nearly two weeks of confrontation and confusing diplomatic exchanges, the Kremlin agreed to withdraw their weapons in exchange for American promises not to invade Cuba and to withdraw obsolete U.S. missiles targeted at the Soviet Union from Turkey. Recently released information suggests that the Soviet leadership did not intend to start a war or provoke a crisis; rather, installing missiles in Cuba was a relatively quick and cheap way to overcome strategic Soviet inferiority.

UNFULFILLED PROMISES

Khrushchev constantly emphasized Soviet accomplishments, and he bragged about plans to catch up and overtake the West in agriculture, science, and industry. At the Twenty-Second Party Congress in 1961, he made the rash promise that the current generation would live under full communism, that is, a society in which there would be no scarcity, no wages, and no markets. He also introduced a new ideological concept, the All-People's State, in which a congenial alliance of the three major social classes (workers, peasants, and intelligentsia) replaced the dictatorship of the proletariat. In practical terms, this meant that greater popular participation was encouraged among the population, but was still under strict Communist Party supervision. Local governments (the councils, or Soviets) were to be reinvigorated. Comrades' courts, staffed by ordinary citizens and empowered to deal with minor criminal cases, were promoted as an example of democracy and socialist legality. Another innovation was the *druzhina*, a people's militia, made up of young (often Komsomol) volunteers who wore armbands and patrolled the streets looking for miscreants.

The aim of these programs was to socialize citizens to more responsible behavior and a stronger commitment to socialism through greater participation in the system. But Soviet politics remained, as Russians frequently observed, like the weather—it came from on high, and most people could do nothing about it. Khrushchev's modest attempts at expanding participation were jettisoned by his successors toward the end of the 1960s and, although they insisted that Soviet democracy was continuing to expand under the rubric of developed socialism, the Brezhnev era (1964–1982) was decidedly less liberal.

By 1964, Khrushchev had managed to antagonize most of the powerful interests in the Soviet Union. Regional and local Party officials resented the frequent personnel changes and the 1962 decision to divide their responsibilities into separate agricultural and industrial portfolios. Government ministers had been alienated by the creation of the regional economic councils. By reducing the standing army and shifting expenditures toward nuclear weapons, while neglecting conventional armaments, Khrushchev had earned the enmity of the USSR's top military leaders. Other annoying traits included his frequent reversals on policy matters, ill-considered experiments in agriculture, and boorish behavior, such as reportedly pounding his shoe on the lectern at the United Nations during a speech by a Philippine delegate. Regardless of whether or not this particular event happened (and Khrushchev biographer William Taubman presents evidence both for and against) the Soviet people were frequently embarrassed by their erratic leader.

In October 1964, the Presidium demanded his resignation. At a special emergency meeting of the Central Committee, Party ideologist Mikhail Suslov charged the First Secretary with violating the principle of collective leadership, mismanaging agriculture and industry, and damaging the Communist Party through his frequent reorganization schemes. Leonid Brezhnev, a rather bland protégé of Khrushchev's who would succeed him as Party leader, criticized his attempts to restore a cult of personality. His enforced retirement was approved by the Central Committee and the 70-year-old Khrushchev retreated to his dacha outside Moscow, where he tended his garden and eventually taped two volumes of memoirs. Aside from occasional references to the purveyor of harebrained schemes, the Soviet press did not again mention Nikita Khrushchev until his death in 1971.

BREZHNEV AND COMPANY

The first order of business for the new regime was to restore stability to Soviet politics. Leonid Ilyich Brezhnev, who assumed the position of General

Secretary of the CPSU at age 58, proclaimed renewed adherence to the principle of collective leadership and assured Party officials that frequent personnel changes were a thing of the past. Communist Party cadres were now allowed to hold their positions for life, barring gross malfeasance. Brezhnev was a bureaucrat of limited intelligence with an interest in agriculture. Born in 1906 in Kamenskoye (renamed Dneprodzherzhinsk under Soviet rule), he attended a classical gymnasium and dreamed of being an actor. Brezhnev joined the Komsomol in 1923, studied agriculture and land management, and graduated from the Dneprodzherzhinsk Metallurgical Institute in the 1930s. During World War II, he served as a political commissar; later, his memoirs, entitled *The Small Earth,* became required reading for all high school students. After the war, he was appointed CPSU First Secretary in Moldavia, and then First Secretary of Kazakhstan. Brezhnev was granted membership in the Central Committee Presidium in 1957, and became a Secretary of the Party Central Committee in 1963.

The new Soviet leaders divided the leading Party and government positions between two individuals; Khrushchev had held both positions since 1958. Alexei Kosygin, chairman of the Leningrad Party organization during the war and the former Minister of Light Industry, became Chairman of the Council of Ministers, or Premier. Most of Kosygin's experience had been in textiles and consumer goods industries, and as Premier, he would assume much of the responsibility for industrial production. Nikolai Podgornyi took over the less influential office of Chairman of the Supreme Soviet, often described as the presidency of the USSR.

Some of Khrushchev's experiments were undone almost immediately. The regional economic councils were abolished in 1965, and centralized ministries were restored under the Council of Ministers. Kosygin, though, understood the need for reform in the Soviet economy. In the mid-1960s, growth rates had declined to 4–5 percent per year from the 7–9 percent rates of the 1950s, and the quality of goods produced through central planning was often shoddy. Soviet economist Yevsei Liberman had first proposed introducing some limited forms of profit making and greater enterprise autonomy in 1962, while reducing the role of the State Planning Committee (Gosplan) in Soviet industry. Some of his ideas subsequently found their way into Kosygin's reforms.

The post-Khrushchev leadership agreed on the need to improve the material well-being of the population and to dampen consumer expectations (or at least avoid the wild promises voiced by their predecessor). Kosygin linked his political reputation to the development of consumer goods and light industry, using a modified version of Liberman's ideas. Brezhnev, who had helped implement the Virgin Lands project in Kazakhstan, stressed massive investment and the expanded use of fertilizer and scientific methods in agriculture. The defense establishment, a powerful vested interest, also received a large share of the budgetary pie. Since state investment favored agriculture, the consumer, and the military, long-term capital investment in heavy industry was slighted. By the 1980s, these priorities had caused economic growth to slow to a crawl.

Structural weaknesses in the Soviet economy paralleled similar problems in Eastern Europe. The more highly industrialized Eastern European countries—East Germany, Czechoslovakia, Poland, and Hungary—experienced a slowdown in growth rates first. These countries struggled to meet the growing aspirations of their people. Under Janos Kadar, Hungary had been gradually reforming since the 1956 revolution; a New Economic Mechanism introduced in 1968 broadened these reforms. East Germany relied on technology and, after 1972, subsidies from West Germany to maintain a relatively high standard of living. Poland's leadership borrowed technology and money from the West throughout the 1970s, and then had to resort to price increases to cover their massive debts. When the Polish government raised prices on basic food items, workers and students took to the streets in protest. Major public disturbances occurred in Poland in 1968, 1970, and 1976. Massive strikes originating in the Gdansk shipyards in 1980–1981 led to the formation of the labor organization Solidarity and forced Soviet officials to recognize that socialism had major structural flaws.

Czechoslovakia under Anton Novotny had combined rigid central planning with neo-Stalinist repression. When Alexander Dubcek replaced Novotny as General Secretary in January 1968, the Czechoslovak Communist Party quickly adopted market reforms, relaxed censorship, permitted the formation of independent political parties and interest groups, and severed links to the Soviet KGB. Soviet leaders watched these developments with growing unease through the spring and summer; Eastern Europe's Communist leaders fretted about the possible spill-over of democratic ideas into their domains. After several attempts at negotiation, the Kremlin ordered Warsaw Pact forces to invade Prague and restore order. Dubcek was bundled off to Moscow, pressured to capitulate, and then forced to retire. His successor, Gustav Husak, steered the country back to the Leninist model of rigid Party control.

The invasion of Czechoslovakia was observed with dismay by the more reform-minded intellectuals in the USSR and Eastern Europe. A tiny, eight-person demonstration took place in Moscow's Red Square, but it was quickly disbanded by the police. Pavel Litvinov, grandson of Stalin's Minister of Foreign Affairs, Maksim Litvinov (1930–1938), was one of the participants. An authoritative article published in *Pravda* articulated what came to be known as the Brezhnev Doctrine—an open declaration of the Soviet Union's right and duty to intervene with force in countries where socialism was endangered. The Brezhnev Doctrine preserved Soviet control over the East European empire; it remained in effect until Mikhail Gorbachev renounced it early in 1989.

Premier Alexei Kosygin's identification with economic reform proved a liability when the Czechoslovak experience demonstrated the political dangers associated with reform. After 1968, his influence in the Soviet hierarchy waned, and the conservative Brezhnev emerged as first among equals. In 1969, he contemplated rehabilitating Stalin, but opposition from the Polish and Hungarian Communist Parties quashed this idea. However, this setback did not deter Brezhnev from creating his own personality cult. By the time of his death, this General Secretary of modest accomplishments had received over 200 medals, including four Hero of the Soviet Union awards and the rank of Marshal of the USSR for his outstanding contributions to building socialism. The 1977 Constitution represented his crowning achievement, the new stage of developed socialism, and was generally known as the Brezhnev Constitution.

Brezhnev, like many chief executives, soon discovered the advantages of being a world statesman. Starting in 1969, the Soviet Union and the United States began discussions on limiting long-range nuclear missiles, the Strategic Arms Limitations Talks (SALT). President Richard Nixon, who had built his political career bashing communism, was now willing to deal with Soviet leaders as equals and even partners. Brezhnev in turn basked in the publicity of summit negotiations: Nixon visited Moscow in May 1972; Brezhnev went to the United States in June 1973; and Brezhnev and Nixon's successor, Gerald Ford, met in the Russian Far East port of Vladivostok in December 1974. In addition to the welcome media attention, summit meetings provided opportunities for Brezhnev to add to his collection of foreign limousines and sports cars, given to him as gifts by fellow statesmen.

This relaxation of tensions, détente, was formalized in the Strategic Arms Limitations Treaty (SALT I), the Anti-Ballistic Missile Treaty (ABM), and the Basic Principles agreement between the United States and the Soviet Union, all signed in 1972. Ostensibly an attempt to cap the arms race, the SALT I negotiations merely established numerical limits on missile launchers, which were then raised in the second round of talks. The Soviet side was unwilling to permit inspections on the ground, so both sides verified the limits through spy satellites. SALT also failed to constrain technology. Both sides quickly developed multiple-warhead, independently targeted reentry vehicles (MIRVs), adding more nuclear weapons to the same number of missiles and further accelerating the arms race. The ABM Treaty limited each side's ability to construct missile defense systems, premised on Mutual Assured Destruction (MAD). The MAD doctrine reasoned that if Soviet and American cities remained undefended, neither power would risk initiating nuclear war since the result would be mutual annihilation.

The Basic Principles agreement, a political document, provided for various economic, environmental, cultural, and technological exchanges, such as the joint Apollo-Soyuz space mission in 1975. Trade expanded as the Soviet Union purchased grain from farmers in the Midwest and in turn exported oil products and Stolichnaya vodka to the United States. Dozens of joint projects on air and water pollution, soil erosion, agricultural runoff, and noise pollution were operating by the mid-1970s.

Soviet-American rapprochement was very much driven by events in Asia. The U.S. presence in Indochina had been expanding since 1964, as Washington supported the anti-communist regime in South Vietnam. Soviet support for the communist regime in North Vietnam also grew, from $50 million in 1964 to nearly $1 billion per year from 1967 to 1972. Soviet support for North Vietnam paid major dividends by forcing the United States to commit troops and money to an increasingly unpopular cause. Moscow's support for North Vietnam was also a component of its rivalry with China. Throughout the 1960s, Beijing had portrayed the Chinese model as better suited to the lesser developed countries, and during the tumultuous Cultural Revolution (1966–1969), invective against the revisionist Soviet Union escalated. When armed forces of the two nations engaged in border clashes along the Amur River in 1969, the Kremlin sounded out Washington about its possible reaction to a preemptive strike on Chinese nuclear installations.

Détente was vitally important to the Soviet Union. First, cordial relations with the United States raised the stakes for China of any potential aggression against the USSR. President Nixon and National Security Advisor (later Secretary of State) Henry Kissinger realized this, and adroitly played the China card to extract concessions from the Soviets. In addition, America was now treating the USSR as an equal, militarily and diplomatically. The Soviet Union had in fact achieved nuclear parity with the United States by the end of the 1960s, as a result of its rapid nuclear buildup. In Europe, conventional Warsaw Pact forces greatly outnumbered NATO in tanks, troops, and aircraft. In 1972, the two alliances entered into the Mutual and Balanced Force Reductions Talks in Vienna, but there was no real progress in conventional arms negotiations until late in the Gorbachev era.

The détente process, coupled with the Soviet military buildup and America's precipitous withdrawal from Vietnam in 1975, gave the impression that the USSR was an ascendant superpower. In 1972, Foreign Affairs Minister Andrei Gromyko proudly proclaimed that no international problem of significance anywhere in the world could be resolved without Soviet participation. In the wake of Vietnam, the U.S. Congress limited American involvement in Africa; Moscow responded by expanding its presence in Yemen, Angola, and Mozambique. Conservatives in the United States quickly became disillusioned with détente, which seemed merely to encourage Soviet adventurism around the world. The December 1979 invasion of

Afghanistan by Soviet forces marked détente's collapse and the beginning of the second Cold War.

SOCIETY

Life for the average Soviet citizen improved considerably during the Khrushchev and Brezhnev eras. For example, the output of consumer goods increased by 60 percent just from 1959 to 1965, and meat consumption rose by over 50 percent. Real wages increased 50 percent from 1967 to 1977. Millions of units of new housing, consisting of high-rise apartments, were constructed in the cities. The quality was poor by Western standards, but these small units were a great improvement over the collective apartments (*kommunalki*) of earlier years, when several families had to share a kitchen and toilet. Families began purchasing refrigerators, televisions, and other durable consumer goods. However, there were long waiting lists for such items, and many households lacked goods that were commonplace in the West. When Vice President Richard Nixon hosted an exhibit of U.S. kitchen appliances in Moscow in 1959, Khrushchev challenged the display as an exercise in American propaganda. The press, which reveled in this clash of systems, dubbed their exchange the "kitchen debate."

Stalin's policies had greatly changed the social composition of the USSR. On the eve of collectivization, about 80 percent of the population lived in rural villages, and only a fifth lived in cities. By the time Brezhnev died in 1982, nearly 70 percent of the population was classified as urban, and only 30 percent as rural. Behind these figures lies a major social transformation. Millions of peasants had either left the countryside for jobs and a better life in the cities, or had starved to death during collectivization. Cities, with their cultural attractions and educational opportunities, lured many young people away from the collective farms. Moving to the city and gaining an education were the two keys to social mobility in the Soviet Union; there were no (legal) business opportunities under socialism. Becoming a member of the Communist Party was not critical to obtaining a better life, but it helped. Party membership was required for many of the more prestigious and higher-paying positions, which were listed on the Nomenklatura.

Officially, Soviet society was classified into two social classes—the workers and the peasants—and an overarching stratum, the intelligentsia, was drawn from both. Peasants worked on the *kolkhozy* and were generally the poorest of the three groups. They were the least educated, lived in the most primitive conditions (many peasant homes do not have running water or indoor plumbing to this day), and were bound to the *kolkhoz* by the lack of an internal passport. An unusually large proportion of the rural population was female;

older men had been killed in the war, and ambitious younger men left for the cities. One distinct advantage of life in the countryside was easy access to food. Peasants supplemented their diets by raising vegetables and livestock on small private plots, and any surplus could be sold in the marketplace for extra income.

Industrial workers, including state farmers (those who worked on the *sovkhoz* were classified as workers—they received a set wage and were granted internal passports), were supposedly the backbone of the Soviet system, and indeed, they lived better than the peasants. Blue-collar wages in 1960 were, on average, 73 percent higher than peasant wages, and about 22 percent higher than those of routine service workers. The wages of the scientific and technical intelligentsia, however, were 50 percent higher than the average worker's wages.

Under Brezhnev, wages became more nearly equal. By 1973, the average intelligentsia wage was only 34 percent above that of a manual worker, and workers' wages were now only 31 percent above those of the peasantry. Highly skilled workers, those in dangerous occupations (coal miners, for example) and those living in Siberia or the Far East, might earn incomes well above those of professionals. The more prosperous workers and intelligentsia might have a small dacha (summer home) with a garden plot outside the city. Usually, they were entitled to vacation once a year with their work group at a resort or sanatorium on the Black or Baltic Sea. But incomes were a very poor indicator of how well an individual lived. Bonuses, access to special shops, subsidized canteens, and other perquisites were far more important than salaries; holding a job where bribes could be extorted was even more important. The expanding opportunities for graft and corruption under Brezhnev made Soviet society highly stratified, although differences in wealth were much smaller than those in American society.

Soviet workers were neither very productive nor very satisfied with their jobs. Labor turnover was high, industrial accidents were frequent, and price increases might come unexpectedly. When the government raised food prices overnight in May 1962, workers took to the streets in protest in several cities. Some 200 were killed when troops opened fire on a large demonstration organized by disgruntled locomotive workers in the southern Russian town of Novocherkassk. Worker protests over prices and working conditions continued sporadically throughout the Brezhnev period. The regime usually responded by removing the immediate source of discontent, arresting the ringleaders, and covering up the incident.

Official ideology glorified the manual worker, but, in reality, it was the intelligentsia—engineers, scientists, professors, writers, and other cultural figures—who received the highest status and extra privileges. Most professionals and skilled workers needed more than their salaries to live well. For example, positions in law schools were in great demand since lawyers could obtain choice bribes. Doctors were severely underpaid, but they often received food or other rewards from grateful patients. Medicine was not a prestigious occupation, and the fact that about 70 percent of Soviet medical doctors were women was more an indication of the low priority accorded to health care than of a commitment to women's equality. Prosecutors, judges, and defense lawyers (*advokaty*), like doctors, were employed by the state, and attorneys' legal fees were set by the state until 1988.

Getting anything or getting anything done in the Soviet Union was usually complicated, bureaucratic, and tiring. Many goods were in short supply or, if there was no demand, items simply piled up on the shelves. To live well, one had to cut corners, and bend or often break the law. One's position, connections (*blat*), privileges, and opportunities for graft were critical in obtaining *defitsit* (scarce) goods. For example, a clerk in a meat store could set aside choice cuts for her family and friends, or exchange them for other *defitsit* items. Dentists might do some quality drilling in exchange for ballet tickets or French cognac. Hotel maids collected tips in foreign money and, at some risk, could purchase Western goods in the hard-currency stores. Those with foreign connections could obtain Italian shoes, American blue jeans, or Japanese electronic equipment and sell them on the black market for huge profits, although speculation was a crime and could be severely punished.

Of course, Party and government officials on the Nomenklatura were best positioned to use their influence to enrich themselves. Top Soviet leaders lived a secretive existence protected from public scrutiny. Those on the Kremlin ration automatically had access to the best food, consumer goods, and medical care. They lived rent-free in huge apartments, had luxurious dachas in the country, and were permitted to travel outside the country. Benefits were pegged to one's level in the Nomenklatura: the privileges accorded to an *oblast* (regional) Party first secretary would be greater than those of a *raion* (district) first secretary; Moscow ministers lived better than union republic officials. Huge bribes were paid for appointments to these positions.

For those interested in public affairs, participation was either conducted through official channels supervised by the Communist Party—the Komsomol, trade unions, conservation clubs, and women's groups—or suppressed as a threat to socialist order. Nonetheless, a small, unofficial dissident movement did emerge during the Brezhnev era, consisting of several factions. One tendency was social democratic in nature, represented by intellectuals like Andrei Sakharov and Roy Medvedev, who advocated a more benign socialism. A second group of dissidents were religious believers, including Baptists, Catholics, and Jehovah's Witnesses. Ukrainian, Lithuanian, Crimean Tatar, and other non-Russian nationalist activists comprised yet a third group, while Jews petitioning to leave for Israel were a fourth. Russian nationalists comprised a fifth dissident strain, albeit one with powerful supporters in the Soviet establishment.

Soviet censorship made it difficult for dissidents to communicate their ideas to a broader audience. One means was through self-published, or *samizdat,* material. Writers would laboriously type copies of their manuscripts using carbon paper, and copies would be passed from hand to hand. *Samizdat* consisted of a few regular underground journals, like the *Chronicle of Current Events,* copies of Solzhenitsyn's and Pasternak's work, religious tracts, and occasional Western novels or political writings banned from the public. Students and intellectuals in the larger cities read *samizdat,* but the average person did not have access to, and was not interested in, such writings. Most Soviet citizens were well educated, but not particularly critical in their thinking; many seemed to agree with the authorities that anyone who criticized the Soviet system was psychologically unstable. Indeed, the Russian word for dissident is "otherthinker" (*inakomyslyashchie*). Under Iurii Andropov's tenure as head of the KGB (1967–1982), the regime often silenced dissidents by incarcerating them in psychiatric hospitals and keeping them drugged.

SOVIET NATIONALITIES

Ethnically, the Soviet Union was one of the most diverse countries in the world. Soviet census figures for 1989 listed over 100 separate national groups with distinct languages, cultures, and religions; Russians, however, made up barely 51 percent of the population (see Table 7.1). In keeping with Lenin's idea of a national-territorial federalism, the USSR was divided into 15 Union Republics for large ethnic groups located on the border, 20 Autonomous Republics, 8 Autonomous Regions, and 10 National Areas for progressively smaller groups. However, Lenin had argued that socialist federalism would be transitional. Centralization and the eventual disappearance of national distinctions was the ultimate goal—communist leaders clearly did not believe in multiculturalism, nor were they willing to allow the regions to share power with Moscow.

By creating distinct territorial homelands for the minorities, Soviet nationality policy unintentionally reinforced separate ethnic identities. Wide variations existed in economic development, education, and urbanization among the republics. The Baltic states—Estonia, Latvia, and Lithuania—were the smallest republics (1 to 3 million in population), the most Westernized, and had the highest standard of living. These peoples had historically been linked to Germany, Finland, and Poland, and were Lutheran (Estonians and Latvians) or Catholic (Lithuanians) in religious persuasion. Forcibly incorporated into the USSR by Stalin during World War II, the Baltic peoples remained fiercely nationalistic and resentful of Soviet domination; armed resistance against Soviet

Table 7.1: Major Nationalities of the Soviet Union, 1989 (those in excess of 1 million)

	Number	Percent of Total
Russians	145,155,000	50.8
Ukrainians	44,186,000	15.5
Uzbeks	16,968,000	5.8
Belorus-sians	10,036,000	3.9
Kazakhs	8,136,000	2.8
Azerbaijanis	6,770,000	2.4
Tatars	6,649,000	2.3
Armenians	4,623,000	1.6
Tajiks	4,215,000	1.5
Georgians	3,981,000	1.4
Moldovans	3,352,000	1.2
Lithuanians	3,067,000	1.1
Turkmen	2,729,000	1.0
Kyrgyz	2,529,000	.9
Germans	2,039,000	.7
Chuvash	1,842,000	.6
Latvians	1,459,000	.5
Bashkirs	1,449,000	.5
Jews	1,378,000	.5
Mordovans	1,154,000	.4
Poles	1,126,000	.4
Estonians	1,027,000	.4
Others	12,142,000	4.2
Total	285,742,000	100.4*

[Source: Figures are from the 1989 national census, in Narodnoe khoziaistvo SSSR v. 1990 g. (Moscow: Finansy I Statistika, 1991), 77. Percentages do not add up to 100 due to rounding.

occupation by guerrilla groups continued well into the 1950s. Furthermore, Estonians and Latvians resented the large numbers of Russians who moved into their republics in the postwar period to assume leading political and economic posts and to man the army units stationed there. By 1989, Estonia's population was 30 percent Russian, and Latvia's 34 percent.

Ukrainians were the second-largest nationality in the Soviet Union at over 40 million. Ukraine, with its rich black-earth region, was the breadbasket of the USSR. It also contained important steel, iron ore, and coal industries and about half of the Soviet Union's nuclear power stations, and was home to the Black Sea fleet. (In a fit of international generosity, Khrushchev unilaterally transferred the Crimea to Ukraine in 1954. After the Soviet breakup, Russia and Ukraine both claimed ownership of the fleet.) Ukraine was the historical center of eastern Slavic culture, and Ukrainians were proud of their traditional costumes and folk dances and their outstanding 19th-century poet, Taras Shevchenko. Nationalist Ukrainian dissidents were active from the 1960s to the early 1970s; central authorities, however, cracked down in the wake of disturbances in neighboring Czechoslovakia. First Secretary of the Ukrainian Communist Party Petro Shelest was demoted in 1972 for tolerating nationalist tendencies in his republic. Russians, who made up over a fifth of Ukraine's population, occupied prominent positions in the republic's government and economy.

Nationalism was also strong in the three republics of the Caucasus Mountains: Georgia, Armenia, and Azerbaijan. Georgians and Armenians were both ancient peoples with distinct languages, and had been Orthodox Christian since the fifth century. Before the Revolution, they looked to the Russians for protection against the Moslem Turks. Armenia's strong nationalism derived from the death of over a million Armenians at the hands of Turkey in 1915, resulting from forced marches and internment in concentration camps. Georgian nationalism is equally powerful—under Soviet rule, nationalist demonstrations occurred there in 1924, 1956, and 1978. Azeris, too, were nationalistic, but unlike their Caucasian neighbors, they are a Shi'ite Moslem, Turkic people. Azerbaijan, though rich in oil, was one of the poorest Soviet republics. Relatively few Russians had settled in these republics—only about 6 percent of Georgia's and Azerbaijan's population was Russian; in Armenia, it was under 2 percent.

The Moldavians had also been incorporated during the war; their republic had once been the Romanian province of Bessarabia. Ethnically Romanian, and Orthodox in religious background, Moldavia was poor and heavily agricultural, with a large peasant population. Belorussia, situated north of Ukraine, was also largely an agricultural region. Most Belorussians did not have a strong sense of nationalism. Russians tended to regard them as a rather backward peasant people, a Slavic little brother lacking the historical distinction of Ukrainians. In the late Soviet era, about 13 percent of the population in both republics was ethnic Russian.

Central Asians ranked lowest among the republics in education, economic development level, and representation in Soviet politics. Central Asians were Turkic peoples, with mostly Sunnite Moslem religious traditions, but beyond these commonalities, they were extremely diverse. Uzbeks were a sedentary people who had built great cities filled with grand mosques: Bukhara, Tashkent, and Samarkand. Kazakhs and Kyrgyz, like their relatives the Mongols, had been nomadic peoples, living in circular tents (yurts) and driving their horses and cattle from the steppes to the mountains in semiannual treks until they were forced onto collective farms during collectivization. Tajikistan, the very poorest of Soviet republics, was divided into a number of tribal societies, most of which were Persian rather than Turkish in origin. Three of the five Central Asian republics—Uzbekistan, Turkmenistan, and Tajikistan—had relatively small colonies of Russians, between 5 and 10 percent, while over a fifth of Kyrgyzstan's population was ethnic Russian.

Kazakhstan was a special case. Encompassing a territory the size of all of Western Europe, Kazakhstan was home to a population of just under 17 million in 1989. It was by far the most diverse of the republics: ethnic Kazakhs made up only about 40 percent of the republic's population, and Russians 38 percent; the remainder was a mosaic of Koreans, Germans, Chechens, Greeks, Ukrainians, Uighurs, and others. Some had migrated there to take jobs; others (the Germans, Koreans, and Chechens) had been deported to this huge region under Stalin for real or imagined political crimes. In addition to agriculture (grain, cotton, and apples), Kazakhstan had huge oil reserves. Kazakhstan also had the distinction of hosting the Soviet nuclear testing range at Semipalatinsk and the Baikonur launching facility for the space program. Soil erosion from the Virgin Lands project, the disaster of the disappearing Aral Sea (drained under Brezhnev to irrigate the Central Asian cotton crop), and years of nuclear tests ruined much of Kazakhstan's natural environment.

Russians dominated Soviet society, government, and the economy, partly by virtue of their numbers, and partly because of a Russian imperial mentality fostered by the state. During the 1960s, a nationalist genre of Russian literature, the village prose school, became popular. Village school authors, such as the Siberian Valentin Rasputin, sympathetically portrayed Russian peasant life and implicitly criticized the dehumanizing aspects of modern industrial society. Other nationalists sought to preserve Russian traditions through the All-Russian Society for the Protection of Historical and Cultural Monuments. This organization, which had high-level supporters in the Party, tried to stem the destruction of Russian Orthodox churches promoted by Khrushchev.

More chauvinistic and anti-Semitic currents existed in the Communist Party and the armed forces; these coalesced into national-patriotic movements after the Soviet collapse.

The Khrushchev and Brezhnev regimes both maintained the fiction that ethnic relations were constantly improving; their long-term goal was for national identities to be submerged into a general Soviet consciousness. In most cases, surface relations among the various nationalities were at least cordial. Open displays of racism were infrequent, and intermarriage was common among some groups. But the strong Russification trend underlying Soviet nationality policies antagonized those with strong national feelings, especially the Baltic and Caucasian groups, and generated resentment even among the two smaller Slavic nationalities, who were condescendingly referred to as the "younger brothers" of Russians. Russian nationalists chafed at the limits that Soviet ideology imposed on their cultural aspirations.

Language is central to any ethnic identity. The Soviet 1959 Education Law allowed parents of minority children to choose their preferred language of instruction in primary and occasionally secondary school, but, in reality, there was considerable pressure to enroll children in Russian-language schools. All students in minority-language schools were required to complete at least eight years of instruction in Russian. Education at a Russian-language school was more prestigious, and a Russian high school education was necessary to matriculate at the best universities and to secure a good job after graduation.

Russification was also promoted by the influx of ethnic Russians into the republics mentioned above. Russians often occupied the most important posts in industry, government, and the military. For example, while the top Party and government offices in the republics were usually staffed by a representative of the titular nationality, more reliable Slavs were given key positions in the republics, such as second secretary of the Party or head of the KGB. In this way, Moscow was able to monitor nationalism among the minorities. Russians also dominated sensitive industries. For example, less than 10 percent of Lithuania's population was Russian, but they comprised 90 percent of personnel in that republic's Ignalina nuclear power station. Likewise, Soviet defense industries and the officer corps of the Soviet army were largely the preserve of ethnic Russians.

SOVIET POLITICS

Soviet politics in the late Brezhnev period were no longer as totalitarian as they were under Stalin, but the country was still one of the most repressive authoritarian systems in the world. Political control over the population was far more pervasive than in non-communist authoritarian regimes. However, the chief instrument of control was now bureaucratic regulation, rather than police terror. The Communist Party remained the nerve center of the system, supervising all government offices and schools, army units and newspapers, factories, and farms. Article 6 of the 1977 Constitution had enshrined the Party as the "leading and guiding force" in Soviet society. By 1982, the Party had grown to some 18 million members out of a total population of 285 million. About 250,000 of these were Party officials at various levels—they were the

Communist Party Structure

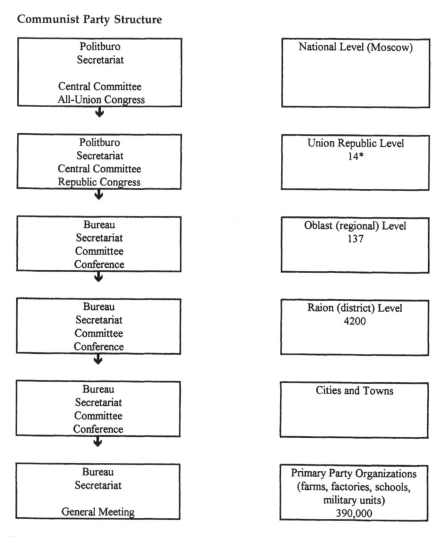

Figure 7.1: Communist Party Structure. Fifteen union republics comprised the USSR, but there was no separate Russian Republic party organization during the Brezhnev regime.

Soviet Government Structure

NATIONAL LEVEL

USSR Presidium -- President USSR Supreme Soviet --Soviet of Union --Soviet of Nationalities	USSR Presidium -- Premier USSR Council of Ministers USSR Supreme Court

UNION REPUBLIC LEVEL

Republic Presidium—Republic President Republic Supreme Soviet	Republic Presidium—Republic President Republic Council of Ministers Republic Supreme Courts

REGIONAL LEVEL

Autonomous Republic Soviets (20)	AR Councils of Ministers—Chairman AR Supreme Courts
Autonomous Region Soviets (8)	Executive Committees—Chairman
National Area Soviets (10)	Executive Committees—Chairman
Oblast (Region) Soviets (123) Krai (Territory) Soviets (6)	Executive Committees—Chairman Regional Courts

LOCAL GOVERNMENT

Raion (District) Soviets (4200)	Executive Committees—Chairman District Courts
Cities, Towns, Village Soviets	Executive Committees—Chairman

ELECTIONS

Figure 7.2: Soviet Government Structure.

ones who exercised power. The top Party leaders, thanks to Brezhnev's promises of stability in personnel matters, often stayed in office until they died. Moscow's rulers grew so old and infirm that Western Sovietologists began to refer to the regime as a gerontocracy—rule by the elderly.

Under Brezhnev, the already large state bureaucracy became even more bloated and sclerotic. The USSR Council of Ministers, roughly equivalent to a Western cabinet, but with several dozen production ministries, reached 110 members by the late 1970s. Soviet planners struggled to keep pace with rapidly advancing technology by using consumer surveys and computer models, but central planning proved to be no substitute for market mechanisms. Although Soviet scientists were among the best in the world, bureaucracy and ideology stifled innovation and productivity, leaving Soviet consumers with shoddy merchandise, poor health care, pervasive shortages, and widespread environmental disasters.

Governments have a tendency to be unresponsive when there is no chance that leaders will be voted out of office. Soviet citizens did vote, but the electoral system was used only for the least powerful of the three branches of the system—the Soviets (the other two were the Party and the government bureaucracy). Despite Khrushchev's rhetoric about the All-People's State and Brezhnev's claims for developed socialism, there was little genuine political participation through these institutions. Candidates for positions on the councils were vetted at each level by the appropriate Party secretariats, and there was only one candidate on the ballot for each position. On election day, voters would receive their ballot, fold it in half, and drop it in the ballot box in full view of officials. Voters had the option of stepping into a booth and crossing the single name off the ballot, but this was regarded as uncooperative behavior and was frowned on. Local Party secretaries were tasked with getting out the vote as a show of support for the regime, and they were very effective—turnout was usually about 99.9 percent!

These three branches of the Soviet system are depicted in Figures 7.1 and 7.2. The Communist Party's primary function was decision making and oversight; the government ministries carried out policies, and the Soviets provided a patina of democracy. Offices frequently overlapped—important bureaucrats like the Minister of Defense, Minister of Foreign Affairs, and head of the KGB were also members of the Politburo, and would routinely be elected to the Supreme Soviet. Local Party secretaries were represented on the executive committees of local Soviets. Virtually all members of the USSR Council of Ministers were also on the Party Central Committee. Unlike in the United States, the various institutions did not provide for checks and balances. Instead, the interlocking system of appointments contributed to a highly centralized framework of political power in the Soviet Union.

General Secretary Brezhnev died in November 1982, leaving a legacy of economic stagnation, cultural mediocrity, and political repression. His rule had been more benign than that of Stalin and more stable than that of Khrushchev. But stability led to stagnation. Problems were mounting that Brezhnev either could not or would not acknowledge. One popular joke of the time has Brezhnev, Khrushchev, and Stalin riding together in a railway car. When the train grinds to a halt, Stalin declares, "I'll fix this," and promptly has the entire crew shot and replaced. The train moves along for a bit, but then stops again. Khrushchev promises to get it going, and immediately reorganizes the entire management. The train starts up, rolls along the tracks for a while, but soon stops yet again. "I know what to do," says Brezhnev. He pulls down the blinds in the car and suggests to the others, "Let's just pretend we're moving." Within three years, the Soviet Union would be taken over by a generation of leaders who would succeed in derailing the train of state.

IVAN THE TERRIBLE.

THE ROMANOFFS.

The first Russian monarch to use the title of czar, Ivan IV was known as Ivan the Terrible. During his long reign, he centralized the Muscovite state and set the stage for future expansion. [Courtesy of the Library of Congress]

Peter I, also known as Peter the Great, ruled the Russian empire from 1682 until his death in 1725. He is renowned for introducing European civilization to Russia and elevating Russia to a recognized entity among the European powers. [Courtesy of the Library of Congress]

Russian czar Nicholas II and his family, ca. 1900. [The Illustrated London News Picture Library]

Vladimir Lenin led the 1917 Bolshevik Revolution, which toppled the czarist Russian monarchy and brought to power a government that was the leader of the communist world for the next 75 years. [Courtesy of the Library of Congress]

Left to right: British prime minister Winston Churchill, U.S. president Franklin D. Roosevelt, and Soviet premier Joseph Stalin at the Yalta Conference in February 1945. [National Archives]

Fidel Castro and Nikita Khrushchev at the United Nations, 1960. [Courtesy of the Library of Congress]

U.S. president Ronald Reagan meets with Soviet leader Mikhail Gorbachev during the Geneva Summit in Switzerland on November 11, 1985. [Courtesy of the Ronald Reagan Library]

Vladimir Putin, President of Russia, speaks at the Kremlin in Moscow. [Courtesy of the Presidential Press and Information Office]

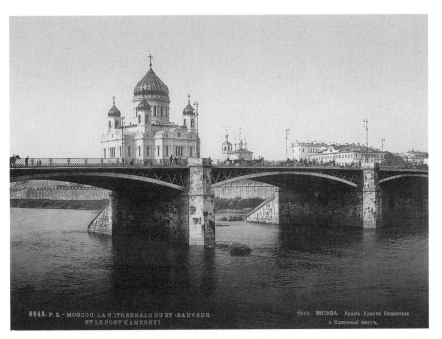

8843. P. Z. - MOSCOU. LA CATHÉDRALE DU ST -SAUVEUR
ET LE PONT KAMENNYI

8843. МОСКВА. Храмъ Христа Спасителя
и Каменный мостъ.

The Cathedral of Christ the Savior, Moscow. [Courtesy of the Library of Congress].

8

Gorbachev, Perestroika, and the Collapse of Communism

The Soviet people are convinced that as a result of perestroika and de-mocratization the country will become richer and stronger. Life will get better. There are, and will be, difficulties, sometimes considerable, on the road to perestroika, and we are not concealing that. But we will cope with them. Of that we are sure.

—Mikhail Gorbachev, *Perestroika: New Thinking for Our Country and the World*

From its birth in the Revolution of 1917 to its demise at the end of 1991, the Soviet Union stood as the chief political, ideological, and military adversary of the Western democratic world. The Western democracies were constitutionally based systems embodying the concept of representative government, holding regular competitive elections for political office, respecting (in general) the rights and freedoms of the individual citizen, and promoting market economies with extensive private enterprise. By contrast, the Soviet Union and its East European colonies rejected the principles of bourgeois democracy as a sham, promoting instead the Marxist concept that the industrial working class should exercise political power without regard for the niceties of democratic procedure. The supposedly transitional phase of the dictatorship of the proletariat under Stalin solidified into a centralized, repressive dictatorship in which all facets of life—political, cultural, and economic—were regulated by the Communist Party and state bureaucracy.

The first indications of the economic problems that would eventually lead to Mikhail Gorbachev's reforms surfaced during Nikita Khrushchev's tenure as General Secretary from 1953 to 1964. Khrushchev's ill-fated attempts at reform alienated much of the Party and government bureaucracy, and his successors, Leonid Brezhnev and Alexei Kosygin, merely tinkered with the Stalinist structure of centralized political control and economic planning. A period of bureaucratic lethargy, which Gorbachev and the reformers would later call the "time of stagnation," supplanted Stalin's terroristic oppression and Khrushchev's poorly conceived experiments. The problems became more acute and obvious to younger, reform-minded Soviet leaders, as the industrial economy could not keep up with the dynamic computer and information-driven economies of Europe, the United States, and East Asia.

MOUNTING PROBLEMS

There was no single factor that brought the Soviet system to a state of crisis. Economic problems were the most disturbing, particularly a steep decline in the gross national product (GNP) growth, to the point where the Soviet economy was expanding at only .5 to 2 percent annually in the early 1980s. If we consider the waste and inefficiency, the routine distortion of production figures, continued population growth, and the fact that much of what was produced was of poor quality or not in demand by consumers, the record is even worse. A black market (underground) economy, comprising about one-fifth of total output, was a measure of the inadequacy of the legal economy. Absenteeism and alcoholism were common among workers. Most state stores closed early, so workers would often leave work early to do their shopping; daily shopping was necessary since there were no prepared foods and most homes boasted only compact refrigerators with little if any freezer space.

Soviet economic problems were complex, and resulted from the inherent difficulties in trying to operate a modern economy through central planning. First, the economy was extraordinarily wasteful—it took more than twice as much raw material and energy to produce finished goods in the USSR as it did in Western industrialized countries. Second, most Soviet goods were of poor quality. They were not competitive in world markets, so most were consumed domestically or exported to Eastern Europe or to developing nations. The only Soviet exports capable of earning hard currency were unprocessed raw materials—oil, natural gas, gold, timber, diamonds—and military weapons. Prices for Soviet goods were set arbitrarily by a State Pricing Committee in the Council of Ministers, and so did not send accurate signals to either producers or consumers about their scarcity and value. Many food items, as well as transportation, education, housing, and medical care, were heavily subsidized. Other goods—luxury items, for example—were overpriced to discourage demand. Soviet consumers had extremely high savings rates because there was so little to buy. Banks offered low interest rates, and there was no Soviet stock market in which to invest, so stashing rubles under the bed was a common practice. State subsidies and the regime's claim that inflation did not exist under socialism meant running large budget deficits and incurring heavy foreign debt.

Strains were also beginning to show in the multinational fabric of the Soviet Union. Latvians, Lithuanians, and Estonians had never accepted their forced incorporation; Baltic émigré organizations lobbied Washington and other Western capitals to put pressure on Moscow. Much of the Soviet Jewish population left the USSR for Israel or the United States in the 1970s—over 50,000 in 1979 alone. In 1978, thousands of Georgian students marched in the capital, Tbilisi, after learning of plans to drop Georgian as the state language of the republic; Soviet authorities quickly gave in to their demands. Another disturbing trend, at least from Moscow's perspective, was a significant decline in birth rates among the Slavic nationalities. Birth rates were highest in Central Asia, where traditional extended families were still common. Demographers predicted that if trends continued, Russians would soon become a minority in the USSR. High population growth in Central Asia led to an imbalance between workers and industry; the jobs were concentrated in European Russia, but the labor supply was located in Central Asia. And an increasing proportion of draft-age recruits for the army came from Central Asia—close to one-third by the early 1980s. These young men were often not well educated, and many had only a weak command of the Russian language.

Another major problem was the economic and human costs associated with environmental pollution. Soviet economic development strategies had taken an extraordinary toll on the natural environment. Most of the major rivers and lakes were severely polluted from poorly treated sewage, industrial effluents, and agricultural runoff. In 1989, fully 75 percent of all surface water in the USSR was classified as polluted. Seventy percent of the volume of the great Aral Sea, which covered an area the size of West Virginia, was drained off to irrigate Central Asia's cotton crop. Cellulose plants built in the 1960s threatened beautiful Lake Baikal in the heart of Siberia, a reservoir for one-fifth of the entire world's supply of fresh water. All major Soviet cities suffered from the polluted air caused by coal-fired power plants and dirty industries. Strict laws on air pollution had been on the books since 1949, but were routinely violated. All of the incentives were geared toward fulfilling quotas—managers were simply not rewarded for conserving raw materials or reducing emissions. Production always trumped the environment.

The costs of this cavalier attitude toward the environment were enormous. The Soviet fishing industry saw its harvests drop precipitously in the polluted lakes, rivers, and inland seas. Water contaminated by oil products, pesticides, and industrial wastes was responsible for hepatitis, cholera, and other water-borne diseases. Air pollution caused high rates of respiratory disease and eye infections in many industrial cities. The liberal use of pesticides and herbicides in agriculture, and heavy industrial emissions, led to increased cancer rates, birth defects, and blood and liver diseases. The Soviet Union, alone among industrial nations, saw its infant mortality rate (an accurate indicator of the general health of a population) rise from 22.9 deaths per thousand live births in 1971 to 25.4 in 1987. Life expectancy among adults, another health indicator, also declined in the 1970s. Pollution, together with poor diet and heavy smoking and drinking, was responsible for this dismal record.

The Soviet economy had provided the population with a modestly improving standard of living ever since Stalin's death, but it could not match rising consumer expectations. Much of Soviet investment went to feed the huge military machine, which absorbed some 20 to 25 percent of the total gross domestic product. As the United States retreated from international commitments following the Vietnam debacle, the Brezhnev regime increasingly resorted to military threats, and occasionally the direct exercise of military power, to achieve its foreign policy goals. In the latter half of the 1970s, Soviet officials confidently asserted that the correlation of forces in world affairs had shifted in favor of socialism and against the capitalist states. By the time Brezhnev died in November of 1982, however, the Soviet Union confronted stubborn guerrilla resistance in Afghanistan (which the Soviets had invaded in 1979), a restive population in Poland (where the Solidarity movement had openly defied the government during 1980–1981), and a conservative Reagan administration in Washington determined to rebuild America's military strength and confront the Soviet Union around the globe. Few Third World countries any longer admired the USSR as a model of development, preferring instead the example of newly industrializing and increasingly wealthy capitalist nations.

In sum, the early 1980s found an aging and unimaginative Soviet leadership facing intractable domestic problems and an increasingly difficult international environment. As the old guard died off or retired, a new generation of leaders, influenced more by Khrushchev's thaw than Stalin's terror, moved into the highest echelons of power. Alexei Kosygin died in office in 1980; the Party's chief ideologist and reactionary, Mikhail Suslov, the gray eminence of Soviet politics, died early in 1982. Leonid Brezhnev died on November 10, 1982, and conservative Politburo members chose Yurii Andropov, chairman of the KGB since 1967, and trained as a barge engineer, to be the new General Secretary. Andropov was clearly not the closet liberal some Western observers suspected (because he drank scotch and preferred jazz), but as head of the secret police, he was well informed about Soviet social and economic problems. By contrast, most of the elderly leadership was insulated from the hardships of everyday life—the endless lines, poor-quality housing, crowded mass transportation, polluted rivers, and surly bureaucrats. Comfortable in their well-appointed Kremlin offices, spacious country dachas, and Zil limousines, Soviet leaders probably believed their own propaganda about how life in the Soviet Union was constantly improving. General Secretary Andropov realized that the Soviet economy was close to a state of crisis, and launched campaigns to improve labor discipline and deal with corruption and alcohol abuse.

However, Andropov died within a year, and the Politburo settled on Brezhnev's nondescript protégé, Konstantin Chernenko, as an acceptable transitional figure. Chernenko was a Party apparatchik of extraordinarily limited intellect and poor health; the more vigorous Mikhail Gorbachev, now second in command, often stood in for Chernenko when he was incapacitated. The Soviet intelligentsia, who had been cautiously optimistic about the possibility for change when Andropov was in power, were appalled. Reform was put on hold as the doddering Chernenko served out a painful 13 months and then died of heart failure, having accomplished nothing. On March 11, 1985, after divisive wrangling, Politburo members appointed the relatively youthful (age 54) Mikhail Gorbachev General Secretary of the Communist Party.

GORBACHEV SUCCEEDS

The dramatic changes that led to the collapse of the Soviet Union and its communist empire cannot be attributed to any one individual or factor. Mikhail Gorbachev certainly deserves much of the credit for initiating the reform process, but Gorbachev is not the entire story. Nor is it accurate to assert, as some prominent American conservatives have, that President Ronald Reagan's confrontational policies and accelerated defense spending, particularly in the form of his Strategic Defense Initiative, or SDI, led to the collapse of the USSR. These factors played a role, but they were overshadowed by the critical importance of internal motivations. So many domestic problems had accumulated under Brezhnev—economic stagnation, technological backwardness, corruption, environmental pollution, growing cynicism and alienation, simmering discontent among the various nationalities—that the need for reform was apparent to all but the most obdurate ideologues.

Born in 1931 in the southern Russian region of Stavropol, Mikhail Gorbachev excelled in high school and entered the prestigious Moscow State University in 1950. Unlike most Soviet leaders, who had received engineering or other technical degrees, Gorbachev studied in the law faculty. He was an ardent believer in communism, and Khrushchev's revelations at the Twentieth Party Congress in 1956 came as a great shock to him, as they did to many other young intellectuals of the time. After graduation, he became head of the Komsomol youth organization for Stavropol city, then for the entire region. Gorbachev was active in Stavropol agricultural work, taking night classes in the subject, and, at age 39, became Party First Secretary for the Stavropol region, the equivalent of a powerful governor. As Party boss, he often hosted the Moscow elite at Mineralnye Vody (Mineral Waters), a spa and resort. In September 1978, Brezhnev stopped in for a visit and was so impressed with Gorbachev that within two months, he was appointed Secretary of the Central Committee in Moscow, with special responsibility for agriculture. The following year, he was made a candidate (probationary) member of the Politburo; in 1980, he was promoted to full Politburo membership.

From the perspective of Gorbachev and like-minded reformers, the economy was the greatest weakness of the Soviet system. Top-heavy central planning, with its focus on generating ever-larger quotas of heavy industrial products, was clearly out of sync with the modern electronic age. Shortly after Brezhnev died, the country's top social scientists had been charged with developing a set of recommendations for economic and social reform. Andropov assigned Gorbachev and Nikolai Ryzhkov, another member of the Secretariat, to head this task force. Many reform proposals looked back to the limited capitalism of the NEP, while others suggested adopting ideas from the Hungarian, East German, or Chinese experiments. Occasionally, these internal debates spilled into the pages of mass circulation journals and newspapers. One of the most prominent voices of reform, Siberian sociologist Tatiana Zaslavskaya, argued that the rigid authoritarian methods of production established under Stalin were no longer appropriate for an educated urban workforce. The recent example of Poland and instances of worker dissatisfaction throughout the USSR and Eastern Europe, she argued in her famous Novosibirsk Report, suggested that alienation, a Marxist concept applied only to capitalist systems until now, was a very real problem in the workers' paradise. The findings in Zaslavskaya's report were quite sensitive; her paper and other frank analyses of Soviet shortcomings were at first restricted to specialists and Party officials.

When the simpleminded Chernenko died in March of 1985, Gorbachev assumed office with literally hundreds of proposals for reform in hand. Of course, there were still conservatives in the Soviet leadership who resisted significant change, so Gorbachev had to proceed cautiously until he could develop a stronger base of support in the Kremlin. Through a series of adroit maneuvers, Gorbachev demoted or retired many of the older generation of policy makers, replacing them with younger, more reform-minded officials. Within three months, he had eased Andrei Gromyko out of his position as Minister of Foreign Affairs, replacing him with the Georgian First Secretary and reformer Eduard Shevardnadze. A new face in the foreign ministry was essential if Gorbachev was to succeed in implementing his new thinking in

Soviet foreign policy. Gorbachev also appointed Aleksandr Yakovlev, an intellectual and former ambassador to Canada who had studied at Columbia University, as his closest advisor. Yakovlev's foreign policy experience was instrumental in drafting Soviet New Thinking, and he actively promoted glasnost (openness) in the media and in politics.

By the middle of 1987, Gorbachev had solidified his political position and had managed to put his ideas for change—most notably, perestroika and glasnost (economic and political restructuring)—at the top of the Soviet agenda. It should be emphasized, however, that neither Gorbachev nor his reformist allies had a grand strategy for change. They were experimenting, trying to reshape a moribund system and yet preserve most of the central elements of that system. It was a strategy that could not succeed.

PERESTROIKA AND GLASNOST

Perestroika, broadly defined as the restructuring of the Soviet economy, was at the heart of Gorbachev's reform program, as outlined in his book of the same title. Gorbachev, who never abandoned his belief in the inherent superiority of socialism, initially sought to modernize the Soviet economy by correcting some of its more egregious failures while leaving the basic structure intact. For the first two years, Gorbachev stressed the importance of accelerating economic performance, improving worker discipline, and attacking alcoholism (which seriously impaired productivity). These measures had been proposed during the brief tenure of Yurii Andropov, who had been a cautious voice for reform and one of Gorbachev's patrons in the leadership. Such palliatives did not get to the root of the problem, however. By mid-1987, it was increasingly apparent that more was needed than simply adjusting the Soviet system of central planning.

One very unpopular reform that Gorbachev pursued and then abandoned was his attack on alcohol. Drinking to excess has a long and honored tradition in Russia. By custom, once a bottle of vodka was opened, it was drained. And for most serious Russian drinkers, a liter bottle was barely adequate for one man. Gorbachev's anti-alcohol campaign consisted of reducing shop hours, destroying vineyards, cutting back on production, and drastically raising prices. Thirsty Russians countered by making homebrew, or *samogon*—one Soviet official told this author that arrests for bootlegging in Leningrad increased tenfold in just a few months. As in the Stalin campaign, communists were to set an example for the rest of the people. Bottles of mineral water were served at official functions, and Party establishments went dry. The results were disastrous: the government lost about 10 billion rubles per year in tax revenue, hundreds were poisoned by moonshine, and Gorbachev was derided as the mineral water Secretary.

At the Twenty-Seventh Party Congress in 1986, Gorbachev had laid out a program of economic reform for the twelfth Five-Year Plan (1986–1990). Specific elements of economic reform included legalizing cooperatives, relaxing central controls over state enterprises, and liberalizing foreign trade. Other features of the economic reform plan included reform of the taxation system and substantial cuts in the bloated defense budget. Gorbachev was also determined to end the practice of subsidizing radical Third World states. The Brezhnev regime had been providing $1–2 billion in annual aid to Vietnam, and nearly $5 billion per year to Cuba, mostly in the form of cheap oil. Other friendly states received concessionary terms on weapons purchases or assistance for industrial projects. Now, politics would no longer be the dominant consideration—even the Soviets' closest allies would have to pay world-market prices for Soviet goods.

The first cooperatives appeared in 1987; by the end of 1991, there were thousands of these small businesses providing much-needed services to the Soviet consumer. Cooperatives were, in actuality, small private businesses—restaurants, taxi services, souvenir stands, car repair shops, dental clinics, dating services, and so forth. In many cases, the legalization of cooperatives simply meant that illegal black market operations could now do business legally. However, limits on their ability to hire labor and the difficulty involved in finding space for shops (virtually all buildings were, of course, owned by the state) hindered their potential for growth.

Making the huge, bureaucratic state enterprises and the state and collective farms more efficient was a far more challenging task. A Law on the State Enterprise was enacted in 1988, granting enterprises greater independence from the central ministries, while requiring them to function on a cost-accounting basis; that is, to cover costs through sales. Enterprises would now engage in wholesale trade among themselves, and would no longer be allocated materials through a central supply committee. Planning would now be less detailed, providing enterprises with general guidance instead of exact quotas. Factories were also supposed to operate with greater input from the workers, who would be empowered to elect their managers. Since the early Stalin era, Soviet enterprises had been organized on the principle of one-person authoritarian management. Factory managers had behaved like 19th-century American capitalist barons. Workers could not strike and had virtually no say in running the plant. Khrushchev, Brezhnev, and Chernenko had each publicly promoted the idea of greater workplace democracy, but these pronouncements had little effect on industrial management practices. Of course, none of these communist rulers really favored genuine factory democracy. Those who governed the workers' state feared the workers, and their grand pronouncements were little more than ploys designed to keep the working class quiescent. Gorbachev's notion of democracy was also tied to a specific goal—improving worker morale and enhancing productivity—rather than being important in its own right.

As political relaxation progressed, Soviet workers began to spontaneously demand that the Party and government address longstanding grievances. In July 1989, tens of thousands of miners from the country's major coal regions—the Kuznets coal basin in Siberia, the Donets basin in Ukraine, Vorkuta in the far north, and Karaganda in northern Kazakhstan—went on strike. Coal miners, one of the elite groups of Soviet labor, worked deep underground in difficult and dangerous conditions. The miners lived in miserable apartments, received only sporadic supplies of poor-quality goods, and had very few benefits. But the ultimate indignity was not having enough soap to wash off the coal dust and grime. Intimidated by this spontaneous uprising of the proletariat, the government quickly provided food, clothing, better salaries, more benefits, and lots of soap.

Gorbachev's reform program had only a marginal impact on Soviet industry. Much of the government's ineffectiveness lay in its inability to enact meaningful price reform. Without real prices, enterprises had no means of gauging their true costs and whether or not they were profitable. Central ministry directives about how much to produce were supposed to yield to lower-level market exchanges, but in the absence of true prices, enterprises continued to receive state orders for their goods. Ministries also continued to take most of enterprise profits, leaving them little independence. The continued presence of state bureaucracies in production also hampered cooperation between new private businesses and state enterprises. A private construction firm, for example, might have ample supplies of bricks to build new houses. However, if lumber could only be obtained through the Ministry of Timber, and all of its production was promised to state enterprises, it would be impossible for the private firm to acquire the needed materials. Partial reform threw the economy into a tailspin.

In agriculture, reform consisted of reducing the subsidies granted to the collective and state farms, encouraging them to turn a profit, and providing incentives for increased output. Under Brezhnev, small-scale family teams had become active in Soviet agriculture, and the private plots had become a vital part of food production. Although these plots comprised only 3 percent of the total arable land, private plots had produced about one-quarter of all food consumed in the USSR. Gorbachev's reforms combined decentralization and profit incentives in agriculture with bureaucratic consolidation at the center. A State Agro-Industrial Committee (Gosagroprom) consolidated five food production and processing bureaucracies into one super-ministry. This typically Soviet effort at reform was a disaster. A popular joke around the time of the Soviet collapse has a CIA agent confiding to his new KGB acquaintance that Gosagroprom was really a plot by U.S. intelligence services to help bring about the downfall of the Soviet Union.

By liberalizing foreign trade, the regime hoped for an infusion of new technology into the moribund Soviet economy. Competition with foreign businesses would provide an incentive for Soviet firms to produce better products. The Ministry of Foreign Trade was stripped of its monopoly position, and by the end of 1988, most ministries, enterprises, and other organizations were allowed to engage in foreign trade. Joint ventures with foreign firms were encouraged, and the government planned to make the ruble a convertible currency within a few years. The Soviet government indicated its intention to participate in international economic organizations—such as the General Agreement on Tariffs and Trade (now the World Trade Organization), the World Bank, the International Monetary Fund (IMF), and the Asian Pacific Economic Cooperation forum—which it had previously denounced as capitalist dominated.

By 1989, Gorbachev had evolved from his initial cautious position on economic reform to accepting the need for the market to be the primary regulator of the Soviet economy. However, more conservative Politburo members, top officials in the military and the KGB, enterprise managers, and the powerful heads of the economic ministries and state committees favored preserving the command economy. For decades, Soviet propaganda had condemned the market as inefficient and exploitative; this conditioning was hard to resist. Perhaps more importantly, adopting a genuine market economy threatened the positions and perquisites of many Soviet officials. The economic ministries had derailed previous reform efforts; now, they severely constrained the reform process.

The second major principle of Gorbachev's reform program, glasnost, was supposed to provide the conditions for more effective economic restructuring. Usually translated as "openness" or "publicity," glasnost was meant to expose the full extent of mismanagement, corruption, and falsification in the economic system, holding both management and workers up to the glare of public opinion. Given the long Soviet (and Russian) tradition of secrecy, most Soviet leaders, Gorbachev included, did not envision completely abolishing the government's control over information. It proved difficult to apply glasnost selectively, however. When Reactor Number 4 at the Chernobyl nuclear power station in Ukraine exploded on April 26, 1986, the Kremlin's treatment of this disaster tested the limits of glasnost. Although the Soviet government at first withheld information on the true extent of the damage, domestic and international concern forced a public investigation that was unprecedented in Soviet history.

Chernobyl encouraged a frightened Soviet populace to demand more honest reporting from their government on a wide range of social, economic, and political issues—environmental pollution, disease, crime, official corruption, accidents, and natural disasters. As censorship weakened, the official Soviet press became increasingly critical of government actions, and the subjects open for public discussion expanded to include nationality relations, military issues, foreign policy, and even the private lives of top Soviet leaders. Encouraged by Gorbachev, the media attempted to fill in the blank spots in Soviet history, events that had been ignored or blatantly falsified in order to portray the Soviet system in a more flattering light. Stalin's bloody dictatorship was reappraised, and such prominent enemies of the state as Leon Trotsky, Nikolai Bukharin (the Party's chief theoretician in the 1920s and an outspoken advocate of the liberal policies of that period), and Aleksandr Solzhenitsyn, the famous dissident novelist and historian of the prison camps, were reevaluated. By the end of the 1980s, even Lenin, who had been virtually deified after his death as a prophet of Marxism and a supposedly infallible ruler, was condemned for having planted the seeds of dictatorship.

Ever since Lenin had convinced other Party leaders to ban opposing factions at the Tenth Party Congress in 1921, political opposition had been punished as a crime against the state. Not only were competing parties illegal, but all social and cultural organizations, from churches to chess clubs, were tightly controlled and monitored by the Communist Party. As perestroika and glasnost evolved, these political controls were relaxed and independent groups began to organize and articulate their demands. Ecology was one prominent issue that captured a great deal of attention, especially after Chernobyl, and many of the earliest informal groups were organized to combat local environmental problems. The Soviet government's abysmal record on the environment, due to careless practices in agriculture, industry, nuclear power, and defense, contributed significantly to the crisis in Soviet health care. Environmental destruction also helped stimulate greater militancy among the Soviet Union's national minorities, who shared the belief that the Soviet government had, in classic colonial style, deliberately located heavily polluting industries in their homelands.

Of course, ecology problems were only one in a long list of resentments held by the national minorities. The elaborate federal structure of the Soviet government theoretically gave the republics, autonomous republics, autonomous regions, and national areas a certain measure of self-determination. In reality, the national aspirations of most minorities were frustrated by centralized Party control and persistent efforts at Russification. Gorbachev and many of the reformers did not realize the strength of nationalism in the Soviet Union. By 1989–1990, National Front movements in the Baltic states, Ukraine, Belarus, and the Caucasus were demanding sovereign control over their internal affairs from Moscow; soon, Lithuania would declare its outright independence from the USSR.

NEW THINKING IN FOREIGN POLICY

A third element of Gorbachev's reform program was his determination to end the Cold War, repair ties with China, revise relations with the Third World, and put Soviet–East European relations on a new footing. The confrontational character of Soviet foreign policy had unnecessarily raised international tensions, provoked bloody conflicts by proxy in places like Nicaragua and Afghanistan, contributed to a costly arms race, and raised the specter of nuclear war between the superpowers. In addition, support for Soviet allies in Eastern Europe and for radical Third World regimes had proved immensely costly, a burden the USSR could no longer afford. Gorbachev and Foreign Affairs Minister Eduard Shevardnadze developed a radically new interpretation of Soviet national security and foreign policy interests more in keeping with perestroika's demands.

Since the end of World War II, Eastern Europe had followed the Soviet lead in political and economic matters. Repeated disturbances in Poland, Hungary, Czechoslovakia, and East Germany indicated that the Soviet model was inappropriate for much of Eastern Europe, and that continued Soviet imperial rule represented an affront to their sovereignty. Gorbachev encouraged Eastern European communist leaders to emulate his reforms, although the new thinking in foreign policy, as it was called, rejected the use of coercion as a tool to ensure compliance with Soviet practice. In his December 1988 United Nations speech, Gorbachev abandoned longstanding Soviet claims of being the only true defender of communist orthodoxy. As Foreign Ministry spokesman Gennadii Gerasimov explained, the Brezhnev Doctrine of limited sovereignty enunciated after the 1968 Czechoslovak invasion had been supplanted by the Sinatra doctrine, letting the East European states "do it their way."

As it became clear that Soviet military forces would no longer intervene to prop up unpopular communist governments, demands for change in Eastern Europe intensified. Cautious reforms were enacted in Hungary and Poland, traditionally the most liberal communist regimes, but leaders in Czechoslovakia, Romania, Bulgaria, and East Germany resisted ceding political power to democratic institutions. Between October and December 1989, however, a wave of revolution swept over Eastern Europe as communist regimes fell and the Berlin Wall was torn down. The summary execution of Romania's brutal dictator Nicolai Ceausescu and his wife on Christmas Day 1989 marked the end of communism in Eastern Europe.

Eastern Europe's liberation provided further encouragement to the movements for greater autonomy in the 15 union republics that comprised the Soviet Union. The Soviet constitution promised self-determination for Ukrainians, Armenians, Uzbeks, Lithuanians, and other major ethnic groups, but did not adequately satisfy the aspirations of the various nationalities. Although some cultural autonomy was permitted, and education in native languages was available, the Communist Party exercised tight central control from Moscow over the republics' affairs. Efforts to promote a unifying Soviet identity became a thinly disguised policy of Russification, antagonizing the 49 percent of the population that was not ethnic Russian. The end of the Soviet Empire in Eastern Europe raised the possibility of independence for the internal empire as well, accelerating demands for sovereignty and, in some cases, complete independence.

Beyond Eastern Europe, Gorbachev's new perspective on foreign policy led to major improvements in relations with the United States, China, and Western Europe, and reversed decades of support for radical Third World causes. Successful domestic reform, Gorbachev realized, could not be achieved in an atmosphere of international hostility. Prior to 1985, no Soviet leader had ever admitted that aggressive Soviet behavior might be responsible for the poor state of East-West relations or for the Sino-Soviet split. New thinking acknowledged that confrontational Soviet foreign policies, based on Lenin's ideas of class struggle, had often proved ineffective or even counterproductive to Soviet national interests. Gorbachev and the Kremlin reformers now spoke of universal human values and a common European home, promised an end to the enemy image and negative propaganda that had characterized Moscow's portrayal of the West, and pledged a reduction of military forces to a level sufficient for an adequate national defense.

Despite initial skepticism in the West, this new thinking produced a sea change in Soviet foreign policy. The first breakthrough—the December 1987 Intermediate-Range Nuclear Forces (INF) Treaty signed by the United States and the USSR—eliminated an entire class of highly destabilizing nuclear weapons. Soviet SS-20 nuclear missiles targeted at Europe had been placed in the western USSR starting in 1978; the following year, NATO decided to deploy Pershing II and ground-launched cruise missiles in Western Europe that were targeted at the Soviet Union. This new generation of weapons was highly destabilizing since the missiles would take only minutes to reach their targets. Peace groups in Europe had vigorously protested this escalation of the arms race, but talks conducted in the early 1980s had gone nowhere. With the INF Treaty, Reagan and Gorbachev concluded the first agreement between the superpowers to eliminate an entire class of weapons, and the first to allow highly intrusive verification of the accords in the form of on-site monitoring of the weapons' destruction.

NATO and the Warsaw Pact countries also began serious negotiations to reduce the huge stores of conventional (nonnuclear) weapons deployed between the Atlantic Ocean and the Ural Mountains. Mutual and Balanced Force Reductions talks between the two sides had been dragging on for years, but the Soviet side was unwilling to make the necessary cuts to bring its forces down to levels comparable to NATO's. Gorbachev broke this logjam, and a major treaty requiring the Soviet Union to undertake asymmetrical cuts in conventional weapons in Europe was signed in 1990 (the Conventional Forces in Europe, or CFE Treaty). In 1991, an unprecedented agreement significantly reducing strategic arms (the START Treaty) was signed by the United States and the Soviet Union.

Gorbachev also moved to repair relations with the countries of East Asia. The Soviet Union maintained a huge military presence in the Asian Pacific that consisted of ground troops and air and naval deployments in the Russian Far East, port rights in Vietnam and North Korea, and over 100,000 occupation troops in Afghanistan. For all this presence, Moscow had very little genuine influence in the region. The Soviet Union was feared and respected, but marginal as an economic power or a cultural influence. It was, as Australian scholar Paul Dibb suggested in his book, *The Soviet Union: The Incomplete Superpower* (Urbana: University of Illinois Press, 1988), an "incomplete superpower," powerful militarily, but weak in all other categories.

Soviet involvement in Afghanistan, like U.S. involvement in Vietnam, weakened Moscow's position in the region and made it more difficult to enact domestic reform. While there were few protests within the USSR, the war drained the Soviet treasury and cost the Soviet army some 13,000 lives. Gorbachev recognized the problem, calling Afghanistan a "bleeding wound." U.S. support for the mujahideen fighters, particularly equipping them with Stinger surface-to-air missiles, had, together with the determined resistance of the Afghan guerrillas, helped deprive Moscow of any semblance of a victory. In addition, their continued presence in Afghanistan poisoned U.S.-Soviet and Sino-Soviet relations. In 1988, Gorbachev announced that all Soviet troops would be withdrawn from Afghanistan within a year; the withdrawal process was completed by late 1989.

Two decades of tensions between the USSR and China had cost Moscow billions of rubles to deploy troops along the 4,000-mile border. At a May 1989 summit meeting in Beijing, the first in 30 years, China and the Soviet Union put an end to 30 years of bitter confrontation. In Beijing, Gorbachev promoted improved economic cooperation between China and the USSR, and announced a reduction of 200,000 Soviet troops in Asia over the next two years. However, the summit was overshadowed by the student demonstrations in Beijing's Tiananmen Square taking place at that time. The student protests were very much inspired by Gorbachev's liberalization of the Soviet Union. Their calls for greater democracy were tolerated by the Chinese authorities during Gorbachev's visit to the Chinese capital, but the occupation of Beijing's largest square was highly embarrassing to the regime. Within two weeks of Gorbachev's departure, the military dispersed the students in a bloody massacre.

China's communist leadership favored improving ties with the Soviet Union, but they were unnerved by the political turmoil on their northern border.

Gorbachev also implemented a major breakthrough in Soviet policy on the Korean peninsula. Since the end of World War II, Moscow had supplied North Korea's totalitarian regime with cheap oil, technical assistance in constructing nuclear power stations, military weapons, and political support. In keeping with Pyongyang's wishes, Moscow did not have diplomatic relations with South Korea, and there was virtually no contact between the two nations. As South Korea developed into an economic powerhouse in the 1980s, this position became increasingly untenable. Initial contacts were explored during the 1988 Seoul Olympic Games, and diplomatic ties were established in late September 1990, over North Korea's strident protests. Gorbachev met with President Roh Tae Woo of South Korea in May 1991 to discuss trade and Korean investment projects in the USSR, and the South Korean government offered a $3 billion aid package to their former enemy.

Although these remarkable developments in foreign policy created the relaxed international climate necessary for perestroika, many influential voices in the Soviet Union were critical of what they perceived as Gorbachev's extravagant concessions to the West and disturbed by the loss of the Soviet Empire. These same conservatives were also disturbed by the increasing disorder and confusion in Soviet society, and resisted efforts to develop private enterprise and a market-oriented economy. As the 1980s drew to a close, political forces in the USSR were polarized between the supporters of reform, who urged a program of genuine democratization, and the critics, who argued Russia's need for an authoritarian form of government.

DEMOCRATIZATION

Radical changes in Soviet political and economic life had polarized opinions, with elites divided between such conservatives as Yegor Ligachev and supporters of more rapid reform, led by Boris Yeltsin and Aleksandr Yakovlev. Gorbachev sought to occupy the middle ground, but it was a difficult balancing act. At first, Gorbachev could not bring himself to question the leading and guiding role of the Communist Party in Soviet society, a position enshrined in the 1977 Constitution. He believed that the Party could democratize, carry out perestroika, and still remain the nucleus of the political system. As early as 1987, experiments were introduced to provide for competitive, secret ballots for local and regional Party offices, and for term limits. However, these attempts to undermine the old, comfortable, and often corrupt system of Nomenklatura appointments by which politically loyal officials secured powerful jobs alienated conservatives in the CPSU.

Gorbachev had brought Boris Yeltsin to Moscow in 1985 from Sverdlovsk oblast (region) in the Ural Mountains, where he had been the Communist Party's First Secretary. Yeltsin was to serve as a member of the Politburo and First Secretary of Moscow—in effect, as a powerful mayor. The gregarious, hard-drinking Yeltsin proved immensely popular as Party Secretary for Moscow. Portraying himself as a genuine man of the people, Yeltsin started riding the Moscow subway and busses, and stood in store lines in order to appreciate the everyday hardships endured by Soviet people. Angered by Yeltsin's constant pressure for faster reform and his public criticism of the leadership, Gorbachev, Ligachev, and other members of the Politburo humiliated him at a 1987 Central Committee meeting. Dragged from his hospital bed, Yeltsin was subjected to repeated denunciations and was relieved of his Politburo position and dismissed as Moscow First Secretary. Few suspected the amazing comeback he would make over the next three years.

The Nineteenth Party Conference of June 1988, which illustrated the strength of conservative opposition to reform within the Communist Party, marked a watershed in political reform. By this point, Gorbachev was convinced that perestroika could not succeed, barring a shift of political power from the authoritarian CPSU to elected governmental institutions. Popular pressure expressed through the electoral process, he reasoned, would compel reluctant officials to support his reform program. The Nineteenth Party Conference adopted resolutions calling for the further democratization of Soviet society, and the Party's Central Committee designed a series of constitutional amendments that created an electoral system and a functioning parliament.

Elections to the new Congress of People's Deputies, held in March 1989, were relatively free by Soviet standards. Although some offices were filled Soviet-style, with only one nominee per office, many had two, five, or even twelve candidates for one position. The most undemocratic aspect of elections to the 2,250-member Congress was the provision of electing one-third of the deputies from social and political organizations—the Communist Party, Komsomol, trade unions, women's organizations, and the Academy of Sciences—thus weighting the vote heavily in favor of the conservative forces that dominated these organizations. Another third would be elected from the national republics and smaller ethnic regions, and the final third by population from electoral districts. Although the outcome was biased against reform candidates, roughly one-fifth of the elected deputies were ardent reformers. Since political parties other than the CPSU were still illegal, candidates ran as individuals, making it difficult to discern their positions on issues.

The Congress, which opened in May 1989, was broadcast live on Soviet television to an entranced audience. Unaccustomed to democracy, deputies to the Congress haggled over procedural issues and traded accusations. Champion weightlifter Yurii Vlasov condemned historic abuses by the KGB. Delegates from Georgia demanded prosecution of the Soviet general who had commanded his forces to crush Tbilisi demonstrators earlier that year; 31 had been killed with sharpened shovels wielded by special forces. The prominent physicist and human rights campaigner Andrei Sakharov delivered an impassioned plea for greater democracy, much to Gorbachev's annoyance. As might be expected, this new Congress could not immediately provide effective governance. Its emergence, however, helped legitimize the concept of representative democracy among an important segment of the population. It also marked the beginning of the end of the Communist Party's monopoly over political power.

Much of the problem in trying to effect reform stemmed from the pervasive influence of the CPSU in Soviet political life. The Party had succeeded, albeit at tremendous cost, in constructing the rudiments of a modern industrial society—an urbanized population base, factories, transportation and communications infrastructure, mass education, and science. As a consequence, Soviet society and the economy had experienced major transformations since the Revolution. The moribund political system, however, had great difficulty adapting to the changing conditions of the late 20th century. The Communist Party's obsession with secrecy clashed with the demands of the information age, its myopic focus on expanding industrial output ignored the worldwide trend toward quality and efficiency, and its centralized approach to political issues could not meet the challenge of creating community out of an increasingly diverse society. Prior to Gorbachev, the Party had resisted granting the population a larger role in governing. Lacking flexibility, the Soviet state maintained the appearance of exercising effective authority right until the point when the system began to collapse.

As Harvard political scientist Samuel Huntington pointed out in his classic *Political Order in Changing Societies* (New Haven: Yale University Press, 1968), a political system with several powerful institutions is more likely to adapt to change than a system with only one significant institution. If one institution suffers a loss of legitimacy, the others can assume some of the weakened institution's functions. Soviet reformers, however, faced the daunting task of creating entirely new institutions—a functioning legislature, independent courts, a responsible executive, and genuine federalism—virtually overnight to replace a rapidly disintegrating Communist Party. As might be expected, there was considerable disagreement over the precise form these new governing institutions would assume.

In all political systems, it takes time for new institutions to acquire legitimacy, or acceptance by the public of their right to make decisions that govern people's lives. The United States, for example, fought a bloody civil war over issues of federal power versus states' rights more than 70 years after the Constitution was enacted. It would be unrealistic to assume that new institutions could be designed, staffed, and functioning smoothly within a few years, especially in the context of exponentially increasing demands from the population. Again, drawing on Huntington's study of transitional societies, political instability in the Soviet Union resulted from the rapid expansion of political participation, coupled with the inability of reformers to organize and institutionalize the means of reconciling conflicting demands. In other words, political change could not keep up with social and economic change.

A genuine constitutional order is essential for democracy. Serious discussion about the need for a state based on the rule of law was introduced at the Nineteenth Party Conference. The Soviet constitutions of 1918, 1924, 1936, and 1977 had functioned more as statements of intent and propaganda devices than binding legal documents outlining institutions' powers and protecting citizens' rights and liberties. Under Gorbachev, the Brezhnev Constitution of 1977 was amended repeatedly by the Supreme Soviet; one-third of the Constitution's articles were amended in 1988 alone. These amendments shifted power from the Party to more representative political institutions, such as the Congress of People's Deputies, created an executive presidency, designed a committee on constitutional supervision to adjudicate disputes at the highest level, and broadened citizens' rights. Early in 1990, Article 6, guaranteeing the Communist Party's leading position, was dropped from the Constitution. These changes did not immediately establish a constitutional government in the Soviet Union, but they were key steps toward a democratic rule of law.

This hodgepodge of amendments yielded a document that was unwieldy and inadequate for an effectively functioning democracy. Late in 1989, Gorbachev appointed a Constitutional Commission to draft a completely new constitution. By this point, however, political events were moving so rapidly that the authorities could not keep up with exploding demands. Relations between the capital and the republics were a major sticking point in the constitutional negotiations. Revelations about official corruption and mismanagement and the obvious failure of Gorbachev's economic reform policies undermined the credibility of central authorities and inspired calls for greater autonomy in the provinces. Toward the end of 1990, Soviet leaders began to reevaluate the sham federalism that had promised cultural autonomy while ensuring centralized Communist Party control over the various national republics. Plans were drawn up for a new Union Treaty to replace the one that had created the Union of Soviet Socialist Republics in 1922. Gorbachev and the reformers were finally willing to draw up a new constitution that would grant significant self-governing powers to the republics. But conservatives, who saw their influence expand in late 1990 and early 1991, argued that the establishment of genuine federalism would undermine the basis of the Soviet communist system. Ironically, the movement toward political autonomy in the republics had progressed so far that even a decentralized system patterned on the U.S.

or Canadian constitution would not satisfy their demands for sovereignty or independence.

CULTURE AND SOCIETY

A key element of reform was freeing the creative energies of Soviet society in publishing, theater, art, music, and political and social activity. Aleksandr Yakovlev, who was promoted to membership in the Politburo in January 1987, was a key architect of glasnost. Convinced that a more open society was needed to rally support for perestroika, Yakovlev used his influence to appoint liberals as editors of influential newspapers and magazines; liberals were also given key positions in the film industry and theater. Vitalii Korotich became editor of *Ogonyok* (Little Flame), a color weekly that became widely read for its biting satire of public affairs. As the new editor of *Novyi Mir,* Sergei Zalygin, an erudite hydraulic engineer, published penetrating political articles, previously banned novels, and environmental exposés.

As censorship controls eased, previously banned works were published—Pasternak's *Dr. Zhivago,* Anatoly Rybakov's *Children of the Arbat,* and Aleksandr Solzhenitsyn's novels. Solzhenitsyn's *Gulag Archipelago,* for which he had been expelled from the USSR, was now available to the general public. Mikhail Shatrov's play *Onward, Onward, Onward,* a critique of the Stalinist repression, was first performed in 1987. But the major cultural event of that year was a film by the Georgian director Tengiz Abuladze titled *Repentance.* The script for the film, an allegory about the evils of dictatorship, was written in 1981, and Shevardnadze, then First Secretary of Georgia, recommended its release when the filming was completed in 1984. But Abuladze did not receive permission to show the film until Yakovlev and Gorbachev personally approved it for distribution. *Repentance* drew huge audiences in the Soviet Union and was quite popular in the United States and Europe.

Glasnost had exposed the extent of the regime's deception and mistreatment of its own people. The revelations about Soviet labor camps, the Molotov-Ribbentrop Non-Aggression Pact of 1939, the 1930s show trials, corruption and mismanagement in government, environmental disasters, and costly foreign policy mistakes led to widespread cynicism and disillusionment among much of the population. Marxist-Leninist ideology was quickly abandoned by all but a few loyal adherents. Many Soviet citizens turned to religion to fill the spiritual void in their lives. Attendance at Russian Orthodox churches ballooned, and groups began raising money to restore churches that had fallen into disrepair. Catholics, Baptists, Seventh-Day Adventists, and other Christian denominations became more active; Hare Krishnas and even more exotic cults became popular. Faith healers, spiritualists, and occult followers dominated Soviet television and filled local news kiosks with their pamphlets.

In one of the many ironies of that period, two societies sharing the same name, but having radically different agendas, appeared on the scene. One, Pamyat (Memorial), formed in 1987, was committed to publicizing the terrible truth about Stalin's rule. Led mostly by young scholars and writers, Memorial's goal was to build monuments and research centers to commemorate the victims of Stalin's Terror. Much like Jewish students of the Holocaust, Memorial wanted the world to know and remember what had happened, so that history would not be repeated. The other Pamyat (Memory) was an anti-Semitic, violently Russian nationalist organization. Formed late in the Brezhnev era to preserve Russian cultural monuments and supported by forces in the military and the Party, Memory claimed that Jews, Westerners, and Zionists were responsible for all of Russia's ills, from AIDS and drugs to alcoholism and rock 'n' roll, and that the Bolshevik Revolution was really a Jewish-led conspiracy that destroyed the true, tsarist Russia.

Liberalization eventually led to a backlash by conservative forces, who were dismayed by the breakdown of order in Soviet society. A strong authoritarian current has long existed in Russian political culture, and these sentiments found an outlet not only in fringe groups, but also in nationalist and communist publications. *Nash sovremennik* (Our Contemporary) and the Party newspaper *Pravda* were two conservative periodicals that decried the reformers' preoccupation with the ills of Soviet society and their attempts to degrade communism's historical achievements. Elderly citizens who had gone through collectivization, the Purges, and the Great Fatherland War found it difficult to accept the notion that their sacrifices had been in vain. One middle-aged chemistry teacher, Nina Andreyevna, expressed her commitment to fundamental Stalinism in a March 1988 article submitted as a letter to *Sovetskaya Rossiya*. The paper's editors, backed by Politburo hard-liner Anatoly Lukyanov, published her article under the title "I Cannot Forsake Principles." Knowledgeable insiders realized that this was a blatant attack on Gorbachev, reflecting the views of Party hard-liners and appearing as it did in one of the Party's flagship papers. Andreyeva's article was timed for publication just as Gorbachev was leaving for Yugoslavia, briefly raising the possibility of a reactionary coup. On his return to Moscow, Gorbachev rallied his supporters in the Politburo. He and Yakovlev penned a defense of perestroika, and this official rebuttal to the Andreyevna article was duly published in the April 5 issue of *Pravda*. The defenders of the old order retreated for the time being.

STRAINS OF NATIONALISM

With glasnost and political liberalization, Soviet people quickly lost their fear of the regime and began forming political organizations. Among the hundreds of informal groups that sprang up were independent labor unions, women's groups, ecology groups, peasant organizations, professional groups, and religious cults. Most of these groups were small and local in nature; many were little more than discussion groups. Such organizations, though, are the very fabric of a civic culture and a responsible and active society that is autonomous from the state, and are necessary in building a successful democracy.

The most potent political demands from the newly active population were for ethnic and national freedom. Contrary to Marxian predictions, nationalism, not class, was the basis for revolution in the Soviet Union. Few Soviet reformers, Gorbachev included, understood the strength of national feeling among the 100-odd ethnic groups that comprised the USSR. Soviet leaders actually seemed to believe their own propaganda that the tsarist prison of nations had been supplanted by a family of nations under communism. For 70 years, the pressures of ideological conformity and the threat of physical force had constrained national aspirations. There were occasional glimpses of discontent bubbling beneath the surface, as in 1986, when Kazakh students took to the streets to protest the appointment of an ethnic Russian as their republic's First Secretary. But few could anticipate the tremendous surge of nationalism that would accompany the relaxation of political controls between 1987 and 1991.

National front organizations first formed in the Baltic states of Latvia, Lithuania, and Estonia; these provided the model for the national fronts that subsequently formed in the other republics. Environmental devastation was an important rallying point for the Balts, as it was for many Soviet nationalities. Estonians resented the open-pit mining for phosphates that scarred the landscape; Lithuanians who were apprehensive about the possibility of another Chernobyl lobbied for the closure of the Ignalina nuclear power station. Ecological demands quickly broadened into more general calls for each republic to exercise sovereignty over its national territory and resources, and then for full independence from the USSR. Even top leaders of the republic communist parties jumped on the nationalist bandwagon. All three Baltic states insisted that since their forcible incorporation had been illegal under international law, they would not request independence from Moscow, but were entitled to secede without negotiations. Soviet troops were sent into Vilnius, Lithuania, and Riga, Latvia, in January 1991 to restore order, but were soon withdrawn amid strident local and international outrage.

Nationalism in the Caucasian republics took the form of internecine struggle, rather than opposition to Moscow, as conflicts broke out among various nationalist factions. In 1988, Armenian nationalists within Nagorno-Karabagh, an autonomous region located entirely within Azerbaijan, but with a population that was 75-percent Armenian, passed a resolution demanding that their region be transferred to Armenian jurisdiction. Armenians in Armenia, Azerbaijan, and Russia supported the resolution, but Azeri nationalists rejected

Armenia's claims, and brutal attacks on ethnic Armenians in Sumgait resulted in the deaths of hundreds. Reprisals against ethnic Azeris in Armenia fed a cycle of suspicion and fear, leading thousands on both sides to flee for their home republics. Both sides obtained weapons from local military units and, in 1989, the Azeris blockaded all road and rail links into Armenia. Desultory fighting continued into 1994. Moscow tried to mediate the dispute, but was viewed as biased by both sides, and its efforts were unsuccessful.

National front organizations formed in Belorussia, Moldavia, and Central Asia, but they were small and weak compared to those in the Baltic and Caucasian republics. Ukraine was a different matter. In Ukraine, writers and intellectuals were concerned about the decline of their native language and traditions, as the Russian language had supplanted Ukrainian in the republic's education system. The Union of Writers of Ukraine demanded reforms mandating increased use of Ukrainian in schools, state offices, and workplaces, and in the media and entertainment. A powerful Popular Movement (Rukh) formed early in 1989, lobbying for linguistic concessions; pressure from Rukh contributed to the ouster of Ukraine's conservative Party First Secretary, Vladimir Shcherbitsky, by September of that year.

The nuclear explosion at Chernobyl, only 70 miles north of Kiev, also stimulated Ukrainian nationalism. The Chernobyl disaster killed 31 people outright, poisoned thousands more with nuclear radiation over the next decade, and contaminated huge tracts of agricultural land. Fully one-half of Soviet nuclear energy plants were located on Ukrainian soil, and Moscow officials controlled their operation, not Kiev. Ukrainian environmentalists organized protests against plans to build additional plants in the republic. Finally, resentment against Moscow was kindled by revelations about the extent of the 1932–1933 famine, which had taken the lives of nearly 5 million Ukrainians. A referendum held on December 1, 1991, in which 90 percent of Ukraine's voters opted for independence, signaled the end of the USSR.

The rebirth of Russian nationalism was critical in the breakup of the Soviet Union. Pamyat was only a fringe element—there were also democratic, ecological, and religious Russian nationalists, and the more authoritarian National Bolshevik strain. Russian writers, including those from the village prose school, lobbied successfully against the proposed diversion of Siberian rivers southward to replenish Central Asia's Aral Sea. The series of canal, dams, and locks needed for such a massive engineering feat, they asserted, would destroy many Russian Orthodox churches. Revitalizing Russia's Orthodox heritage was high on the agenda of many nationalist groups. Russian Orthodox churches were restored at an astonishing rate: only 10 new parishes were registered in 1986, but this had ballooned to 2,185 in 1989. Russian nationalists were often intolerant of other faiths and ethnic groups. Writers such as Valentin Rasputin and Aleksandr Solzhenitsyn called for Russia to shed its internal empire, freeing the Soviet nationalities and making Russia more purely Russian. At the same time, Russian nationalists were deeply divided over their preferred form of government. National Bolsheviks, for example, promoted a national form of communism; other nationalists urged the revival of tsarist autocracy.

Political decentralization, which resulted in the formation of independent republic legislatures in 1990–1991, provided a powerful boost to the Russian national movement. Competitive elections were held for a new Russian Federation legislature in March 1990. Roughly six candidates stood for each of the 1,068 seats, and turnout was fairly high at 77 percent. Boris Yeltsin received over 80 percent of the vote on the first ballot from his home town of Sverdlovsk (now Ekaterinburg), and in May 1990, he was elected Chairman of the Russian Parliament. Under his leadership, the Russian Federation declared sovereignty, began to conduct foreign policy, and, in general, acted as a state within a state. The following June, Yeltsin's legitimacy was greatly enhanced when he became Russia's new Executive President. Competing against Gorbachev's Prime Minister Nikolai Ryzhkov and the flamboyant Russian nationalist Vladimir Zhirinovsky, the leader of the Russian Liberal Democratic Party, Yeltsin won a direct popular election with nearly 60 percent of the vote.

COUP AND COLLAPSE

Conservative forces had been gathering strength in the latter part of 1990 and the first half of 1991. Foreign Minister Eduard Shevardnadze cautioned against the possibility of a right-wing coup in December 1990, when he resigned his position. The other prominent advocate of reform, Aleksandr Yakovlev, had warned Gorbachev that he was surrounded by enemies just before his resignation in July. Yakovlev was admonished not to exaggerate. U.S. Ambassador Jack Matlock met with Gorbachev in June 1991 and passed along to him intelligence reports about a possible coup. The stubborn General Secretary refused to take these warnings seriously and left with his family for a vacation in the Crimea in early August. On August 19, a group known as the State Committee for the State of Emergency, composed of government hardliners, announced that Gorbachev was incapacitated and sent tanks into the streets to preserve order.

The proximate cause of what was called the August Coup was the new Union Treaty scheduled to be signed on August 20. This treaty would have revised the Soviet Constitution, establishing a genuine federal system for the first time in Soviet history. Soviet hard-liners understood that transferring authority from Moscow to the republics would lead to the disintegration of the

Soviet Union, and they decided to act before the treaty was signed into law. The coup leaders included Vladimir Kryuchkov, head of the KGB, as well as Defense Minister Dmitrii Yazov, Interior Minister Boris Pugo, Prime Minister Valentin Pavlov, and Chairman of the Supreme Soviet Antoly Lukyanov. It was decided that Vice President Gennadii Yanayev, a timid alcoholic of limited abilities, would assume Gorbachev's duties to preserve the illusion of legality. A delegation was sent to the Crimea to demand that Gorbachev cooperate with the State Committee for the State of Emergency, the ruling committee set up by the plotters. He refused and was held there under house arrest. Coup leaders then released a statement asserting that he was ill and could not carry out his presidential duties.

Fortunately, the coup instigators had neither the ability nor the ruthlessness necessary to consolidate their grasp on power. Key democratic leaders—Yeltsin, Russian republic Prime Minister Aleksandr Rutskoi, Supreme Soviet Chairman Ruslan Khasbulatov, and Leningrad Mayor Anatoly Sobchak—were not arrested. Full control over the media eluded the plotters. Although heads of the power ministries (Defense, KGB, and Interior) organized the coup, they were unwilling to use sufficient force to crush the democratic forces. Coup resisters led by Yeltsin, Khasbulatov, and Rutskoi had barricaded themselves in the White House, the white marble seat of the Russian republic government on the bank of the Moscow River. Students, housewives, new businessmen, and Afghanistan vets flocked to the White House to help in any way they could. Elite army units from the Taman division who were called in to surround the building were persuaded to join the democrats. The defining moment of the coup came when Yeltsin mounted one of the T-72 tanks and delivered an impassioned denunciation of the reactionary and unconstitutional actions of the Emergency Committee, and appealed to all Russian citizens to resist.

Reactions to the attempted takeover illustrated the highly fragmented character of public opinion about the changes taking place in the USSR. Many courageous individuals rallied to support Russian President Boris Yeltsin at the parliament building. The demoralized Soviet army was divided—some officers ignored orders to march on Moscow and St. Petersburg, while others commanded tanks in the streets of the capital. A few regional leaders condemned the coup; most cautiously waited for the situation to crystallize before committing themselves. Within three days, by August 21, the coup had collapsed. Gorbachev and his wife Raisa immediately flew back to Moscow. By this point, however, Gorbachev's indecisiveness and poor judgment, and Yeltsin's heroic resistance at the White House, had decisively shifted the balance of power toward Yeltsin. In addition, Yeltsin's direct election as Russia's President conferred a legitimacy that Gorbachev, who was indirectly elected, did not possess.

Gorbachev attempted to hold the USSR together in a looser arrangement, but his authority and credibility had been so tarnished that he was doomed to fail. For the minority republics, the conservatives' bid for power and Gorbachev's apparent inability to grasp the significance of the August events following the coup confirmed their worst fears. In this climate, full independence seemed the best guarantee against Moscow reestablishing centralized political control. Yeltsin, unlike Gorbachev, had encouraged the non-Russian republics to assert their sovereignty. "Take as much as you can handle," he advised. Latvia, Lithuania, and Estonia took his advice; they appealed for international diplomatic recognition and were granted it. One by one, the other republics declared their independence from the Soviet Union. The death blow came with Ukraine's December 1 referendum, in which 90 percent of the population voted in favor of independence.

With the failed coup, the most powerful Soviet institutions were no longer able to exercise control over this vast territory. The Communist Party had been thoroughly discredited, and in November, Yeltsin issued a decree ordering it banned altogether. In early December, Yeltsin, Ukrainian President Leonid Kuchma, and Belarusian Supreme Soviet Chairman Stanislav Shushkievich met in Minsk and formed the Commonwealth of Independent States (CIS), a weak confederation, to replace the USSR. Two weeks later, eight other republics joined the CIS; Georgia and the Baltic states refused. Gorbachev's resignation on Christmas Day 1991 marked the end of the 74-year Soviet experiment to create a communist utopia.

Many factors played a role in the collapse of the Soviet Union. The most important seem to have been internal, although international pressures, many of which were linked to Moscow's inept foreign policies, also deserved some credit for the collapse. Domestic factors included the increasingly poor economic performance of the centrally planned economy, technological backwardness, a stifling and repressive political system that discouraged creativity, excessive military spending, extraordinary bureaucratic inefficiency, a catastrophic ecology record, and insensitivity to the national interests of the Soviet Union's diverse minorities. Confrontational foreign policies, influenced by the ideology of class struggle, alienated many Soviet allies and brought the capitalist world together in an effort to contain the perceived communist threat.

The accumulation of domestic problems and international pressures coincided with a major generational change in Soviet leadership. Gorbachev was central in planning and promoting reform, but it should be remembered that he was supported by younger officials for whom the terror of the Stalin era was only a vague memory. This generation was better educated and more critical of Soviet achievements than the Brezhnevs, the Suslovs, and the Gromykos, whose careers were built over the graves of the Old Bolsheviks. Lastly, we should not forget the Soviet people, who were disillusioned and impatient with a corrupt, repressive system that refused to acknowledge their humanity. The revolution that brought about the collapse of the Soviet Union may have started with the Party elite, but it ended with an extraordinary display of public affirmation that dictatorship could not be restored.

9

Russia's Search for Democracy: The Yeltsin Era

Sooner or later, I will leave political life. I will exit according to the rules, the Constitution, and the law. I would definitely like to make that contribution to the history of Russia, to set the precedent of a normal, civilized, orderly departure from politics.

—Boris Yeltsin, *The Struggle for Russia*

The death of the USSR gave birth to 15 new, independent countries—the former union republics. Russia was left with about half the population of the former Soviet Union at 147 million and three-fourths of its territory. Russia and the other republics were still bound together by transportation links, economic interdependency, and some common security considerations. Independent Russia was much more homogeneous than the former Soviet Union—82 percent Russian and 18 percent various non-Russian nationalities (see Table 9.1). Of great concern to Russian nationalists was the fact that about 25 million ethnic Russians now lived outside their homeland: 10 million of these in Ukraine, 7 million in Kazakhstan, and the remainder scattered throughout the other newly independent states. The Commonwealth of Independent States (CIS) was formed late in 1991 to preserve some political, economic, and security links among the newly independent republics, but this organization was very

Table 9.1: Major Nationalities of the Russian Federation, 1989 (those in excess of 500,000).

	Number	Percent of Total
Russians	119,866,000	81.5
Tatars	5,522,000	3.8
Ukrainians	4,363,000	3.0
Chuvash	1,774,000	1.2
Bashkirs	1,345,000	0.9
Belarusians	1,206,000	0.8
Mordovans	1,073,000	0.7
Chechens	899,000	0.6
Germans	842,000	0.6
Udmurts	715,000	0.5
Maritsy	644,000	0.4
Kazakhs	636,000	0.4
Avars	544,000	0.4
Jews	537,000	0.4
Armenians	532,000	0.4
Others	6,524,000	4.4
Total	147,022,000	100.0

Source: Figures are from the 1989 national census, in Rossiskii statisticheskii ezhegodnik 1994 (Moscow: Gostkomstat Rossii, 1994), p. 33.

weak, and optimistic expectations that over time, it might function like the European Union were not borne out. Over the next few years, the former republics of the Soviet Union would drift further apart.

The new Russian Federation faced several daunting tasks. First and most pressing was the need to enact major economic reform—privatizing the state enterprises, freeing domestic and foreign trade, liberalizing prices, and in general creating a market economy from a centrally planned system. Second, Russia needed to continue the process of democratization by designing a new constitution and creating new political institutions, a new legal system, and a democratic political culture. Third, the economic and political transformations that followed the collapse of communism generated pressing social problems, among them unemployment, poverty, declining health care, and crime. Fourth, Russia had to create a new foreign policy identity to replace the self-designated Soviet role as leader of the world communist movement. Finally, Russia would need a system of spiritual or philosophical values to replace the bankrupt ideas of Marxism-Leninism. Addressing each of these issues simultaneously is a tall order, and the process has not been a smooth one.

ECONOMIC REFORM

The first order of business in Russia was to enact radical economic reform. President Boris Yeltsin and his acting prime minister, Yegor Gaidar, adopted a program of shock therapy involving the abrupt deregulation of prices, the privatization of state-owned enterprises, and the shift to a market economy. At first, many Russians believed that capitalism would bring instant riches. However, freeing prices brought about hyperinflation: 2,500 percent in 1992, 840 percent in 1993, and 200 percent in 1994. Many lost their savings virtually overnight, and wage increases quickly fell behind the cost of living. Russia was inundated with a flood of foreign goods—American Coke and Pepsi, Chinese toys and children's clothes, German Mercedes and BMW automobiles, Japanese and Korean electronics, British cigarettes, and Swiss chocolates. Many resented this flood of foreign goods, particularly Snickers candy bars, which seemed to be everywhere.

In late 1991, Yeltsin had surrounded himself with a group of young radical reformers who were determined to bring capitalism to Russia as quickly as possible—Yegor Gaidar, Anatoly Chubais, and Aleksandr Shokhin. Foreign economists Jeffrey Sachs of Harvard and Anders Åslund of Sweden served as advisors to the government. A program of price liberalization and financial stabilization was enacted at the beginning of 1992, premised on rapid transformation of the old command economy. Speed was deemed necessary to break the hold of the old Soviet Nomenklatura, who were resisting reform, and to achieve results before patience wore thin with the sacrifices of reform. Politically, they reasoned, weakening the Nomenklatura would make a return to communism impossible. In actuality, most of the new business elite, the wealthy New Russians, were former Communist Party and government officials who were ideally positioned to take advantage of the economic transition. Similarly, there was a great deal of continuity in the political world. About four-fifths of the politicians in the Russian Congress of People's Deputies were former Party and government officials. The ranks of these communist-era holdovers were augmented by ambitious, politically reformist, and entrepreneurial young Russians.

Russia's middle-aged elites were survivors, but certainly not innovators. In spring 1992, the Supreme Soviet adopted a privatization program over strong protests. The job of privatizing Russia's economy was given to Anatoly Chubais, an economist and former university professor in his thirties. In the summer of 1992, Chubais introduced a system of vouchers, giving each Russian citizen 10,000 rubles to invest in newly privatized companies. Given the high rate of inflation, 10,000 rubles, which in the Soviet era would have been the equivalent of four years' salary for a well-paid worker, was now worth only a few dollars. Some invested their vouchers; others sold them at a discount rate to speculators. Factory workers and managers were given the opportunity to purchase one-quarter to one-half of their enterprise's shares; these were usually allocated based on the employee's rank within the enterprise. Of course, that meant that factory executives were ideally positioned to obtain the bulk of the shares, and many became wealthy overnight.

Much of the Russian economy was privatized within the first five years. Nearly 47,000 small businesses were privatized in 1992 alone, and by the end of 1994, well over 100,000 enterprises had been privatized. Small businesses employed just over 10 percent of all workers by 1996 and accounted for 11–12 percent of total production. Mid-size and large enterprises were privatized more slowly; only 18 were auctioned off in 1992, but by 1995, that number had risen to nearly 18,000. To placate the political opposition, defense industries, health care systems, and other strategic or sensitive enterprises were retained under state ownership.

Very few Russian citizens became investors in the newly privatized economy. Russians were slow to buy stocks, bonds, or mutual funds, and most distrusted banks, preferring to put their cash under a mattress instead of depositing it in a savings account. Many wealthy Russians did not trust their country's business environment, preferring to invest their money in the more stable countries of Western Europe. The European Bank for Reconstruction and Development estimates that by the mid-1990s, Russians had invested $40–50 billion outside Russia, while foreign investors were putting only $1–2 billion per year into the Russian economy. Furthermore, Russian managers and workers were suspicious of investment by outsiders—either foreigners or Russian mafia—and many refused opportunities to attract much-needed capital investment for their firms. Because of conservative management strategies, many firms avoided restructuring, which was necessary in order to turn a profit. One group of Western and Russian economists estimated that as of 1996, three-fourths of Russia's enterprises still needed radical restructuring to be profitable—only one-fourth could operate profitably in the new market economy.

Even before the collapse of communism, officials in the Communist Party, the Komsomol, and the ministries had arranged deals with their friends and relatives to buy state and Party property at bargain prices. These assets were then resold for huge profits, spawning millionaires almost overnight. These New Russians acquired foreign luxury cars, huge homes, and expensive clothes, and surrounded themselves with beautiful young women. They frequented glitzy nightclubs and restaurants, paying exorbitant sums for lavish meals and entertainment. Many hired small armies of bodyguards—former police, army, or KGB agents—for protection against competitors. Average Russians despised the newly rich and the robber baron form of capitalism they practiced. Anatoly Chubais and Yegor Gaidar, the architects of Russia's market economy, were held responsible for these ills and soon became the most hated politicians in Russia.

For most Russians, privatization meant a decline in living standards. Beggars, usually older women, sat outside subway stations and churches pleading for money. Street markets sprang up where people would bring old pairs of shoes, toys, vegetables from their garden plots, tools, books, and anything else they could sell. The more successful vendors sold goods out of small kiosks— newspapers, liquor, candy bars, soft drinks, pornography, watches, fruit—and paid protection money to the ubiquitous gangs that roamed the streets. Some hawked souvenirs for the tourist trade—colorful scarves, *matryoshka* dolls, lacquer boxes. Thousands of aspiring businessmen and women engaged in shuttle trade. The shuttlers would fly to Istanbul, Bangkok, Warsaw, Berlin, or Seoul, buy up clothes, electronic goods, or food, and bring them back to Russia to sell at greatly inflated prices. In the Russian Far East, used Toyotas and Hondas flooded the streets of Vladivostok, Khabarovsk, and smaller cities. Since the Japanese drive on the left side of the road, and Russians drive on the right side of the road, as do Americans, these imports made for some exciting traffic.

Russia's economic reforms disrupted the lives of many workers. For the majority of them, wages did not keep up with price increases. The government's tax burden on firms was so great that many could not afford to buy raw materials, pay their taxes, and pay workers. too. By the mid- to late 1990s, workers frequently did not receive their wages on time; some had not been paid in over a year. Strikes increased dramatically during the years 1994–1997, with miners and teachers among the most disaffected elements of the labor force. Some of the more desperate teachers took part in hunger strikes. The more politically astute workers took advantage of the 1996 presidential elections to extract promises of aid from President Yeltsin as he campaigned across the country. Russian organized labor also made the payment of overdue wages its primary demand. However, organized labor, weak as it was in the post-communist environment, impeded the reform process. The Independent Federation of Trade Unions of Russia, successor to the communist-dominated labor unions of the Soviet era and claimant to 95 percent of all organized workers, lobbied to keep unprofitable mines and businesses open. This kept workers employed in the short term, but jeopardized the long-term viability of their firms.

The agricultural sector was in even more dire straits than industry or services. Technically, all of the collective and state farms had transformed themselves into joint-stock companies, but most continued to operate as they had before—inefficiently, and at a loss. Communist and Agrarian Party members in Parliament refused to legalize the private ownership of farmland. Without a legal guarantee of property, few farmers were willing to strike out on their own. A few thousand entrepreneurial types had tried private farming early in the 1990s, but given the absence of credit, fertilizer, and technical support, as well as the active hostility of much of the Russian peasantry, many abandoned the effort. By the late 1990s, Russia, a potentially rich agricultural country, was importing fully half of its food from abroad.

Perhaps the biggest problem in economic reform was the explosion of organized crime and the links between these mafia gangs and politicians. Even at its most impressive, the Soviet government had never managed to eliminate the criminal underworld, whose Russian, Chechen, Tatar, and Central Asian variants existed in the labor camps and on the fringes of Soviet society. With the breakdown of order in the early 1990s, the old gangs began to operate openly, and hundreds of new ones formed. Reflecting the Russian tendency toward absolutism, complete subservience gave way to total freedom. Russia's mafia gangs were involved in smuggling gold, diamonds, and other valuable minerals out of the country, and computers, electronic goods, and other items into the country (thus avoiding customs duties); selling military weapons to clients abroad; operating extortion and protection rackets; smuggling drugs; and stealing cars. Some of the more powerful criminal bosses set up operations abroad, including in the United States, leading the FBI to establish close working relations with Russian law enforcement.

Organized crime had been closely linked to Soviet officialdom, and these ties carried over into the post-communist period. In the latter stages of perestroika, the Soviet elite had plundered the state and secreted billions of dollars in bank accounts abroad. Ambitious young bureaucrats set themselves up as consultants, using their connections with government to help prospective businessmen evade taxes, regulations, and other red tape. The most powerful new businessmen (and virtually all were men) controlled huge conglomerates that encompassed banking, mass media, oil and gas, and real estate. By the late 1990s, these financial tycoons were referred to as "the oligarchs"—prime movers and shakers in Russian business and politics. Among the most influential were Vladimir Gusinsky, chairman of MOST bank; Boris Berezovsky, automobile magnate and banker; and Vladimir Potanin, head of Uneximbank. These financial barons had amassed huge profits through the loans for shares program in which the banks lent money to the government in exchange for shares in major Russian industries.

While some Russian entrepreneurs became super-rich, many other Russians remained mired in poverty, and the development of a stable middle class, essential for a successful democracy, proved elusive. At the heart of Russia's economic troubles was the country's failure to evolve into a genuine market economy. Many of the large, inefficient industrial firms were not allowed to go bankrupt—the state propped them up with subsidies and allowed them to continue operating without paying their tax bills. Those firms that did pay taxes often could not afford to pay workers, so wage arrears were widespread. The problem, as economists Clifford Gaddy and Barry Ickes point out in an article in the journal *Foreign Affairs* (1998), is that so many enterprises—possibly as many as three-fourths—were simply not profitable. They did not produce goods or services that would attract cash buyers; instead of paying money for supplies, firms compensated by using elaborate bartering arrangements. Cash shortages meant that workers either were not paid or received some products in kind from their employer, which they in turn tried to sell in the open-air markets. The entire economy was based on the pretense that value was being added to products during the manufacturing process; in reality, factories often made products that were worth less than the resources that went into them. Gaddy and Ickes called this a "virtual economy."

Of course, in a true market economy, firms that operated on these principles would quickly go bankrupt. Theoretically, inefficient Russian firms should have gone under and been replaced by profitable businesses. That is what happened in Poland during that country's shock therapy, and by the mid-1990s, Poland was posting impressive growth rates of 5 percent per year or better. Russia, by contrast, suffered through eight straight years of economic decline. The pretense of Russia's virtual economy burst late in 1998 when the ruble lost much of its value and the Russian stock market dropped by nearly 90 percent. Since many products were imported, the devaluation of the ruble meant that prices for many items skyrocketed. As Russia's economy collapsed, Yeltsin and the Parliament wrangled over his choice for Prime Minister. In September 1998, the President tried to reappoint Viktor Chernomyrdin, whom he had replaced with the youthful Sergei Kiriyenko earlier in the year. Yeltsin eventually was forced to compromise and appoint Yevgeny Primakov, Minister of Foreign Affairs, former head of the Foreign Intelligence Service (successor to the KGB), and a survivor from the Soviet era. But Primakov, an accomplished and erudite diplomat, had little knowledge of economics. His ability to guide Russia toward economic prosperity, the Prime Minister's chief responsibility, would have to be complemented by extraordinary political skills in addressing the serious social problems that had accompanied economic change. Primakov proved to be a very skillful politician—so good, in fact, that an increasingly unpopular Yeltsin fired his Prime Minister in May 1999, replacing him with Minister of the Interior, Sergei Stepashin, who served a brief three months. In August, Yeltsin fired Stepashin and replaced him with a little-known former KGB lieutenant colonel and head of the Federal Security Service (FSB), Vladimir Putin.

SOCIAL PROBLEMS

For many Russians, one of the most traumatic consequences of the collapse of communism was the loss of the comprehensive social welfare programs that had made life safe and predictable, if not affluent. The rights to a job, a free education, free health care, and a guaranteed pension were taken for granted during the Soviet period. In the brave new world of emerging Russian capitalism, these entitlements were placed in jeopardy.

Soviet ideology held that unemployment was an evil of capitalism, unthinkable in the more humane socialist state. Of course, the inefficient planned economy concealed massive underemployment in which surplus employees were paid for less than a full day's work. Russia's new capitalist system threw many of these redundant workers out on the street. By 1997, official unemployment had reached 10 percent; however, the reluctance of many of the old state enterprises and newly privatized monopolies to shed excess workers meant that the actual unemployment figures were much higher. Compounding the problem, the government was unable to pay adequate unemployment benefits due to the massive state debt.

Education had been one bright spot in an otherwise dismal Soviet record. The communist system had provided a solid basic education for each child, with particular strengths in math, science, geography, and languages. Entrance to the best universities, like Moscow State and Leningrad, was highly competitive, and their graduates were the equals of those at Harvard or Oxford. Less talented students matriculated at small universities or polytechnic schools. Engineering was by far the most popular major at Soviet universities and polytechnics; science, math, and literature were also well represented. Education was free, and students were guaranteed a job after graduation. They were also expected to work for at least three years at an assigned job after receiving their degrees.

Education experienced drastic changes in the 1990s. The censorship and discipline of the Soviet era were replaced by open inquiry and individual expression, while business and economics became the majors of choice for college students. Russian high schools offered a variety of educational experiences, including gymnasiums (highly competitive college preparatory schools), vocational-technical schools (also competitive), and independent and religious schools, which were usually funded by churches and businesses. Since the government was forced to slash education budgets, even students in state schools were asked to pay for tuition and books. Most state schools were dilapidated, and teachers were paid only $80–$120 per month, if they were paid at all. Teachers periodically went on strike to demand back wages. The youngest and most capable teachers left to go into business, where they could earn a decent wage.

Russian education quickly came to reflect the emerging social divisions between haves and have-nots. Private elementary and high schools opened to educate the children of wealthy New Russians, and by 1997, approximately 300 private colleges and universities, many incorporating business studies, were operating. However, less than half of those were licensed, and many had questionable academic standards. A hefty bribe could often secure an academic degree. The wealthiest of the New Russians sent their children abroad to be educated in Switzerland, France, Britain, or the United States. President Yeltsin was roundly criticized for sending his 15-year-old grandson to an exclusive private school in England, which charged $23,000 a year in tuition.

In the late perestroika era and the early years of post-communist Russia, many young people abandoned higher education as useless in Russia's emerging capitalist economy. The prospect of spending five years or more in college was far less attractive than the ready money that could be made through creative business activities on Russia's mean streets. By the late 1990s, however, educators detected a trend: young people were beginning to return to the university, with most seeking degrees in economics, law, finance, and accountancy, and a few pursuing language or environmental studies. The total number of college students rose from 583,000 in 1990 to 748,000 in 1997. Higher education was still very elitist, though, when compared to that of the United States, where 52 percent of high school graduates went on to college.

Health care in the former Soviet Union functioned on two levels: excellent modern treatment for the elite, and universally available but poor-quality care for the average patient. Post-Soviet medicine was also bifurcated, based on those who could pay for treatment at the new private hospitals and clinics, and those who continued to rely on government medical services. Russia's population is not healthy by Western standards. Alcoholism is acute among males, and about 70 percent of men smoke, as do 30 percent of women. Drug abuse became widespread among Russian youth, and the practice of sharing needles contributed to a growing AIDS problem. High levels of stress, crime, and environmental pollution raised morbidity and mortality rates. In some regions, cholera, tuberculosis, and hepatitis were major problems.

The extent of Russia's health care crisis in the 1990s is apparent in the following statistics. Life expectancy for Russian men in 1995 was on average only 57 years; in 1987, it had been 64.9 years. By comparison, the average life expectancy for males in the United States was 73; for women, it was 79. Russian men died more frequently in industrial and automobile accidents, and frequently drank themselves to death, often from consuming poisoned moonshine. In addition, Russia's birth rate was declining, probably due to low living standards and the uncertainties of life in post-communist Russia. Women simply were not bearing enough children to offset the large number of deaths in the population. A study by the Russian State Statistics Committee in 1995 predicted that these trends would continue, and Russia's population would decrease by 5.1 million over the next decade. According to the Russian State Statistical Service, the population had declined from 148.6 million in 1993 to 143.5 million in 2005, and dropped to 142 million by the end of 2008.

The environmental situation in Russia also contributed to the poor state of Russians' health. As noted in Chapter 8, the Soviet record on the environment was abysmal. Soviet communism left a legacy of polluted water, fouled air, eroded agricultural land, and piles of radioactive waste. Lake Baikal's pristine waters had been contaminated and, in Central Asia, the great Aral Sea's waters had been depleted to irrigate cotton for hard-currency exports. The dissolution of the USSR left some of the problems to the newly independent states; many others, however, remained to plague Russia itself.

Environmental protection did not improve notably after the collapse of communism. Some benefits were realized from the steep decline in industrial production—closed factories were no longer polluting the air and water. Strapped by huge budget deficits, Moscow and the regional and local governments did not have the funds to clean up polluted lakes and rivers, deal with soil erosion, or properly dispose of radioactive wastes, nor did they have adequate means of enforcing environmental laws. Russia's new entrepreneurs were intent solely on making money, and cared little about their environmental records. Environmental interest groups had formed as early as 1987, but Russian environmental activism peaked over the next three years and then declined markedly after the collapse of communism. Many ecology groups remained active through the 1990s, but most were small, and few had the resources to lobby effectively for environmental protection.

Russia's military was responsible for much of the country's environmental destruction. In the closed military research city Tomsk-7, a 1993 explosion released a plume of radioactivity across northern Siberia. The Russian navy dumped nuclear waste from decommissioned submarines off the Russian Far East coast, angering the Japanese, who fished in these waters. National security arguments continued to be used to justify withholding information about nuclear contamination. When a retired captain, Aleksandr Nikitin, co-authored a report with a Norwegian ecology organization on extensive nuclear waste dumping in the Arctic Ocean, he was charged with espionage by the FSB. A St. Petersburg judge dismissed the charges against Nikitin in 1998, ruling that they were based on insufficient evidence.

Women had experienced informal discrimination in the Soviet period; still, many women held prominent positions as factory managers, scientists, Communist Party and government officials, and professors. A quota system ensured that women were well represented in the Supreme Soviet and local soviets, the elected but relatively impotent legislatures. After the communist system collapsed, women found their position in society eroding. Virtually all of the financial and business elites were men, while some 70 percent of the newly unemployed were women. Businesses openly engaged in discriminatory practices in hiring, and there were few protections against sexual harassment. The Russian Orthodox Church and conservative politicians urged women to return to traditional domestic roles in the home.

In 1993, a coalition of three women's organizations formed the Women of Russia electoral bloc to promote women's political interests; they secured 8.1 percent of the party vote in that year's December parliamentary elections, giving them a total of 21 seats in the Duma. In all, 60 women were elected to the 450-seat lower house, giving them a total representation of 13.5 percent. Women of Russia had campaigned for a socially responsible state—a government that would provide consumer goods, child care, and housing at reasonable cost. The bloc also called for the observance of human rights and attention to the rule of law.

The end of the Soviet quota system for women meant that a smaller proportion of women were now represented in politics, but with more opportunities for genuine democratic participation. Women were most prominent in the Duma, the lower house of Parliament. At the beginning of 1996, women made up only 10.4 percent of the Duma, about the same proportion of women as there were in the U.S. House of Representatives. Women's representation declined after the December 1995 parliamentary elections, when the Women of Russia electoral bloc failed to garner at least 5 percent of the vote required for proportional representation, and secured only 3 district seats. Only 1 woman was serving in the Federation Council, the upper house, out of 178 deputies, and only 1 of 89 regional governors was a woman. There were 3 women (out of 19) on the Constitutional Court, and 19 of the 115 Supreme Court justices were women. Tragically, Russia lost one of its most outstanding reformist politicians, Duma member Galina Starovoitova, when she was gunned down outside her St. Petersburg apartment in November 1998.

By the end of the 1990s, Russia's economic transformation had divided society into roughly three groups: the numerically small but very wealthy New Russians engaged in the banking, business, and government sectors; a small but growing middle class consisting of mostly young, urban small business people and traders; and the great majority of Russians in the working class and rural areas, who struggled to maintain a decent standard of living. Retired people, soldiers, farmers, and those on fixed incomes comprised the 25–35 percent of the Russian population living in poverty, defined in 1998 as having an income under $32 per month. The most pathetic of the poor were beggars, usually elderly women, and homeless teenagers abandoned by unemployed or alcoholic parents, who roamed the city streets. In 1996, Moscow

Mayor Yurii Luzhkov ordered thousands of the city's homeless population, many of whom had flocked to the capital in search of jobs and apartments, rounded up and deported.

While Russia's economic crisis consigned over a quarter of the population to poverty, it also limited the government's ability to provide relief to its most destitute citizens. Modest pensions were sufficient during the Soviet era, when food and rents were highly subsidized, but $20 per month did not go far in a Moscow that was now more expensive than New York. The state's inability to collect taxes meant that only minimal public support could be provided for medical care, education, orphanages, and homeless shelters. Many regions in Siberia, northern Russia, and the Russian Far East had received subsidized food and fuel under the Soviet regime and high wages for their work in sensitive defense factories. Now these regions, virtually abandoned by Moscow, had to endure brutal winters without adequate supplies of hot water or food. The International Monetary Fund and other Western economic institutions aggravated the situation by insisting on government cost-cutting measures as a condition of assistance to Russia. This policy caused a great deal of resentment, generated support for the communists and nationalists who blamed the West for Russia's troubles, and complicated Russia's efforts to build a viable democracy.

BUILDING DEMOCRACY

Russia had no prior experience with democracy, and so had to build it from scratch after the collapse of the USSR. Russia's leaders were faced with the multiple tasks of rebuilding the state apparatus, reinventing a sense of Russian nationhood, and restoring feelings of pride and confidence in government at the same time that they were transforming the economy. Under Yeltsin, the Russian Federation had a record of mixed progress toward the establishment of formal democracy. Reasonably fair parliamentary and presidential elections were held under conditions of universal suffrage. Citizens of Russia enjoyed formal constitutional guarantees, including free speech, a free press, freedom of religion and movement, and equality of the sexes. The police and military were under civilian control, a single-party monopoly gave way to multiparty competition, and individuals had the right to form various political, cultural, and social organizations free from government control.

Despite these remarkable achievements, Russia was distinctly different from the more fully consolidated representative democracies. Russia under Yeltsin was what Notre Dame political scientist Guillermo O'Donnell, in an article in the *Journal of Democracy* (1994), called a "delegative democracy"—formally democratic because of free and fair elections, but with strong and often arbitrary presidential leadership, combined with ineffective legislative and judicial institutions and a weak civic culture. The Russian state was too weak to exercise an effective rule of law throughout the territory of the Russian Federation. Like many new democracies, Russia had achieved the first, formal stage of democratization, but had made only marginal progress toward "deepening" its democracy by encouraging greater citizen participation and entrenching democratic attitudes and practices throughout society.

In Russia's super-presidential political system, much depends on the personality and leadership ability of the chief executive. As President, Yeltsin played a vital role in Russia's transition from communist dictatorship, but his poor health, his often contradictory pronouncements, his sometimes questionable decisions, and his tendency to abuse alcohol weakened his authority and hindered the full consolidation of democracy. Born in 1931 in the village of Butka, Sverdlovsk oblast, Boris Nikolaevich Yeltsin was a bright student but also something of a troublemaker who often challenged his teachers. He was expelled from school in the seventh grade, but later finished high school with excellent marks. Yeltsin attended the Ural Kirov Technical College, studying engineering and construction. For recreation, he played tennis and coached girls' volleyball. While serving as chief engineer of a factory in his native Sverdlovsk, Yeltsin spent a full year learning each of the 12 major trades practiced in the plant. He joined the Communist Party in 1961 and moved rapidly through the ranks. He was appointed First Secretary of Sverdlovsk oblast in 1976 and served in that position until his transfer to Moscow in 1985.

Politics in Yeltsin's Russia was marked by recurrent and occasionally violent conflict between the executive and legislative branches of government. Yeltsin's direct election as Russia's first democratic President, the early cooperative relationship established between the presidency and the Russian Supreme Soviet, and Yeltsin's commitment to judicial reform and a market economy augured well for the development of democratic institutions in the post-communist era. However, Yeltsin's actions in the wake of the August 1991 coup did little to strengthen nascent democratic institutions. For example, he resisted calls for new elections to formalize his authority in this radically changed environment. A commitment to radical economic reform and fear of opposition from the remaining Nomenklatura were used to justify Yeltsin's assumption of unified executive powers, including the right to rule by decree through 1992. The President's advisors, led by First Deputy Prime Minister Gennadi Burbulis and Deputy Prime Minister for Economics Yegor Gaidar, implemented a program of shock therapy based on Western neoliberal economic theory. The reformers expected ordinary Russians to endure a brief period of painful transition before the full benefits of the new market economy would be realized. As the transitional period dragged on into the

21st century, many people became impoverished while a few grew immensely wealthy. Russians soon became disgusted with the ineffectiveness, corruption, and indifference of their new democratic government.

A healthy democracy embodies the concept of competition among political parties for votes and offices. However, this competition must take place according to certain rules, including loyalty to the basic system and renouncing violence as a means to achieve one's goals. Yeltsin's commitment to radical shock therapy and his tendency to exclude politicians who were not committed to his program from the governing process thrust Parliament into the role of a confrontational opposition body. The Speaker, Ruslan Khasbulatov, had been closely allied with Yeltsin during the August Coup. In 1992–1993, though, Khasbulatov quickly became disillusioned with Yeltsin's reforms and rammed through a series of amendments designed to transform Russia into a parliamentary system in which the institution of the presidency would be transformed into a mere figurehead. For his part, Yeltsin frequently ignored legislation passed by the Parliament, issuing decrees that were in turn ignored by Parliament and by Russia's regions. Regional leaders were drawn into the struggle between President and Parliament, and were able to enhance their autonomy by encouraging central authorities to bid competitively for their support. This resulted in a peculiar form of asymmetric federalism in which the more resource-rich and influential regions acquired special status through treaties negotiated with the President.

As tensions mounted between the President and Parliament in 1993, Yeltsin engineered a referendum on the President and the government's policies, which was held in April. Four questions were posed to voters in the referendum: Did they have confidence in Yeltsin as president? Did they support his economic and social policies? Should early elections be called for the presidency? Should early elections be called for the legislature? The administration asked Russians to vote yes, yes, no, and yes; in effect, they were forcing voters to choose between the two institutions. Although Yeltsin won on all four questions, encouraging him to press ahead with a new constitution that favored strong presidential rule, his subsequent use of undemocratic methods to preserve Russia's new democracy generated deep cynicism among the public.

The question of a new constitution had been on the agenda since the collapse of the USSR. Russia was still using the Russian Soviet Federated Socialist Republic (RSFSR) Constitution from 1978, which had been greatly amended but was still clearly inadequate in a radically changed environment of transition toward democracy and a market economy. At least four different constitutional versions had been debated during the summer of 1993. The conflict over what form a new Russian constitution would take left the country deeply divided. On one side were the advocates of market reform—Yeltsin's close advisors and the democrats in Parliament who supported President Yeltsin, centralized presidential power, and close cooperation with the West. On the other side were Yeltsin's critics in Parliament, primarily the communists, agrarians, and conservative nationalists, led by Speaker Khasbulatov and supported by Yeltsin's own Vice President, the former Army hero Aleksandr Rutskoi. This group vigorously criticized the human costs of reform and opposed the Western-oriented foreign policy pursued by Yeltsin and Foreign Minister Andrei Kozyrev. Yeltsin's poor health and drinking problems also encouraged opposition. In essence, a sort of dual power (*dvoevlastie*) reminiscent of 1917 emerged in Moscow. Several constitutional variants were advanced during 1993, as the conflict between the President and Parliament heated up.

Faced with intractable opposition, Yeltsin dissolved Parliament on September 21, 1993, and called for new elections in December. The conservative-nationalist members of Parliament refused to accept Yeltsin's decision. Rutskoi, Khasbulatov, and a mélange of communists and fascists barricaded themselves in the Parliament building, the so-called White House on the banks of the Moscow River. Armed with light weapons and waving the Soviet flag, the parliamentary rebels appealed to the country to rise up against this "anti-constitutional coup." Moscow officials turned off electricity and phone service to the White House to ratchet up the pressure. On October 3, the conservatives attacked the neighboring Moscow mayoral offices and marched on the Ostankino (national radio and television) studios. Yeltsin responded by sending heavy tanks to shell the rebels into submission, leaving the white marble edifice blackened and smoking and the rebels in jail.

Muscovites, and the rest of the country, were dismayed by this factional violence, which resulted in over 100 deaths, and were disgusted with politicians on both sides. Public confidence in Russia's political structure, particularly the presidency, was seriously eroded. Public opinion surveys conducted by British and Russian political scientists Richard Rose and Vladimir Tikhomirov in 1993 and 1995 (*Trends in the New Russia Barometer, 1992–1995,* University of Strathclyde, 1995) found Russians to be increasingly critical of presidential power. When asked whether Parliament should be able to veto presidential actions, those answering "strongly agree" or "somewhat agree" increased from 50 percent in 1993 to 64 percent in 1995. However, the Russian public distrusted most governmental institutions. Surveys conducted by Richard Rose in 1995 found that Parliament was the least trusted institution in Russia—only 4 percent of the public trusted this body. Six percent trusted the government, meaning then-Prime Minister Chernomyrdin and his cabinet, and 8 percent trusted the President. In contrast, 47 percent listed the Orthodox Church as the most trusted institution; the armed forces and mass media were second and third, at 24 and 21 percent, respectively.

Popular disillusionment with the course of Russian democracy was reflected in the December 1993 elections, in which Yeltsin's version of the constitution was put to a vote and 450 members of the new Russian Parliament (the Duma, or lower house, with the Federation Council, the upper chamber) were elected. Turnout was 54.8 percent, and of those who voted, 58.4 percent approved the draft constitution. Assuming the figures were accurately reported, this means that only 31 percent, or less than a third of eligible voters, voted in favor. In addition, a large percentage of Russian voters cast their ballots for conservative-nationalist parties. Vladimir Zhirinovsky's Liberal Democratic Party (LDP), which was neither liberal nor democratic, received the largest share of the party list vote at 26.2 percent, and gained a total of 64 seats in the Duma. All told, the LDP, the Communist Party of the Russian Federation, and the Agrarian Party received just over 43 percent of the vote. Russia's complicated electoral system, however, enabled democratic parties (Yabloko and Russia's Choice) and independents to win over 50 percent of total Duma seats. The Russian people, like Russia's politicians, were deeply divided over the preferred course their country should take.

Federalism was a controversial political question in post-communist Russia, as it was in the newly independent United States over two centuries ago. In 1990–1991, various territories within Russia had conducted a War of Laws with Moscow, resisting directives from the capital and asserting sovereignty over their population and natural resources. At that time, Yeltsin had urged the regions to take as much sovereignty as they could handle, since decentralization strengthened his hand while weakening Gorbachev's position. Once Russia became independent, Yeltsin sought to reestablish Moscow's authority through a new Union Treaty with the 89 constituent territories. Two—Chechnya and Tatarstan—refused to sign the treaty when it was promulgated early in 1992. Other provinces (the nonethnic oblasts) unilaterally sought a higher status within the new federation by declaring themselves republics. These oblasts, or regions, of which there were 50, resented being assigned a secondary place in the federation, behind the 21 ethnically based republics.

In the December 1993 Constitution, each of the 89 units was granted 2 seats in the upper chamber of Parliament, the Federation Council. But through a series of individually negotiated treaties, Moscow granted special privileges to certain regions that were denied to others, and resentment of disadvantaged regions complicated national unity and legitimacy. For instance, one major concession to the country's non-Russian ethnic groups was the retention of the 21 autonomous republics, which were granted higher status within the Russian Federation. These autonomous republics were allowed constitutions (rather than legal charters), and their native languages were guaranteed co-equal status with Russian. These provisions were enough to cause resentment among Russians in the nonethnic oblasts (regions) and *krais* (territories), but were often insufficient to placate the country's minority ethnic groups. One republic, Chechnya, attempted to secede from the Russian Federation, resulting in a bloody civil war during 1994–1996.

Chechnya is a small republic of mostly Turkic Muslim peoples located in the Caucasus Mountains in southern Russia. Chechens had fought bitterly against 19th-century Russian conquerors. After the Soviet collapse, the Chechen-Ingush republic divided into its respective parts and Chechnya asserted its independence from Russia. Moscow tolerated the situation for three years, but a combination of circumstances—popular resentment of the powerful Chechen mafia, the importance of oil pipelines and rail links running through the republic, and Yeltsin's need to reassert central control over more recalcitrant members of the federation—led to an invasion by Russian armed forces in December 1994. Yeltsin may also have resented the fact that his chief rival in Parliament, Speaker Ruslan Khasbulatov, was an ethnic Chechen. The Russian armed forces were poorly trained and inadequately equipped, but they did manage to destroy the capital, Grozny, inflicting heavy casualties on the civilian population. Chechen guerrillas, aided by Islamic volunteers from Afghanistan, Iran, and elsewhere, fought back fiercely. The violence continued until presidential candidate Aleksandr Lebed negotiated a ceasefire in August 1996. Yeltsin had appointed Lebed to head the National Security Council after the tough-talking general placed third in the first round of the 1996 presidential elections. Yeltsin needed Lebed's 15 percent of the voters to defeat Communist Party candidate Gennadii Zyuganov in the second electoral round. Shortly after brokering the Chechnya cease-fire, Lebed was fired by Yeltsin. Shortly thereafter, Lebed ran for and was elected governor of the Siberian province of Krasnoyarsk.

Although many of Russia's regions have pressed for greater autonomy, Chechnya is the only one whose demands have been violently suppressed. Two republics in north and central Russia—Tatarstan and Sakha (formerly Yakutia)—are more representative of how Moscow and the regions have interacted. The Tatar republic also declared independence in 1991, under pressure from a strong nationalist movement, and refused to sign the Federal Treaty in March 1992. Roughly half of the population is ethnic Tatar, Muslim descendants of the Mongols who invaded Russia in the 13th century, and about half is ethnic Russian. The major issues in Tatarstan's drive for more autonomy have been the language issue (would Tatar or Russian be the official language, or would they have equal status?), citizenship (could republic residents hold Tatar citizenship in addition to citizenship in the Russian Federation?), and the nature of the relationship between Kazan and Moscow. Tatarstan exports oil and has a relatively strong industrial base, and the Tatar leadership wanted maximum control over oil revenues and taxes. The President of Tatarstan, Mintimer Shaimiev, used the support of both Tatar nationalists and Russians to negotiate a compromise with Moscow in 1994, providing equal status to both of the major languages, dual citizenship, and extensive republic control over its economy.

Like Tatarstan, approximately half of Sakha's (formerly Yakutia) population is comprised of Russians sent to work the gold and diamond mines, and the natural gas wells and coal mines, in this huge northern territory. About 40 percent are ethnic Yakuts, a people closely related to Alaskan Inuits. For residents of Sakha, the major issue was control over the region's vast natural wealth. Nationalism was not very strong among the Yakuts; there were relatively few Yakut intellectuals, and many had been assimilated to Russian customs. Instead, the dispute with Moscow was more economic. Sakha signed the Federal Treaty, but President Mikhail Nikolaev negotiated a treaty giving the republic considerable authority to exploit its natural resources. For example, in the late 1990s, Sakha was negotiating directly with South Korea to develop natural gas pipelines that would run from north-central Siberia southward to Korea and Japan.

A second problem with Russian federalism is that the center has not ensured that federal units will not abuse their authority in the area of civil rights and liberties. This is similar to what happened in the American South during the first half of the 20th century; the result was pockets of authoritarianism. Initially, Yeltsin had appointed the regional governors under decree powers granted to him by Parliament. However, all of Russia's governors had stood for popular election by early 1997, and their greater independence from Moscow made it possible for some to continue to rule in the style of Soviet-era Party bosses. In the tradition of the imperial Inspector General, satirized in Nikolai Gogol's brilliant novel, Yeltsin appointed presidential representatives to serve as his eyes and ears in the republics. As one might imagine, these envoys were greatly resented by local politicians, who did not want their behavior reported back to Moscow. Many preferred to rule as feudal lords, unconstrained by central authorities, regional legislatures, or public opinion. Criminals found the lax controls in the regions ideal for business. Some even stood for election to local and regional councils in order to secure immunity from prosecution. In short, Russia's developing federalism limited potential authoritarian abuses by Moscow, but created new regional obstacles to democratic consolidation.

Federal constitutions can only provide the basic outlines of power sharing. Practice and judicial rulings over time more clearly delineate the respective spheres of authority. In new democracies that adopt federalism, an extended period of adjustment is to be expected. Russia's experience with federalism has been chaotic in part because of a long tradition of highly centralized authority (notwithstanding the formal appurtenances of federalism during the Soviet period) and a deeply divided political culture. Many regions benefited from Moscow's subsidies, while refusing to send tax receipts to the central government. This contributed to the federal government's budget deficit and complicated the government's ability to pay for education, health care, pensions, and unemployment benefits.

Judicial reform was also an important component of Russia's early democratization. Courts in the Soviet period had little power and were often manipulated by Communist Party and government officials. In postcommunist Russia, the court system was reorganized based on Western principles of the rule of law, including the subordination of all governmental institutions to the Russian Constitution and legal protections for civil rights and liberties. A three-tiered structure of courts was established at the national, regional, and local levels, and the concept of a trial by jury was introduced. Previously, cases had been decided by a professional judge and two lay assessors. A Supreme Court was to serve as the final court of appeal for civil, criminal, and military cases, while a commercial court would deal with economic disputes. A Constitutional Court was created to adjudicate disputes between the executive and the legislature and between Moscow and the provinces, and to ensure constitutional protection of citizens' rights.

The Constitutional Court was designed as an impartial arbiter of constitutional questions, similar to the U.S. Supreme Court (although it is actually modeled more closely on the German Constitutional Court). In 1993, the Constitutional Court became politicized when its Chief Justice, Valerii Zorkin, condemned Yeltsin's dissolution of Parliament as unconstitutional and supported Khasbulatov and Rutskoi. Zorkin was dismissed by the President (this was itself an unconstitutional action), and the Court was not reconstituted until 1995. The Court gradually rebuilt its reputation as a respected legal arbiter, resolving disputes among various branches of the national government, delineating the powers of regional authorities, and ruling that President Yeltsin was ineligible to run for reelection in the year 2000. In 1996, the Constitutional Court ruled on a number of cases involving presidential authority, parliamentary immunity, federalism, and citizenship issues, but according to the U.S. State Department, it has experienced difficulty enforcing its decisions. Judicial independence evolved slowly under Yeltsin, but the courts' authority has been constrained by inadequate funding and uncooperative government executives. Under Vladimir Putin, the courts became increasingly politicized, responding to the wishes of the presidential administration. (For a breakdown of Russia's judicial branch, see Figure 9.1.)

Presidential systems embody an invitation to struggle between executive and legislature. Political scientist Juan Linz, in *The Failure of Presidential Democracy* (Baltimore: Johns Hopkins University Press, 1994), has argued persuasively that for this and other reasons, presidential regimes are ill suited for new democracies. The principle of territorial representation on which legisla-

Russian Federation Government

Legislative Branch	Executive Branch	Judicial Branch
Federal Assembly Two chambers: **Federation Council** (178 Deputies, 2 from each of 89 regions)	**President** (popular election, 4 year term) Security Council Defense Council	**Constitutional Court** (19 judges)
and **State Duma** (450 Deputies, 225 from party lists, 225 from single-member districts, elected for 4 year terms)	Presidential Administration Government **Prime Minister** Cabinet Ministers	**Supreme Court** (criminal, civil, and administrative cases) **Court of Arbitration** (economic issues)

Figure 9.1: Russian Federation Government.

tures are based gives them a social and political composition that is quite different than that of presidents. Legislatures, particularly bicameral ones with regionally based upper chambers, are disproportionately representative of small towns and rural areas, and rural populations tend to be conservative. Presidential supporters, on the other hand, tend to be concentrated more in the capital and in large urban areas, and are more reform-oriented.

The 1996 Russian presidential campaign and the two rounds of elections (Russia uses runoff elections if a candidate does not receive an absolute majority on the first ballot) made it clear that Russian politics was highly polarized. Ten names were on the first ballot, but the real contest was between President Yeltsin and Communist Party leader Gennadii Zyuganov, who represented reformism and anti-reformism, respectively. Yeltsin placed first with 35.3 percent of the vote, Zyuganov was a close second with 32 percent, and Lebed received 14.5 percent. Much of the Russian media, alarmed by the possibility of renewed censorship under communist rule, characterized their runoff election as a choice between democracy and dictatorship. Yeltsin's American campaign advisors counseled a polarizing strategy, while campaign leaflets and television ads suggested that a communist victory would return the country to the worst excesses of Stalinism. Yeltsin won the second round of balloting, with 53.8 percent to Zyuganov's 40.3 percent; turnout was a healthy 68.8 percent. Five percent of the electorate voted against both candidates.

In 1996–1997, Russia's legislative-executive relations moved toward a vague semblance of normality. The presence of a majority opposition in the Duma and the adoption of numerous laws by Parliament narrowed Yeltsin's ability to rule through presidential decree. In October 1997, a potential crisis in the form of a parliamentary vote of no confidence was averted by compromise on both sides. Opposition from the communists and Yabloko over the budget and tax code late in the year forced the government to compromise on key parts of its legislation. In 1998 and 1999, legislators continued to challenge the President by advancing motions for his impeachment. Very little was accomplished in this atmosphere of vitriolic confrontation.

New democracies need to have an adequately functioning state. The Soviet state was extremely powerful and thoroughly penetrated Soviet society; by contrast, the Russian state under Yeltsin was extremely weak and exercised at best questionable authority over much of its vast territory. Large and diverse democracies must often resort to federalism as a means of dealing with potential state problems—that is, ensuring the government really has the authority to make and enforce laws. Implicit in the idea of a federal constitution is the recognition of and acquiescence to different regional identities. Ideally, concessions to regional identities should make it easier to build national consensus. This does not always work, though. Canada's many concessions to the French-speaking Quebecois have not dampened the enthusiasm of Quebec nationalists for independence.

There is one factor that should favor Russia's democratic consolidation. Unlike many other new democracies, Russia does not have a politically powerful military. In South America and Spain, for example, powerful military officers influenced the pace and agenda of democratic transitions. The former Soviet regime, by contrast, kept tight political control over the military. Although under Yeltsin, political control over the military loosened, the Russian military demonstrated a reluctance to become involved in politics. Military involvement in politics was sporadic and small-scale, limited primarily to the defense of the White House during the August 1991 coup and to assaulting the White House in October 1993. In each case, military leaders were reluctant participants in essentially civilian conflicts. It was not until Vladimir Putin's presidency that the heads of the power ministries (the *siloviki*) would come to dominate Russian politics.

There has been political activism among certain segments of the army, but these actions are targeted largely toward meeting the most basic needs of officers and soldiers—for housing, decent pay, and so forth. Some disgruntled military leaders threatened political action against the Yeltsin government unless their demands for better treatment of the armed forces were met, but little came of these threats. One activist army officer and member of the Duma, General Lev Rokhlin, created the Movement in Support of the Army, Defense Industry and Military Sciences to lobby the government for increased military funding and better treatment of officers and enlisted men. Curiously, Rokhlin was killed in the summer of 1998, apparently by his wife. Under Yeltsin, Russia's officer corps was fragmented, and it lacked the ability to challenge the civilian leadership.

POLITICAL CULTURE AND RUSSIAN DEMOCRACY

New political institutions can be designed relatively quickly during a democratic transition. Political culture may be equally important in democratic consolidation, yet it is far less subject to conscious reconstruction. Political culture is defined as the attitudes, values, and beliefs of a population about government, politics, and fellow citizens. Just as every country has a unique culture (art, music, literature, social customs), each country also has its own distinct political culture. American political culture, for example, was influenced by the ideas of British political thinkers and the frontier experience. Americans tend to be strongly individualistic, believe in the rule of law and equal treatment for everyone, join interest groups in large numbers, oppose government interference in the economy and in people's private lives, and are extremely religious. Russian political culture, by contrast, has often been characterized as authoritarian. Russians, supposedly due to their long tradition of repressive government, are unfamiliar with or indifferent to the rule of law, favor a strong role for government in the economy (instead of private enterprise), don't join groups and political parties, and are collective-minded rather than individualistic. Is this portrayal accurate?

Political scientists generally use public opinion surveys to gain insights into a country's political culture. Surprisingly, surveys conducted in postcommunist Russia have found that overall, there is a high degree of support for basic democratic ideas. For the most part, the Russian public favors individual rights like freedom of speech, the right to form political associations, and freedom of press and religion. Russians are tolerant of most groups (with the notable exceptions of homosexuals and fascists), value the right to vote in free and fair elections, and want their country to develop a political system based on the rule of law. One study found that Russians living in and around Moscow were not much different from West Europeans in their commitment to democratic rights.

Of course, Moscow is the capital of Russia, and Muscovites are more educated and more politically sophisticated than people in the provinces. Voting results from the parliamentary and presidential elections of the 1990s indicated the existence of a red belt of support for the Communist Party, Agrarians, the Liberal Democratic Party, and other nationalists in the rural areas of southern Russia and in the Far East. These voters were less democratic in their orientation. In addition, most Russians tend to favor a stronger role for government in the economy, probably a residual of the communist welfare state mentality. For example, 64 percent of respondents to one 1994 survey by the Russian Institute of Public Opinion said that a guaranteed education and social security were, in their opinion, the most important human right. Nearly half (49 percent) said a well-paying job was the most important, while one-third said a guaranteed minimum standard of living was. Only 18 percent listed freedom of speech as the most important right; 9 percent said the right to elect public officials was most important to them (Yuri Levada, *Democratic Disorder and Russian Public Opinion Trends in VCIOM Surveys, 1991–95,* University of Strathclyde, 1995).

The problem is that the average Russian does not believe that he or she can influence the government in any meaningful way. A 1998 survey by the Russian Bureau of Applied Sociological Research (*Nezavisimaya gazeta,* August 6, 1998) found that fully 60 percent of people did not think they could influence public affairs by voting. Only 23 percent of the respondents thought they could influence politics through elections. Russians had a very low opinion of the Yeltsin government. They viewed it as corrupt and unresponsive, even if it was far more democratic than during the Soviet period. People were concerned with the weakness of governmental authority because the government was unable to stop crime, improve the economy, or deal effectively with the social problems discussed earlier in this chapter.

Much of the blame for this disgust with Russia's government rested with Russia's new leaders, who failed to manage either the political or economic transition successfully. During democratic transitions in Spain and Latin America, influential elites worked out pacts or agreements among themselves that set ground rules for everyone to follow. In Russia, however, no comparable types of arrangements were concluded. Negotiated pacts on the future of various major groups (business elites, military, police, and others formerly in privileged positions) are important because they reduce uncertainty and make a painful transition easier. In the absence of pacts, democratic transitions can easily become what political scientists call a zero-sum game, where one side's gain is always a loss for the other side. This clearly happened in the immediate post-Soviet period. President Yeltsin and his reformist team, Yegor Gaidar and Anatoly Chubais, approached politics from a confrontational standpoint. Their opponents, the former Soviet Party and government bureaucrats, were perceived not as a loyal opposition, but rather as enemies. Those who did not support the administration's economic reform program were excluded from any meaningful participation. The administration's Western-oriented foreign policy contributed an additional divisive element to Russia's political debates.

One major problem in Russia's transition was the absence of clearly identifiable social or political groups with which the fledging Russian government could form pacts. Authoritarian regimes that tolerate social and political pluralism improve the chances of a successful democratic consolidation, for groups such as trade unions, women's organization, farmers' groups, and civic associations often play a responsible role in democratic transitioning. A complex fabric of social, cultural, and political organizations made democratic transition easier in the cases of Spain, South Korea, and Taiwan. By contrast, the Communist Party's monopolization of political power in the former Soviet Union and repression of all types of independent social groups retarded the development of civil society in Russia.

In the Yeltsin era, Russia's post-communist political leaders were deeply divided on political issues and often behaved irresponsibly. Russia's fragmented political culture was reflected in the party system. Russia's political spectrum in the 1990s was polarized along a single dimension: between supporters and opponents of reform, broadly defined. There were no other major issues to bridge the gap that separated Russians holding radically different opinions. This deep divide was apparent in both the 1993 and 1995 Duma elections. Moreover, most Russians could not identify with any philosophy or belief system that would unify the country. The 1998 Bureau of Applied Sociological Research study found only a handful of Russians who thought that communist or socialist ideas could unify Russian society. Only 2.5 percent thought religion was a unifying force, and democracy as an idea was mentioned by just under 6 percent. By far the largest number (35.3 percent) cited reviving Russia as a great world power. Nationalism is certainly a potent unifying force around the world, and promoting Russia as a great power was popular among politicians in the 1990s—there was even a Great Power Party led by former Vice President Aleksandr Rutskoi. But it would be Vladimir Putin who would succeed in rallying Russian nationalism to restore the country's great power status in the first decade of the 21st century.

Organized political parties are an important part of any successful democracy, but not all parties are democratic in their orientation. In addition, the strength and appeal of parties tells us a great deal about the political belief systems in a country. If a large segment of the population votes for a fascist party, for example, we may conclude that support for fascism is fairly strong. Russia's political spectrum in the 1990s, as viewed through the prism of voter support for parties, was highly fractured. Two of Russia's political parties— the Communist Party–Russian Federation, led by Gennadii Zyuganov, and Vladimir Zhirinovsky's Liberal Democratic Party—advocated ideas that called into question their commitment to democratic values. The leaders and supporters of these parties claimed that they accepted and supported Russia's democratic constitutional order. But studies by Western political scientists suggest that Communist and Liberal Democratic Party supporters have, at best, a weak attachment to democratic norms. In public opinion surveys conducted before the 1996 presidential elections, Russians who intended to vote for Zyuganov or Zhirinovsky for President were somewhat more intolerant of non-Russian ethnic groups than supporters of President Yeltsin, Prime Minister Viktor Chernomyrdin, or the democrats Gregorii Yavlinsky and Yegor Gaidar. Supporters of these two parties tended to favor state intervention in the economy and held more anti-Western attitudes. More importantly, supporters of the Communists and Liberal Democrats were significantly more opposed to democratic competition and were far more willing to support an effective leader, even if democracy was subverted in the process. For them, democracy was not terribly important in and of itself.

Over time, undemocratic parties may come to accept democratic processes, as in the example of Italy's Communist Party. Participation by the Russian Communist Party and the LDP in two rounds of parliamentary elections and, even more significantly, their electoral success, should have tempered their anti-democratic inclinations. The Communist Party's decision in the fall of 1997 to abandon a no confidence vote against the government, and the Party's participation in the trilateral commission negotiations on the 1998 budget, suggested the mainstreaming of Russia's communists as an opposition party. It also bears noting that leaders of the more radical communist factions—Viktor Anpilov of Workers' Russia, Viktor Tyulkin of the Russian Communist Workers' Party, and Anatolii Kryuchkov of the Russian Party of Communists—accused Zyuganov of selling out to the government, as did more radical elements within his own party.

The Communist Party's superior organization and more effective national network of supporters also gave it an edge over its democratic counterparts in the 1990s. This, together with the loyal support of older Russians who were nostalgic for the stable communist past, resulted in the communists winning 35 percent (157) of the Duma seats in the 1995 elections. Paradoxically, it seems that Russia's democratic electoral system favored an organization with less than democratic inclinations and history. By contrast, the Liberal Democratic Party was both the creature and the victim of the unpredictable Vladimir Zhirinovsky. Over time, his nationalist platform was co-opted by more moderate parties, while Zhirinovsky's clown-like antics (punching out fellow legislators, posing for magazines in his underwear) discredited him as an individual politician and contributed to the weakening of the LDP. This may explain the decline in LDP seats from 63 (14.2 percent) in 1993 to 51 (11.3 percent) in 1995.

Russia's democratic parties did not fare well in the new democratic environment of the 1990s. Ideological, policy, and personal disputes kept the democratic movement fractured and divided. Gregorii Yavlinsky's Yabloko Party was attractive to intellectuals and young urbanites, but this party gained only ten percent of the seats in the 1995 Duma elections. Yavlinsky preferred criticizing Yeltsin's reform program to cooperating with the President. Yeltsin himself refused to be aligned with any party, although in 1995, he did sanction Prime Minister Viktor Chernomyrdin's formation of Our Home Is Russia, a centrist, pro-reform party to support the government. Our Home Is Russia was the second-largest faction of the four major parties after the 1995 election, with 55 seats.

The fact that the 1995 parliamentary elections and the 1996 presidential contest were relatively clean and nonviolent (at least compared with the events of fall 1993), and produced a divided government, suggested that political competition in Russia was evolving in a more moderate direction. The major critics of reform, the communists, were faced with the dilemma of either accommodation with the system or extinction. The party's supporters in the 1990s were largely elderly—a 1995 survey by American political scientists found that only 16.3 percent of those intending to vote for Zyuganov in the 1996 presidential elections were under age 40, compared with 45 percent for Yeltsin, 53.2 percent for Gaidar, and 42.9 percent for Yavlinsky. As older voters die off, and younger voters more inclined toward democracy fill the gap, one would expect support for the Communist Party to decline. The Communist Party did survive into the Putin era as an opposition party, albeit one that was seriously weakened and unable to offer a credible alternative to the pro-presidential parties.

While Russia's leaders in the 1990s may not have been whole-hearted converts to democracy, neither were they willing to jettison basic democratic principles. When Yeltsin's popularity ratings hit the single digits in early 1996, some of his hard-line advisors, most notably Aleksandr Korzhakov (his bodyguard and tennis partner), seriously considered canceling the elections scheduled for June. Yeltsin's more democratic-minded staff prevailed, but his victory was achieved through a campaign that witnessed the massive use of government money to support Yeltsin (and General Aleksandr Lebed, whose 15 percent showing in the first round siphoned votes from Yeltsin's prime opponent, Communist Party leader Zyuganov), the manipulation of state television, and some extraordinarily negative advertising. The crisis atmosphere generated during the presidential campaign, the choice posed in the runoff election between the reformist status quo and a return to some form of communist dictatorship, and serious campaign irregularities suggested that Russia was not yet a normal democracy.

Yeltsin's commitment to democracy was further compromised in the fall of 1997 by rumors that he might consider running for a third term in 2000. Presidential spokesman Sergei Yastrzhembskii suggested that since Yeltsin was initially elected under Russia's old constitution, he might not be bound by the two-term limit of the new constitution. Yeltsin later discounted the rumors, which prompted an appeal for a Constitutional Court ruling from members of the Duma. This incident seemed typical of Yeltsin's tendency toward authoritarian maneuvering. This behavior seems to be characteristic of presidents in delegative democracies, who frequently extend their tenure through extraconstitutional means or by securing appointment to another influential position. In late 1998, the Constitutional Court ruled that Yeltsin was ineligible to run for another term. By that point, however, his continued ill health made another four years seem highly improbable.

Russia's problems in consolidating democracy may in part be a function of the duration of the totalitarian experience, and in part a function of Russian political culture. The communist experience made transition to a functioning market economy extraordinarily difficult and emasculated all possible contenders for political power. When communism collapsed the Yeltsin administration, instead of building consensus and integrating society and the state, pursued a political discourse of conflict and division. Communist and nationalist opposition forces in the Parliament left him little room for compromise. The government's economic and political policies did not discredit supporters of the old order, but instead cemented the division between reformers and reactionaries that had emerged under Gorbachev. With the Parliament under the influence of fundamentally undemocratic forces, constructive interaction between executive and legislature proved difficult to achieve. Russia's painful economic transition, conflict over basic constitutional provisions, and the polarization of Russian society stymied the development of a web of complementary democratic institutions needed for true representative democracy.

The thorough penetration of society by Soviet party-state structures and the extension of this apparatus into all areas of economic, social, and cultural life meant that civil society had been almost completely repressed. Russia lacks a strong network of social and political organizations capable of involving citizens in civic life. Public opinion surveys conducted in 1995 found that only 1.2 percent of Russians belonged to political parties, 1.6 percent to church groups, 2.4 percent to business associations, and 4.3 percent to professional groups. Although 44 percent belonged to trade unions in 1993, this declined to 33.4 percent in 1995, most likely due to privatization and increasing unemployment. This atomization of Russian life inhibited the development of a civic culture that is so important in sustaining democracy.

While strong and continuous economic growth generates favorable conditions for democratic consolidation, economic crisis can undermine a new democracy. The process of simultaneous economic and political transitioning that led to Russia's economic free-fall exacerbated social stratification, polarized the country's politics, and relegated women to more traditional roles. Russia's transition to a market economy yielded deep class divisions, rather than the solid middle class that many political theorists argue is critical for democracy. According to the World Bank, in 1993, the highest 20 percent of income earners in Russia received 53.8 percent of all income. The ability of Russia's small political and business classes to enrich themselves in the midst of a severe economic crisis led to public disgust with the newly wealthy, commonly regarded as criminals, and with the system that created them.

In new democracies, political movements and parties are needed to integrate social fabrics strained by the transition process. The Soviet Communist Party prohibited all other political groups and any type of political opposition—there were no alternative institutions that could play an important role in consolidating democracy. The Russian Orthodox Church could bring the country together, as the Polish Catholic Church did in the 1980s, but Russian Orthodoxy has a history of supporting or at least tolerating authoritarian governance. The Orthodox clergy's authoritarian streak was manifested in the Church's strong support for Russia's restrictive religious law, enacted in 1997.

Russian political parties have made only modest contributions to democratic consolidation. The problem is that Russians tend to distrust all political parties. Data collected by Richard Rose's New Russia Barometer II survey (Centre for the Study of Public Policy, University of Strathclyde) in 1993 indicated that 93 percent of Russian respondents distrusted parties. Government offices and political parties were justifiably perceived as sinecures for personal gain, rather than vehicles for the legitimate fulfillment of societal interests. Identifying with political parties helps citizens in a transitional democracy to develop more coherent belief systems. To the extent that political parties are weak, citizens' political beliefs may prove more susceptible to change in response to volatile economic or social conditions, making them more easily mobilized by political extremists.

Finally, Russia's weak judicial system hindered the development of civil society and, by extension, the consolidation of democracy. The ability of interest groups to use the courts to hold public officials accountable, a common tactic of environmental and women's groups in the United States, is very poorly developed in Russia. Other factors have impeded the formation of effective interest groups in Russian society—a lack of resources, perceptions of the government as unresponsive, and general apathy—but the absence of effective judicial institutions is critical.

RUSSIA IN THE WORLD

The humiliation of the Soviet collapse, the loss of influence in Eastern Europe and the Third World, and the rapid growth of poverty wounded the national pride of many Russians. The so-called national patriots—groups like Vladimir Zhirinovsky's Liberal Democrats and the more extremist Russian National Union, headed by Aleksandr Sterligov, a former KGB officer—were enraged that Russia was no longer a superpower. Many detested the democratic ideals and parliamentary systems of Western Europe and the United States. Highly xenophobic, they feared the influence of the World Bank, the International Monetary Fund, Jewish banks, and other Western organizations on Russia's economy and politics. In his book *Last Thrust to the South,* Zhirinovsky argued that Russia's destiny lay east and south, with the Asian and Middle Eastern nations. According to him, it was Russia's historical mission to rule in Asia; Russian troops should wash their boots in the warm waters of the Indian Ocean. Zhirinovsky was born in Alma Ata, the former capital of Kazakhstan, and exhibited the classic Russian imperial mentality. Not only did he declare his intention to recapture much of the former USSR for Moscow, he also on occasion threatened to take back Alaska!

The outrageous claims of Russian extremists masked a deeper problem: how would a non-communist Russia define its place in world politics? The Soviet communist state had a definite mission and identity, namely the promotion and leadership of world communism. Moscow may have paid only lip-service to this ideal through most of Soviet history, but at least the country had a clear *raison d'être.* New Russia suffered from an identity crisis. Some, particularly the democratically minded reformers, wanted their country to take its place among the modern European nations. Others argued that Russian values and traditions had little in common with Europe or America, that Russia's historical influences came from the East, and that Russia could play a role as a unique bridge between Europe and Asia.

If Soviet foreign policy was shaped by a Marxist-Leninist worldview and the pursuit of military hegemony or dominance, Russian foreign policy in the Yeltsin era was driven mostly by economic considerations. Russia borrowed heavily from the IMF, sought loans and investment from Western and Asian nations, and in general tried to integrate into the world economy. Russian citizens were free to travel around the world on business, for vacations, or to emigrate. Russia no longer subsidized radical Third World movements. This turnaround in foreign policy transformed the United States and Russia from former enemies into partners on many fronts, if not the warmest of allies. However, as successor to the USSR, Russia was owed billions of dollars by Iraq, Iran, North Korea, and others the United States considered rogue nations. Moscow's opposition to U.S. air strikes against Iraq and Serbia, and its nuclear power deals with Iran and India, antagonized Washington. The United States was also concerned about Russia's arms sales to the People's Republic of China, which totaled about $6 billion from 1992 to 1998. But for Russian defense firms hard hit by the economic collapse, these weapons deliveries, which included modern Su-27 fighters, were a lifeline.

A priority of the United States and its NATO allies in the 1990s was to encourage and support the progress of newly democratizing states in Eastern Europe, to facilitate Russian troop withdrawals from Eastern Europe, to ensure orderly reductions of Russia's massive weapons stores, and to support Russia's new democracy. NATO's Partnership for Peace program was one means of linking the post-communist states to the Western democracies. Military cooperation between Russia and the United States, unthinkable a few years earlier, became commonplace. But some tensions remained. For example, Russian politicians loudly protested NATO's plan to admit Poland, Hungary, and the Czech Republic as members; however, all three did become members of NATO in 1999. Russian Duma deputies resisted ratifying the START II agreement, signed in 1993, which would reduce the nuclear stockpiles of both countries to about 3,000 warheads each. They feared this would give the United States a significant advantage in conventional weaponry, although most Russian generals argued that the treaty would benefit Russia as much as it would America. In early 1999, Washington's fears of ballistic missile attack from terrorist states led it to seek a renegotiation of the 1972 ABM Treaty, a proposal that was vigorously opposed by Moscow. Finally, Russian nationalists roundly condemned NATO's use of force against Serbs to protect Bosnian Muslims and Kosovar Albanians in former Yugoslavia.

Yevgeny Primakov, Foreign Minister from 1996 to 1998 and then Prime Minister from 1998 to 1999, was a vocal advocate of restoring Russia's position as a great world power. Trained as a Middle East specialist, Primakov was far more experienced and savvy than his youthful predecessor as Foreign Minister, Andrei Kozyrev. Respected in Western capitals as a tough negotiator, Primakov favored cooperating with the West, while remaining determined to protect Russia's national interests. The political climate in Russia at the close of the 20th century virtually guaranteed that Primakov's successors, and Yeltsin's, would need to pursue policies aimed at making Russia once again a powerful world presence. Putin adroitly stepped into the void.

The major foreign policy concerns for Russia in the 1990s and into the 21st century included the unstable arc along Russia's southern border—the Caucasus, Turkey, Iran, Iraq, Afghanistan, Pakistan, and India. Russia maintained troops in Georgia and Tajikistan, and preserved defense arrangements with the Central Asian states through the CIS. China was critical to Russian foreign policy, in part because of the money earned from arms sales, but also because China's position in world affairs was growing rapidly. South Korea's investments in the Russian Far East and other areas of the country, and the prospects of energy cooperation, ensured a mutually beneficial relationship between the two nations. Toward the end of Yeltsin's presidency, there was a flurry of Russo-Japanese diplomacy aimed at resolving the long-standing dispute over the Northern Territories and concluding a peace treaty, which could strengthen Russia's position in the Asian-Pacific, but an agreement proved elusive.

Russia, for all its pretensions, was not taken very seriously in world politics in the 1990s. Europe and Asia might include the Russian Federation as a courtesy in regional meetings, but Russia seldom commanded attention or respect. In large part, this was due to Russia's weakened economy, whose size was comparable to that of the Netherlands, and the economic collapse that gutted Russia's once-powerful military. In the late Soviet era, there were 5 million men under arms; by 1999, the Russian military had been reduced to 1.2 million. In the 1990s, draft evasion and desertion were rampant, conscripts suffered from hazing and malnutrition, and many of the best officers had left for the private business sector. Ships rusted in ports, and pilots were grounded because of fuel shortages. Perhaps most disturbing from the perspective of Western governments, chaos in the armed forces raised the possibility that Russian nuclear weapons or weapons-grade fuel could fall into the hands of terrorists.

As Russian military sociologists pointed out, the military reflected larger trends in society. In both, discipline had broken down, suicides were up, corruption was rampant, and there was little confidence in the future. At the end of the 20th century, Russia was a nation in crisis, economically, militarily, culturally, and politically. More optimistic observers could point out that the country was far more open than at any time in its past, and it appeared to be moving, however fitfully and imperfectly, toward a market economy and a form of democracy. Pessimists, however, focused on the chaos and disorder of the dual transition, noting the Russian penchant for a strong leader during a time of troubles. This time, the pessimists were right.

10

Return to Authoritarianism: Putin and Beyond

Our entire historical experience shows that a country like Russia can live and develop within its existing borders only if it is a strong nation. All of the periods during which Russia has been weakened, whether politically or economically, have always and inexorably brought to the fore the threat of the country's collapse.

> —Putin's annual address to the
> Federal Assembly, May 2003

We live today in an open and independent country, a country developing in full accordance with the spirit and the letter of the Russian Constitution. Presidential power in Russia will always be the consistent guarantee of the Constitution and our citizens' rights, and it will continue to serve the Russian people and protect our country's sovereign interests.

> —Putin's remarks on the unveiling of a monument to
> Boris Yeltsin, April 22, 2008, from presidential Web site.

The collapse of the Soviet Union was the greatest geopolitical catastro-
phe of the 20th century.

—Putin's annual address to the Federal Assembly,
April 2005.

POLITICS AND GOVERNMENT

On December 31, 1999, a physically ailing Boris Yeltsin, modern Russia's
first elected President, resigned from office and appointed his Prime Minister
and chosen successor, Vladimir Putin, Acting President. Putin, a young, obscure former lieutenant colonel in the secret police (Committee for State Security, or KGB), had served as advisor to the reformist mayor of St. Petersburg,
Anatoly Sobchak in the 1990s. Putin was tapped by the Yeltsin administration
in 1998 to head the Federal Security Service (FSB), the successor organization
of the feared KGB, and after he had served in the position for a just over a year,
Yeltsin appointed him Prime Minister, replacing Sergei Stepashin, who had
only been in the post since May 1999. Russian political analyst Lilia Shevtsova
argues that the Kremlin insiders close to Yeltsin were searching for a replace-
ment that would be loyal and easily controlled, not threatening the considerable interests of the Family, which consisted of Yeltsin, his daughter Tatiana
Dyachenko, bodyguard Aleksandr Korzhakov, oligarch Boris Berezovsky, and
a few other intimates.

Putin's elevation to head of government came at the end of a catastrophic
decade characterized by falling living standards, political mismanagement,
crime and corruption, and general social anarchy. It also coincided with a series of apartment bombings in Moscow and elsewhere that killed several hundred, and the invasion of Dagestan by Chechen rebels. Putin moved quickly
and forcefully in September 1999 to suppress the Chechen uprising, promising
in his earthy way that Russia would "waste the terrorists in the outhouse." In
contrast to the first Chechen war (1994–96), the Russian people rallied around
the new Prime Minister and his approval ratings soared.

Putin inherited more than unrest in the Caucasus. In 1998, the Russian
economy had suffered a meltdown. The Russian state was deeply indebted,
having floated billions in short-term bonds (GKOs) and accepted a $22 billion
loan from the International Monetary Fund. The government defaulted on its
bonds, declaring Russia bankrupt and allowing the ruble to collapse, along
with the savings of millions of ordinary citizens. The oligarchs who were so
closely allied with the Yeltsin regime, however, were largely able to protect
their vast wealth.

There was a widespread longing for order after the chaos of the Yeltsin years.
Opinion polls conducted in fall 1999 found that above all, Russians wanted a

strong leader and a strong state—few were interested in building democracy or protecting civil rights and liberties. In the months prior to the December 1999 Duma elections, the Kremlin created a new party of power, Unity, designed to provide legislative support for Yeltsin's political heir. Unity had no discernable platform—its primary function was to rally Russia's political forces behind Putin and to negate support for the Fatherland All-Russia party (OVR) of Moscow Mayor Yurii Luzhkov and former Prime Minister Evgenii Primakov. Oligarch and Yeltsin Family member Boris Berezovsky orchestrated the campaign, pressuring the country's governors to line up behind the movement. Unity secured 23 percent of the popular vote, just shy of the 24 percent gained by the Communist Party. Fatherland-All Russia received 13 percent of the vote, the democratic Union of Right Forces nine percent, Vladimir Zhirinovsky's misnamed Liberal Democratic Party six percent, and Grigorii Yavlinsky's Yabloko party secured five percent of the vote. The election was not an unqualified victory for Unity, but it did establish a loyal political machine that would serve Putin well in the coming years. More importantly, though, the Putin administration established an alliance with the Communists that co-opted their support (Communist Party leader Gennady Seleznev became Speaker of the Duma) while marginalizing them as a political force. The Communists, who had been the dominant faction and spoilers for Yeltsin in the 1990s, were brought under control by Putin.

Since the political transition from Yeltsin to Putin was stage-managed, rather than following institutionalized democratic procedures, the new President was obliged to consolidate his authority by building a power base and weakening the influence of potential political rivals. Putin did not advance any tangible program, but rather sought to convey an image of strength and resoluteness. This strategy, together with the administrative resources of loyal governors and bureaucrats who had already fallen into line behind the acting president, ensured Putin a comfortable margin of victory in the March 2000 presidential election. Putin received just over 52 percent of the vote, enough to avoid a runoff with his closest challenger, Communist Party head Gennady Zyuganov.

Once elected, Putin set into motion a process of recentralizing political power, pledging to strengthen the "power vertical." In Putin-speak, this meant reining in the independent-minded governors of Russia's 89 regions, bringing the rich and powerful oligarchs under Kremlin control, ensuring that top bureaucrats would toe the line, and, in general, concentrating the bulk of political authority in the hands of the president. Putin appointed Mikhail Kasyanov as his first Prime Minister, following the model of a strong President with a weak premier.

Shortly after his inauguration, Putin decreed the formation of seven administrative regions (*okrugs*) as part of his strategy to weaken the powers of the

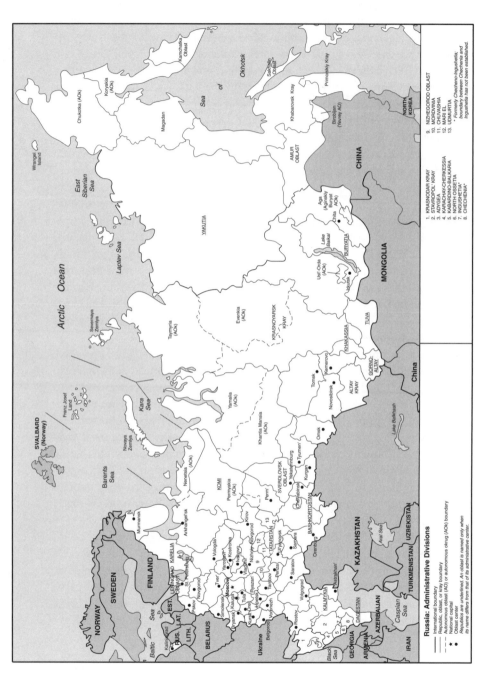

Map of Russia. [Cartography by Bookcomp, Inc.]

governors. Five of the seven heads were from the military or police services (the *siloviki*), and had close ties to Putin. In addition, Putin weakened the Federation Council (the upper house of the legislature) by decreeing that representatives to the chamber would no longer include the governors and top legislative officials of the regions; instead, representatives now would be selected by the regions' legislative and executive branches. Since Unity (and its successor United Russia) quickly established control over most regional governments, the Federation Council became a compliant body that overwhelmingly supported Putin's initiatives. As in the lower house, real discussion and debate became more the exception than the rule.

The *siloviki*—elites from power ministries such as the FSB, defense and interior ministries—would become some of Putin's most loyal supporters, though the *siloviki* themselves were often deeply divided. Putin appointed many of his St. Petersburg friends from the FSB and military to high positions, but he also appointed liberal technocrats in the areas of economics and finance, such as German Gref and Anatoly Chubais to be Minister of Economics and Director of Unified Energy Systems (the state electric power company), respectively. A large proportion of the reformers in Putin's administration were lawyers and economists from St. Petersburg, Putin's home town, rather than from Moscow.

Putin was determined to bring the powerful oligarchs who were despised by average Russians under Kremlin control. The oligarchs had amassed huge fortunes during the privatization phase of the 1990s, using their positions as former members of the Communist *nomenklatura* to acquire state assets, or by building previously illegal operations into massive empires once perestroika sanctioned their activities. As Wellesley economist Marshall Goldman has pointed out, while America's 19th-century robber barons at least created wealth, Russia's oligarchs merely appropriated it. Putin did not seek to divest the oligarchs of their wealth, but he did make it clear that Russia's newly rich should use their fortunes to strengthen the state. Early in his first term, he promised the oligarchs they could keep their business empires as long as they refrained from intervening in politics.

An event in the early months of Putin's leadership gave him the pretext to move against one of the most powerful oligarchs, Vladimir Gusinsky. On August 12, 2000, a defective torpedo on the Kursk nuclear submarine exploded and the boat sank in the Barents Sea, with the loss of all 118 crew members. Russia's government botched the rescue attempt and, in a fit of nationalist pride, rejected offers of assistance from the British and Norwegians. President Putin, showing little compassion for the sailors, compounded matters by refusing to cut short his Black Sea vacation, and then attacked the media for criticizing his leadership and the military over the tragedy. A special target of Putin's anger was Gusinsky's media empire, particularly NTV, which had been critical of his management of the crisis. Putin also resented NTV's irreverent puppet show, *Kukli* ("Puppets"), which unmercifully satirized the new president. The government brought criminal charges of embezzlement and non-payment of debts against Gusinsky, briefly arrested him, and finally confiscated his Media-MOST and NTV empires, transferring the assets to state-owned Gazprom. In exchange, Gusinsky was permitted to emigrate to Spain.

Two other oligarchs—Boris Berezovsky and Mikhail Khodorkovsky—made the mistake of challenging Putin in his first term. Berezovsky, who amassed his wealth through trading companies, Aeroflot (the Soviet state airline), oil and automobiles, turned against Putin in 2000. Berezovsky tried to create an opposition party, while launching attacks on the President through his newspapers and ORT television station. The government brought embezzlement charges against Berezovsky, and he eventually sought political asylum in the United Kingdom. From the Kremlin's perspective, Khodorkovsky, who built his empire around the energy company Yukos, was guilty of keeping a strategic national resource (oil) under his private control, funding opposition parties, and even contemplating running for the presidency. In 2003, Khodorkovsky was arrested on charges of fraud and tax evasion, and was sentenced to nine years in prison. Authorities levied billions in tax penalties against Yukos; its assets were seized and the bulk of its properties were auctioned off to state-owned oil company Rosneft.

Khodorkovsky's arrest and imprisonment, and the state takeover of Yukos, sent a strong signal that challenges to the Kremlin would no longer be tolerated. The remaining oligarchs fell in line. Roman Abramovich, a protégé of Berezovsky's, for example, obligingly served as governor of the remote Chukotka region in the Far East, reportedly pumping nearly $1.3 billion of his own money into the province. In turn, Abramovich was allowed to keep his fortune (he ranked 15th on Forbes' list of the world's billionaires in 2008), along with his aluminum empire and the soccer club in Chelsea, England. Abramovich also continued to live in England during most of his term as governor.

Unlike Yeltsin, Putin was convinced the state must control the mass media, either through intimidation and censorship, or through partial or full ownership. Russia's mass media, which consisted of television, radio and newspaper outlets controlled largely by various oligarchs, had functioned independently in the Yeltsin era. The great majority of Russians get their news from television, and by the 2003 parliamentary elections, the Russian government had established control over all central television outlets, ensuring that criticism of the government would remain muted. Russians could obtain critical coverage from newspapers and magazines, but the Putin administration brought major dailies, such as *Rossiskaya gazeta, Izvestiia* and *Komsomolskaya pravda*, under its influence, usually though large state-owned companies like Gazprom (which controlled *Izvestiia*) or friendly oligarchs (such as Vladimir

Potanin, who owned *Komsomolskaya pravda*). Use of the Internet by Russians grew faster than elsewhere in Europe during the late 2000s, with an estimated 14 percent having access by mid-2008, mostly through the workplace. While some Russians used the Internet to seek out alternative information, social networking sites like *Odnoklassniki.ru* (the Russian version of Facebook) were more popular than political Web sites.

Unlike in the former Soviet Union, censorship is more subtle, and media control is focused more narrowly on restricting coverage of certain government actions or policies, most notably the second Chechen war. In the first war the media had better access to Chechen rebels; in the second conflict, the Kremlin and the military managed the news coming out of the Caucasus. Self-censorship became the norm. Negative reporting was viewed as virtually treasonous, and a number of reporters lost their lives covering the war. The best known was Anna Politkovskaya, a courageous writer for the independent *Novaya gazeta*, who traveled frequently to the region and was a blistering critic of Vladimir Putin and his protégé gangster president of Chechnya, Ramzan Kadyrov. Politkovskaya was gunned down in her Moscow apartment hallway in October 2006; the government charged two Chechen brothers, a former police officer and a FSB agent, with the murder, and the trial was held in a closed Moscow military court.

Politkovskaya was only one of many Russian journalists who lost their lives in Putin's violently nationalistic Russia—in 2007, the Committee to Protect Journalists rated Russia the third-deadliest country in the world for journalists, behind only Iraq and Algeria. A young reporter working for *Novaya gazeta*, Anastasia Baburova, was gunned down along with human rights lawyer Stanislav Markelov in January 2009. The following day, Russian nationalists celebrated at the murder scene with champagne. Few murders of journalists are ever solved, and officials seem to lack the political will to prosecute such cases. Journalists have also been harassed or jailed for reporting on sensitive issues, such as ethnic tensions, foreign arms sales, environmental pollution, or protest demonstrations. Overall, press freedom in Russia compared very poorly with the rest of the world—the Reporters without Borders Worldwide Press Freedom Index for 2008 placed Russia 141st out of 173 countries.

By the 2003 Duma elections, the Kremlin had made considerable progress in eliminating genuine political competition. Presidential aide and Kremlin ideologist Vladislav Surkov—who articulated the concept of sovereign democracy—engineered a convincing victory for United Russia, pressuring regional politicians and business leaders to fall in line behind the pro-presidential party. While United Russia secured only 37.6 percent of the vote, the party captured about half of the single member district seats outright, and many who ran as independents subsequently joined the United Russia faction in the Duma. In the end, United Russia controlled over 300 of the 450 seats, giving Putin a clear, loyal majority of deputies. A Surkov-inspired party named Rodina (Motherland), formed to draw disaffected votes away from the Communists and nationalists, gained nine percent of the vote, reducing the Communist total to 12.6 percent. Zhirinovsky's Liberal Democratic Party, capitalizing on the surge of Russian nationalism, gained a respectable 11.5 percent of the vote.

Rodina later fractured, making it incapable of challenging United Russia, and one of its leaders, Dmitry Rogozin, was appointed by Putin as Russia's ambassador to NATO. The two democratic parties—Yabloko and the Union of Right Forces—failed to surmount the required five-percent threshold. United Russia's victory gave it control of all 29 Duma committees, and 8 of 11 seats on the Duma Council, which manages Parliament's agenda. Observers from the Organization for Security and Cooperation in Europe (OSCE) described the elections as "free but not fair," largely due to bias of the state-controlled media in favor of United Russia, and limited coverage of opposition parties. Clearly, United Russia's overwhelming victory reflected Putin's popularity, as well as the Kremlin's effective strategy of neutralizing the political opposition.

The success of the Kremlin's strategy became evident with the 2004 Presidential elections. Putin's approval ratings had held steady at about 70 percent, and the opposition acknowledged that he could not realistically be challenged for the office. Some liberals, led by former world chess champion Gary Kasparov, formed a Committee 2008 calling for a boycott of the elections, but their appeal had little effect. The Rodina party fractured; co-leader Sergey Glazev broke with his party to run for president, while Dmitry Rogozin became Rodina leader in the Duma. The Communist Party also fragmented—former Agrarian Party leader Nikolai Kharitonov stood as presidential candidate for the Communists, but gained only 14 percent of the vote. Putin won easily with 71 percent of the vote. Irina Khakamada, a three-term deputy to the State Duma and former co-chair of the liberal democratic Union of Right Forces (SPS) party, charged Putin's regime with botching the 2002 Nord-Ost theater hostage crisis. She received only 3.8 percent of the vote. Russia's political clown and virulent nationalist, Vladimir Zhirinovsky, appointed his bodyguard to run as the LDP candidate. Turnout was a respectable 64 percent but, as in the Duma elections, media coverage was (in the words of OCSE observers) "clearly biased" in favor of the incumbent.

By 2004, it was clear that the country was moving in a more authoritarian direction. Civil society, which had flowered during the perestroika era but never found deep roots in Russian society, faced harassment from the authorities and indifference from most of the population. The Public Chamber, formed in 2005, illustrated the Kremlin ideal of co-opting non-governmental organizations to support the government line. One-third of the Chamber's 126 members are selected by the President and one-third are chosen by civil society organizations, with the original members selecting the final third. Designed as a consultative body to the President, the Public Chamber functioned as part of the power vertical, a sort of government-controlled umbrella organization for non-governmental organizations (NGOs). Staffed with prominent personalities from the fields of science, law, sports, medicine, youth groups, and journalism, the Public Chamber was tasked by Putin to review legislation being considered in the Duma, counter extremism, and support the government's national priority projects. In reality, it has proved to be largely ceremonial.

The Kremlin's position on social and political organizations, as in politics and economics, was that these groups should not be allowed complete free rein, but rather should support the goals of the state. Groups that had ties to or received funding from foreign NGOs, such as Greenpeace International or Amnesty International, or from disloyal oligarchs like Khodorkovsky, were especially suspect, as were organizations that were critical of the Kremlin or its policies. Groups that were insufficiently patriotic, or which defended human rights too energetically, might be accused of collaborating with foreign intelligence services or have their tax records audited. Putin's concept of state-society relations was paternalistic, with the state guiding and controlling society, in contrast to the Western idea of an autonomous society that could challenge the state.

On September 1, 2004, Russia suffered a brutal terrorist attack that served as a pretext for further tightening of social controls. On this traditional opening day of school, several dozen Chechen militants seized a school in the town of Beslan in the southern Caucasus republic of North Ossetia, holding 1,100 children, teachers, and parents hostage. After three days of negotiating, a bomb exploded inside the school, the authorities attacked the building, and some 330 hostages and terrorists died. The authorities' handling of the situation recalled the Nord-Ost tragedy two years earlier. Chechen terrorists had seized some 850 hostages at a theater in Moscow, and when Russian special forces used a powerful gas to subdue the terrorists, at least 129 hostages lost their lives. In both cases, Putin denied any official responsibility for the tragedies, seeking instead to use the events to rally public opinion against terrorism. In the Beslan events, a parliamentary commission found evidence of gross incompetence by local officials in contrast to the Procurator General's report, which had exonerated the police and security forces. A support group, Beslan Mothers Committee, was set up to lobby for a more complete investigation of the circumstances surrounding the tragedy, with little success.

Putin took advantage of the Beslan massacre to further tighten the Kremlin's grip over Russia's regions. Employing questionable logic, the President decreed that as part of an anti-terrorism strategy governors would no longer be directly elected, but would instead be appointed by the President. In addition, the Duma would no longer be elected half by single-member district and half by party list. Instead, all 450 deputies would be elected through pure proportional representation, with a seven-percent electoral threshold to reduce the chances of extremist parties gaining representation.

Chechnya and the North Caucasus provide an exemplar of Putin's approach to governance and to center-periphery ties. Between 2002 and 2004, Russia had suffered a number of terrorist attacks emanating from the North Caucasus—the Nord Ost theater crisis, airplane bombings, the Beslan tragedy—and Putin's goal of solidifying a strong state capable of protecting its people seemed distant. By 2006, however, the situation in Chechnya had stabilized, with Russian troops, aided by Chechen collaborators, securing control of the major cities, although the rebels continued to harass the troops from their mountain hideouts. With Moscow's support, former rebel and moderate Muslim Akhmad Kadyrov became President in October 2003, through stage-managed elections, only to be assassinated in May 2004, when a bomb exploded under a reviewing stand where he was observing the Victory Day parade. A caretaker president served until Ramzan Kadyrov, Akhmad's son, turned 30 years of age, at which point Putin named him to the republic's highest office. Ramzan Kadyrov rules Chechnya gangster-style, using his personal security force to terrorize and intimidate opponents, while living in luxurious estates and encouraging a cult of personality around him. Since Kadyrov has brought a measure of (brutal) stability to the war-torn province, Moscow is satisfied. Putin funneled money into Chechnya to rebuild the capital Grozny, and even awarded Kadyrov the Hero of Russia medal for his role in stabilizing the region.

To strengthen the central state apparatus, Putin implemented a series of reforms that severely weakened the autonomy of the regions. Under Yeltsin, Russian federalism was embodied in the constitution, but the relationship between Moscow and the 89 federal units was poorly defined and regulated by ad hoc arrangements, including treaties granting special privileges to the wealthier or more strategically important regions. From the beginning, Putin rejected the idea of bargaining with the regions. Seven plenipotentiary presidential representatives (*polpreds*) were appointed to head the newly established federal districts, which corresponded with the Interior Ministry's troop structure. The presidential representatives were tasked with overseeing resource transfers to the center, and spending the federal funds allocated to the regions. The backgrounds of the appointees, who were mostly officers from the military or police, signaled Putin's intent to restore central control over the independently minded republics and oblasts. During his first year in office, Putin decreed that governors and heads of regional parliaments would no longer automatically be members of the Federation Council, but would be required to select representatives to the upper chamber. As a concession, the regional executives were granted membership in a new State Council, an advisory body to the President, but Putin reserved to the presidency the authority to control its leadership and the agenda. Putin granted regional governing parties (namely United Russia) the right to nominate candidates, while reserving to the president the right to appoint or dismiss governors. The effect of Putin's reforms was to make regional officials less responsive to the public, and more dependent on the president.

The ability to raise taxes is a critical power for any government. In Russia under Putin, new tax laws gave the center greater control over revenues and expenditures. A number of federal ministries and agencies, including the Tax Police, Interior Ministry, Criminal Police, Ministry of Natural Resources, and others, set up new structures in the seven federal districts to monitor and enforce national laws. This development not only strengthened central control over the regions; it also enhanced the power of the government bureaucracy as a political force in Russia, laying the foundation for a bureaucratic authoritarian state. In addition, several of the smaller autonomous regions were merged into larger units, reducing the number of federal subjects from 89 to 84.

The impact of Putin's various initiatives regarding Russian federalism was to end much of the chaos of center-regional relations in the Yeltsin years. Indeed, the cumulative impact of these reforms effectively emasculated Russian federalism, returning the state to a centralized entity reminiscent of Soviet or Tsarist times. While federalism is not necessary in a democratic system (many unitary systems, like France and Norway, are good democracies), hyper-centralized polities erode the potential for regional self-governance and experimentation. In Russia's case, extreme centralization has historically been seen as necessary to preserve order and protect national security, but it has also stifled initiative and given central authorities the power to repress democratic freedoms.

Changes in electoral law under Putin, though ostensibly designed to strengthen the party system and eliminate the pernicious influence of small extremist parties, in reality merely augmented United Russia's position. In late 2002, the Duma passed a bill raising the threshold from five to seven percent for parties competing on the party list system, which would be applied in the December 2007 elections. As part of the government's tightening following Beslan, the Duma enacted legislation shifting from the mixed single-member district/proportional representations (PR) system to a pure PR system based on party lists. Party list proportional representation electoral systems enhance representation, but eliminating electoral districts with readily identifiable representatives reduces the accountability of politicians, particularly in geographically large territories. Other laws enacted under Putin prohibited the formation of electoral blocs, making it even more difficult for smaller parties to surmount the seven-percent threshold. The rationale of these electoral changes was to strengthen the party system by marginalizing the tiny fringe parties that had run candidates in the 1990s. However, the real effect was to strengthen the pro-presidential United Russia party at the expense of all others. Criteria for registering parties were tightened, and Russia's Central Electoral Commission frequently refused to register opposition parties, often on questionable technical grounds.

The impact of these electoral changes was evident in the December 2007 contest for the Duma. Only 11 parties were approved by the Central Electoral Commission, down from 23 in 2003 and 29 in 1999. In an interesting twist, Putin agreed that he would have his name placed at the top of the United Party list for the elections, while refusing to formally become a member. United Russia adopted a vague, non-controversial platform, whose themes included resistance to encroaching Western influence (the color revolutions in Georgia, Ukraine, and Kyrgyzstan), and fear that internal forces (such as communists, Yeltsin supporters, and those linked to foreign powers) would weaken the Russian state. Russian nationalism and anti-Americanism was also evident in the run-up to the elections. Turnout was respectable at 63 percent, but only 4 parties made the 7-percent cutoff. United Russia was the clear winner with 64.3 percent of the vote and 315 of 450 seats. The Communist Party—the only genuine opposition party in Russian politics—received 11.54 percent of the vote, which translated into 57 seats. Zhirinovsky's Liberal Democrats, who tend to vote with the Kremlin on most issues, took 8.14 percent of the vote and 40 seats, while the new party For a Just Russia, created by the Kremlin, gained 7.74 percent of the vote and 38 seats in the Duma. Women won an unprecedented 63 seats in the 2007 Duma, 14 percent of the total—a figure roughly comparable to the representation of women in the U.S. Congress—but the significance of this accomplishment was nullified by the Kremlin's emasculation of the legislature.

The improvement in living standards, a more aggressive foreign policy stance, and Putin's decisive leadership combined to give most Russians the feeling that their country was once again a great power, a force to be reckoned with in world affairs. Putin's popularity had held steady, with approval ratings at or above 70 percent for most of his two terms, and many Russians were reluctant to see him go. Pressure for Putin to change the Constitution and run for a third term mounted in 2007, a clear indication that strong leadership was valued more highly than the rule of law. Putin, though trained as a lawyer, had never shown particularly high regard for legal niceties. But for whatever reason, he rejected a third term as too blatant a manipulation of the political system. Instead, Putin spent much of 2007 searching for a successor. Those in contention for the position included Deputy Prime Minister and former Defense Minister Sergey Ivanov, Chairman of the Duma Boris Gryzlov, Governor of St. Petersburg Valentina Matveyenko, and head of the Russian Railway system Vladimir Yakunin. Putin was also seeking an ideal formula by which he could retain power while formally relinquishing the office of President.

By December, Putin had made his choice, designating his protégé and First Deputy Prime Minister Dmitry Medvedev as his successor. Medvedev, like Putin, was from St. Petersburg and like Putin, he had been trained as a lawyer. He had worked in the international relations department of the St. Petersburg Mayor's office in the 1990s, as a subordinate of Putin's. Considered a moderate, Medvedev had served on the board of Gazprom, and in 2005, was tasked with overseeing Russia's national projects—education, health care, housing and agriculture. Medvedev demonstrated his loyalty before the election by pledging to implement Putin's plan of rapid economic development and diversification and, in his first speech as president-designate, promised that if elected, he would appoint Vladimir Putin to the post of Prime Minister. Based on the French model, Russia's mixed presidential-parliamentary system, with a president as chief of state and a prime minister as chief executive, is a structure that can lead to either the executive dominating the government, or to a structure of shared executive power. Considering the unfortunate history of dual power (*dvoevlastie*) in Russia, most notably the split between the Petrograd Soviet and the Provisional Government in 1917, and the contest between Boris Yeltsin and the Supreme Soviet in 1993, it is unlikely that Putin envisioned sharing power with Medvedev. By late 2009, it seemed apparent that Putin intended to continue exercising broad authority from the office of Prime Minister, overshadowing his constitutional superior.

In the months prior to the March 2008 presidential elections, the Russian media blanketed the country with positive coverage of Medvedev, often showing him with Putin. Medvedev refused to debate the other three candidates who were registered by the Central Electoral Commission: Communist Party leader Gennady Zyuganov, LDP head Vladimir Zhirinovsky, and newcomer Andrei Bogdanov, head of the newly formed and pro-Putin Democratic Party. Regional and local officials, along with the leaders of United Russia, For a Just Russia, the Agrarian party, and Civic Force, all jumped on the bandwagon to support Putin's choice.

With the government's considerable administrative resources dedicated to ensuring a Medvedev victory, the outcome was never really in doubt. The OECD's Office of Democratic Institutions and Human Rights declined to monitor the elections due to the restrictions imposed on it by the Russian government. As in the 2007 Duma elections, there were charges of ballot box stuffing, voter intimidation, the use of regional government offices to turn out a favorable vote, and other irregularities. In the end, Medvedev received an impressive 70.3 percent of the vote, far ahead of Zyuganov's 17.7 percent. Zhirinovsky managed to win just under ten percent of the vote, while Bogdanov received just over one percent.

By Western standards, the election was clearly not democratic since there was no realistic chance of any opposition figures winning. The most prominent opposition candidates—liberal former governor of Nizhni Novgorod Boris Nemtsov, former chess champion Gary Kasparov, and Putin's first Prime Minister Mikhail Kasyanov (2000–2004)—were constantly harassed by the authorities, and the Central Electoral Commission refused to approve their registration. Patriotic, Kremlin-financed and supported youth groups Nashi ("Ours," which follows a program designed by Kremlin ideologist Vladislav Surkov), Youth Guard (the youth wing of United Russia), and Locals, a creation of the Moscow regional government, demonstrated aggressively in favor of Putin and Medvedev, while harassing and intimidating critics of the Kremlin. Their targets included foreign critics of the Kremlin—the British ambassador and representatives from the Baltic states—who were personae non grata in Russia. Nationalist youth movements also conducted election patrols to preempt any Orange-style popular protest, as had occurred in Ukraine in 2004.

Medvedev assumed the presidency, promising to combat Russia's extensive corruption, which permeated the state and economy. Corruption is embedded in Russia's culture. Policemen extort bribes from motorists; officials purchase positions as ministers, Duma deputies, and governors; students bribe administrators for entry into universities and then bribe professors for grades; judges receive bribes to reduce sentences; and patients bribe doctors in order to receive quality treatment. The communist experience left Russians with a sense of entitlement and the belief that it was acceptable to defraud the state. Oil wealth also provides a temptation for corruption in any country, and Russia is no exception.

Despite Putin's promises to root out corruption, the situation actually worsened on his watch. In 2000, Transparency International ranked Russia 79th out of 91 countries surveyed on its Corruption Perception Index, tied with Pakistan and Ecuador (with a score of 2.3). In 2008, the CPI ranked Russia 147th out of 180, with a slightly poorer score of 2.1. Russia's high level of corruption placed it on a par with Kenya and Syria; by comparison, the United States ranked 18th, Estonia 27th, and Ukraine 134th. Oil-rich Kazakhstan was marginally better than Russia at 145 and Uzbekistan was one of the few postcommunist states rated more corrupt than Russia at 166 (Denmark was ranked the least corrupt country, with a score of 9.3). Many factors encourage corruption. In Russia's case, there is historical tradition, the unregulated gangster capitalism of the postcommunist period, the sudden influx of oil and gas wealth, and the absence of a genuine rule of law. Under Putin, government control of the media, the weakening of elective offices, the growth of a powerful bureaucracy with no legislative oversight, and the general move toward a more authoritarian and less transparent style of governing have exacerbated the problem.

Such extensive corruption negatively impacts both governance and economic performance. Corruption lowers economic productivity and growth rates, hinders foreign investment, and presents obstacles for new businesses seeking to enter the economy. It is extremely difficult to create a small or medium-sized business in Russia, given the complex bureaucratic regulations and competition from large firms. Add in the payoffs to government officials and protection money that must be paid to organized crime and it becomes clear why few Russians aspire to start their own businesses. Corruption also undermines the legitimacy of the political systems, in addition to the economy. A 2006 Gallup opinion poll found 80 percent of Russians agreeing that corruption was widespread in government, and 75 percent thought corruption was higher today than in Soviet times. The perception that government is corrupt lowers confidence in officials, undermines the rule of law, and makes it harder to build democratic institutions.

ECONOMY AND SOCIETY

Throughout Boris Yeltsin's presidency, the Russian economy declined steadily as the government wrestled with the immense challenge of transitioning from the failed centrally planned and state-owned economic system of the communist period toward a modern, privatized, market-driven economy. The privatization of state assets had primarily benefited a select few, the oligarchs, while nearly a third of the population remained trapped in poverty. Overall, the rule of law was weak, and this was reflected in weak economic institutions, such as banks, stock and bond markets, and monetary regulation. The government was unable to collect more than a fraction of the taxes it was owed, leading it to float high-interest, short-term bonds (the GKOs). Illiquidity in the economy meant many enterprises dealt in barter rather than cash, failing to pay wages on time. The prices for goods and services did not reflect their real costs.

It was only in 1997 that the Russian economy posted the first positive growth rate in GDP since the collapse of communism; then, in 1998, the economy crashed. The causes of the crash included the decline in oil and commodity prices on which government revenues depended, and the impact of the 1997 Asian financial crisis. These problems were compounded by the government's failure to enact tax reform, institute adequate bankruptcy laws, and guarantee property rights. The government defaulted on its debts in August, and devalued the ruble by the end of the year, wiping out many Russians' savings. While the crisis was a tremendous shock to the population, the ruble devaluation reduced expensive imports, stimulating domestic production and making exports more competitive.

Putin's tenure as Prime Minister and then President coincided with a steady improvement in the Russian economy, for which he was accorded much of the credit. In his first term, Putin enacted a series of economic reforms that provided a more solid foundation for economic growth. He reduced the number of taxes and simplified the tax structure, introducing a flat 13 percent tax in place of a graduated income tax. The Duma passed an agricultural reform law in 2003, and in the same year, the government implemented an insurance deposit program to encourage savings. Nearly 38 percent of the population had been living below the poverty line in 1999; this figure dropped to only 16 percent by 2007. The Russian economy grew at a rate of between 6 and 8 percent annually from 2000 to 2008. Personal income was up substantially, especially in large cities. Moscow, once a gray, bleak city, now boasted glitzy boutiques and lively night clubs, where the country's newly rich partied. In 2007, per capita GDP reached $14,800 (in purchasing power parity), only about one-third that of the United States, but more than double Ukraine's. Unemployment rates dropped to a low of 6.2 percent in 2007, though underemployment was still a problem. Total GDP in that year was $1.3 trillion, compared with a low of $200 billion under Yeltsin.

Not all of these successes should be directly attributed to government policies. Putin benefited from circumstances beyond his control, chief of which was a major increase in oil and gas prices. Despite official plans to diversify the Russian economy, it remained heavily dependent on the production and sale of a few raw materials—oil, natural gas, nickel, aluminum. In the early 2000s, Russia was the second-largest exporter of oil after Saudi Arabia, and it holds the world's largest reserves of natural gas. Russia supplied about 20 percent of Europe's oil, and one-quarter of its natural gas; in addition, Russia continued as either a major energy supplier to former republics or as a transit route for energy producers such as Kazakhstan and Turkmenistan.

Oil and gas account for about two-thirds of the value of Russian exports; taxes on these commodities provided about 60 percent of the government's total budget in 2007, and two-thirds of its export revenues. While Putin demonstrated a commitment to the idea of a market economy, he attached special importance to using state power to promote national champions in the Russian economy. This concept, contained in his 1997 dissertation on strategic resources, asserts that the most important sectors of the economy—oil and gas, other minerals, armaments, nuclear power—should be fully or partially state-owned, or at least under state influence. These national champions include Gazprom (the state-owned gas monopoly), Rosneft (oil), Alrosa (diamonds), Rosoboroneksport (weapons exports), and Rosnanotach (State Nanotechnology Corporation). The government sought greater influence over privately owned empires like Rusal, the giant aluminum company owned by oligarch

Oleg Deripaska, while Khodorkovsky's oil company, Yukos, was appropriated outright.

Under Putin, top Kremlin officials served on the boards of the largest companies—his successor as President, Dmitry Medvedev, for example, was chairman of the board of Gazprom, while Igor Sechin, deputy head of the presidential administration, was chairman of Rosneft. Putin, apparently, was unconcerned with potential conflicts of interest. In fact, one prominent Russian expert, Stanislav Belikovsky, claimed that Putin himself had amassed a $40 billion fortune during his eight years in office, largely from hidden shares in oil and gas companies. In Russia, the commanding heights of the economy are under control of the state and are meant to serve the state in what can be described as a neo-mercantilist system. At the same time, officials with links to these companies find many opportunities to enrich themselves.

Some scholars, most notably Marshall Goldman, have described Russia as a *petrostate*. Generally, petrostates like Saudi Arabia, Kuwait, Venezuela, and Nigeria are heavily dependent on energy exports, they tend to be authoritarian rather than democratic, and they are characterized by high levels of inflation and corruption. While Russia is less dependent on oil and gas exports than many petroleum producers, it does suffer from many of the maladies that plague petrostates. Under Putin, Russia invested the enormous revenues from the oil bonanza into a sovereign wealth fund, which mitigated some of the most serious consequences of over-reliance on a single commodity. Russia's oil fund topped $580 billion by the summer of 2008, but with the financial crisis in the second half of that year, the government was forced to draw heavily on its reserves.

Although most of Putin's economic reforms were concentrated in his first term, in September 2005, he announced plans for major investments in four National Priority Projects—housing, education, health care, and agriculture. The windfall in oil and gas revenue provided the government with the financial resources to tackle these long-neglected areas. Initially, the government allocated about $6.4 billion for all four projects, with much of it targeted toward raising the salaries of teachers, doctors and nurses. In agriculture, the plan was to expand meat production and encourage small-scale farming, which had lagged during most of the post-communist era. In education, the government proposed the creation of world-class business schools in St. Petersburg and Moscow, and the establishment of a number of merit-based scholarships for top students. More affordable quality housing was also a goal. Critics charged that the plans were unrealistic, given the scope of Russia's problems and the relatively modest sums allocated. By the end of 2008, approximately $12 billion had been spent on the projects, but the Duma's planned budget for 2009–2011 anticipated a 23 percent decline in spending to about $9.1 billion.

Of these four policy areas, the one most seriously in need of improvement is health care. Russia's demographic situation in the first decade of the 21st century was arguably the worst of any industrialized nation, and constituted a severe constraint on its economic and military power. Mortality rates were on par with those of developing countries—male longevity was only 59 years, while that for women was 73 (compared with 75 for males and 81 for females in the United States). The chief causes of early death in Russia were cardiovascular diseases, accidents, murders, suicides, and poisoning (drug- and alcohol-related). AIDS cases were concentrated among the young and spread primarily through intravenous drug use—infections grew an astounding 54 percent in one year, from 2005 to 2006, while deaths from AIDS increased 39 percent over that period. Each year since the collapse of communism, Russia's population has declined, shrinking from about 148 million in 1992 to just under 142 million in 2008. United Nations demographers estimate that Russia's population will barely exceed 128 million in 2025. Putin's administration identified the health and demographic crisis as a critical factor limiting Russia's potential to retain its status as a great power.

In 2004, the government, led by Prime Minister Mikhail Fradkov, outlined a plan to monetize benefits; that is, to transform in-kind benefits for pensioners, veterans, students, and the disabled (such as transportation subsidies, medical discounts, free telephone service, and discounts on housing and utilities) into monetary payments of between $10 to $50. This market-oriented reform would presumably reduce bureaucracy and save the government money, but as a result, many disadvantaged Russians would pay more for the same or reduced services. A wave of protests spread across the country in early 2005, the largest demonstrations of discontent since Putin had taken office. Governors in the remote Far East sent a letter to Putin asking him to suspend the monetization process, as did Patriarch Alexei II. Opposition parties, including the National Bolsheviks, Communists, Yabloko, and Rodina, exploited the social unrest to strengthen their position, criticizing United Russia for creating policy without consulting or working with other political forces. Putin deflected attention from his own role in the fiasco by shifting blame to Finance Minister Alexei Kudrin and other officials, a tactic he used frequently during his presidency.

Agriculture has always been the Achilles heel of the Russian economy. Russia has eight percent of the world's arable land, but accounts for less than four percent of total global crop production. In 2003, after a great deal of opposition by the Communist and Agrarian parties, whose members resisted the idea of private agricultural land, the Duma passed a land law that permits the free sale and purchase of land designated as agricultural, although some restrictions were placed on land purchases by foreign nationals. Farmers can mortgage land and bequeath it to their heirs, but in reality, large corporate operations control about two-thirds of Russian agricultural land, while small peasant farms account for only about eight percent. The tiny household plots (at the dachas) still produce a large proportion of fruits, vegetables, and eggs, as in Soviet times, though they hold little more than five percent of the land. High food prices worldwide stimulated a wave of domestic and foreign investment in Russian agriculture in 2008, driving up land prices, but much of the growth occurred before the economic collapse in the second half of the year.

Russia's rapidly growing economy made it a magnet for immigrant labor from the poorer former republics of the Soviet Union, especially the Central Asian states of Tajikistan, Uzbekistan, and Kyrgyzstan. There were also large numbers of Georgians and Azeris in Moscow and other large cities, while Chinese migrants could be found throughout Russia. The Federal Migration Service estimated that in 2007, there were ten million illegal immigrants in Russia, or about seven percent of the population. A law passed in that year restricted foreign immigration, imposing controls on foreign traders who dominate Russia's markets, and establishing quotas on the number of Central Asian, Caucasian, and Chinese migrants who would be allowed into the country. As Russia's economy slowed dramatically in the latter half of 2008, popular sentiment turned against the immigrants.

Initially, the Kremlin claimed Russia was immune from the world financial crisis of 2008–2009. Russia did not suffer a mortgage meltdown, as did the United States, but the precipitous drop in the price of oil, from about $145 per barrel in June 2008 to less than $40 in early 2009, hit the Russian economy hard. The stock market dropped by nearly 80 percent, and by late 2008, the government had allocated nearly two hundred billion dollars from its sovereign wealth fund to prop up banks and major corporations, about 20 times the amount budgeted for the national projects. In a reversal of the 1990s loans for shares deal, the government now appeared poised to re-acquire major assets from the hard-pressed oligarchs. Some Russian analysts warned of the potential for massive popular unrest as the economy slowed.

Under Putin, the Russian Orthodox Church strengthened its role in Russian political life. Russian Orthodoxy is an integral component of Russia's national identity, and about three-fourths of ethnic Russians claim ties to the Church, though few actually attend services regularly. The church itself has been active politically, lobbying for religious education in the schools, promoting family values, and opposing gay activism. Government ministries adopted Orthodox patron saints, and a number of prominent government officials, including President Putin, endorsed a larger cultural and political role for the church. The government also helped restore church buildings and, at Patriarch Alexei's urging, re-established Orthodox chaplains in the armed forces. In turn, the Church supported Putin's program, for example, by condemning Washington's plans to install missile defense shields in Eastern Europe.

Alexei II, who had succeeded Patriarch Pimen I in 1990, presided over the restoration of Church influence in Russia, promoted conservative and nationalist values (though he also condemned anti-Semitism), and in 2007, effected a historic reconciliation with the Russian Orthodox Church Outside Russia, which had long criticized the domestic church for collaborating with the Communists. Mending this rift strengthened ties to the Russian diaspora community, and the move received Putin's strong support. When Alexei II died in December 2008, tens of thousands of the faithful filed past his body at the Church of Christ the Savior in Moscow. Prime Minister Putin and President Medvedev were among those in attendance.

Russian Orthodoxy is perhaps the sole unifying ideology in a state that is now grounded firmly in pragmatism. But making Orthodoxy a quasi-state religion risks alienating the fifth of the population that is non-Russian—most notably, the Tatars (the second-largest ethnic group after the Russians), Chechens, Ingush, Bashkirs, and many others who are Muslim. Intolerance of foreigners and hate crimes increased under Putin. Skinheads and youth gangs attacked immigrants from the Caucasus and Central Asia who had come to work in the booming construction industry, or to sell produce in the markets. Foreigners were also targeted for attacks, Americans and British were condemned, and anti-Semitic rhetoric became commonplace. Few perpetrators of hate crime were arrested or brought to trial. The government did not openly encourage these attacks, but defensive and intolerant rhetoric on the part of top officials created a climate of xenophobia. Police routinely stopped and searched dark-skinned people on the streets or in the metro on the presumption that they might be Chechen terrorists. Racial profiling was not an issue.

Education, one of the national projects, was targeted for major improvements in Putin's second term. In 2007, the government increased compulsory secondary schooling from nine to eleven years. Prior to the economic collapse of 2008, the government had planned to increase educational spending, which was a meager 3.5 percent of GDP in 2006 (the U.S., by comparison, spends 7.4%). To strengthen higher education, Russia had joined the Bologna Process, a multi-national plan to coordinate educational degrees among the European nations, in 2003. Specifics of the plan included introducing a standardized Unified State Exam (similar to the SAT) in place of oral and written examinations. The national education project also included plans to improve the overall quality of education, increase teacher salaries, upgrade facilities, and provide new textbooks and computers. However, corruption remained pervasive, and fewer than 40 percent of students in higher education received public assistance.

Overall, education under Putin was more nationalistic and less critical of Russian politics or society than it was in the 1990s. A new history manual written under the supervision of Kremlin ideologist Vladislav Surkov and released in 2007 stressed patriotic education in the classroom, praised Putin's leadership, played down negative aspects of the Soviet past (such as Stalin's purges, mass deportation of minorities, and the horrors of collectivization), and was sharply critical of American foreign policy and society. Educators who failed to endorse Putin's program were frequently subject to pressure from the authorities. In February 2008, for example, the European University at St. Petersburg was closed on the pretext of fire safety violations; in reality, the institution had fallen into disfavor with the Kremlin when academics received a one million dollar grant from the European Union to monitor Russia's elections and advise political parties on how to prevent vote-rigging. Following a wave of international appeals and petitions, a district court allowed the university to reopen in April, well after the presidential elections.

Expanding government controls over education furthers Putin's goal of a stable society that will uncritically support the government. Indications are the strategy is working. The Putin Generation, as it is called, is more politically active, more supportive, and more patriotic than the youth of the 1990s. Today's Russian youth may be more active politically, but it is less informed about and less critical of the past. A survey of Russian youth by the prestigious Levada Center in 2007 found that fully half viewed Stalin positively. Surveys conducted between 2003 and 2005 by Sarah Mendelson and Thomas Gerber found that 51 percent of young Russians agreed Stalin was a wise leader, while 56 percent thought he did more good than bad. What was most striking, according to Mendelson and Gerber, was the general ignorance of the Soviet past among Russian youth.

FOREIGN POLICY

Vladimir Putin made the restoration of Russia's status as a great power a key goal of his administration. With all its faults, the Soviet Union had at least been a superpower, feared and respected around the globe. Under Mikhail Gorbachev and Boris Yeltsin, Russian foreign policy had centered on the West, but Russia was weakened to the point that it was not an equal partner of the West, nor could it adequately defend its interests. Many Russians became convinced that the United States in particular sought to dictate to them, to marginalize and humiliate their country. America had flooded their country with its consumer goods, expanded NATO into Eastern Europe and the Baltic states (after promising not to expand eastward), acted with impunity in the Balkans, promoted color revolutions in the former Soviet republics, and piously lectured Russia on the inadequacies of its democratic experiment. Putin was determined that Russia should protect its vital national interests: preserve the country's sovereignty and territorial integrity; provide conditions for strong economic growth and Russian integration into the world economy; ensure stability along Russia's periphery; contain instability and terrorist threats along Russia's borders while ensuring the existence of friendly states; enhance Moscow's influence among the former Soviet republics while containing U.S. and European influence in the region; and, in general, make Russia once again a powerful and respected actor in world politics.

The evolution of Russia's foreign policy is reflected in the personas of the foreign ministers who served under Yeltsin and Putin. Yeltsin's first foreign minister, Andrei Kozyrev (1990–96), was criticized for kow-towing to the West. Yevgeny Primakov (1996–98) was known as a pragmatic national-ist, who reoriented Russia away from the West and more toward the Mid-dle East and Asia. Igor Ivanov (1998–2004) followed the philosophy of Sergei Gorchakov, the Minister of Foreign Affairs under Alexander II, who rebuilt Russia's international position following the trauma of the Crimean War. Ivanov implemented a foreign policy that positioned Moscow in opposition to Washington's global hegemony, and continued Primakov's confrontational Balkans policy. Foreign Minister Sergey Lavrov (2004–?) worked assiduously to strengthen the multilateral component in Russia's foreign policy, pursued a multi-vectored diplomacy (that is, a broad range of ties with various coun-tries), and diligently promoted Putin's goal of restoring Russia's great power standing in world politics.

As in the domestic economy, much of Putin's success in foreign policy was due to the steady growth in energy prices from 1999 to mid-2008. Rev-enues from oil and gas exports enabled Russia to pay off its foreign debts, realize budget and trade surpluses, and allocate more funds for the military and foreign assistance. Russia's leverage vis-à-vis Europe grew as oil prices increased—Europe imports one-fifth of its oil from Russia, and one-quarter of its natural gas. An energy-based foreign policy also worked well for Russia in Central, South and East Asia. Russian resources were attractive to policy mak-ers to fuel the rapidly growing but resource-poor economies of China, Japan, South Korea, and India. Landlocked Central Asia is energy-rich, but virtually all export routes run through Russian territory. Moscow adroitly used state companies Gazprom, Rosneft, and Transneft, in tandem with private firms such as Lukoil, to leverage a stronger international position for Russia.

Putin often used confrontational language in foreign affairs, much of which appeared to be for domestic consumption. In a February 2007 speech to the Munich security conference, Putin vigorously condemned nations (that is, the United States) that snubbed international law and were quick to use military force unilaterally or through NATO. Under Putin, Russia consistently pro-moted a stronger role for the United Nations and advocated multilateral ap-proaches to international issues, not because of any high ideals or because the Russian elite truly believed in the rule of law (far from it), but rather because through the U.N., Russia would be able to block Washington by exercising its Security Council veto. Despite differences on some issues (such as energy), Russia and China developed a strategic partnership in opposition to an American-dominated unipolar world. Russia increasingly advocated the idea of a BRIC alignment (Brazil, Russia, India, and China) of the most dynamic emerging economies. Moscow sought to portray itself as a leader in the global realignment of forces, as economic and political power waned in Europe and the United States. In 2008, Russia also accelerated its efforts to develop the Gas Exporting Countries Forum, a natural gas counterpart to the Organization of Petroleum Exporting Countries cartel, which would keep gas prices high and promote the interests of gas exporters. Since Russia has the largest natural gas reserves in the world—about one-third of the total—Moscow naturally seeks to develop this important advantage.

Russia under Putin appeared to become more defensive, retreating into a fortress-like mentality that did not appear justified by genuine security threats. NATO's expansion eastward was frequently cited as one of the greatest threats to Russian security. Although Putin had grudgingly accepted NATO's incorporation of the Baltic states of Latvia, Lithuania, and Estonia in 2004, the prospect of Ukraine and Georgia entering the Atlantic Alliance set off alarm bells in Moscow. Russian leaders believed the democratic color revolutions experienced by Georgia (in 2003) and Ukraine (2004) were orchestrated by Western intelligence agencies with the intent of weakening Russian power; indeed, a color revolution in Russia itself was thought to be the ultimate goal. Russia had backed the losing candidacy of Viktor Yanukovych in Ukraine in the 2004 elections, and Moscow and Tbilisi had clashed repeatedly after Mikheil Saakashvili came to power in Georgia's Rose Revolution. Saakashvili's ill-advised attempt to restore control over South Ossetia in August 2008 gave Russian troops the pretext to move into that break-away region and also into Abkhazia, which had been outside Tbilisi's control since 1992. The five-day war highlighted weaknesses in Russian military equipment, but it was a decisive victory nonetheless, and proved that Moscow would indeed use force to defend its interests in the former empire.

Putin's foreign policy accorded greater attention to the near abroad of former Soviet republics, a region that had been neglected during most of Yeltsin's presidency. Putin made it clear that those countries along Russia's western and southern periphery were in Moscow's legitimate sphere of influence. In security terms, the southern arc, stretching from the Caucasus through Central Asia to the Russian Far East, was a zone of instability where radical Islam, narcotics smugglers, and simmering ethnic conflicts threatened Russian national interests. Moscow's energy-oriented foreign policy dictated a keen interest in controlling the export routes for oil from Kazakhstan and Azerbaijan, and natural gas from Turkmenistan and Uzbekistan. Finally, there were some 25 million Russian expatriates in the former Soviet republics outside Russia at the time of communism's collapse. Several million migrated to Russia in the 1990s, but the remainder chose to stay on, with the bulk living in Ukraine, Belarus, Kazakhstan, and Uzbekistan. Putin's nationalistic approach accorded a high priority to protecting the interests of ethnic Russians residing outside the homeland.

The Commonwealth of Independent States (CIS) had been set up as an amicable divorce agreement in 1991, but it proved to be a poor mechanism for integrating the increasingly divergent interests of the former Soviet republics. In the 2000s, the Shanghai Cooperation Organization (SCO) emerged as a regional counterweight to the increased role of the United States in central Eurasia, particularly after the terrorist attacks of September 11. Comprised of Russia, China, and four Central Asian states (Kazakhstan, Uzbekistan, Tajikistan, and Kyrgyzstan), the SCO had formed in the mid-1990s to settle border disputes among the members. A decade later, it had assumed a broad range of interests, chief of which was preserving stability in this volatile region, by opposing terrorism, separatism, and Western-inspired democracy movements. After Kyrgyzstan's May 2005 Tulip Revolution, a chaotic popular uprising against President Askar Akayev heralded in the West as another in the series of color revolutions, the member states urged an end to America's military presence in the region (at that time, the U.S. had bases in Kyrgyzstan and Uzbekistan). Uzbekistan's President Islam Karimov did terminate his base agreement with Washington, but the U.S. retained its air facility at Manas, Kyrgyzstan, until early 2009, when the Kyrgyz government, encouraged by a promised aid package of $2.15 billion from Moscow, ordered U.S. forces to leave within six months (Bishkek subsequently relented). Shanghai Cooperation Organization members also held joint military exercises on a biennial basis, raising Sino-Russian military cooperation to a new level. Moscow stressed the security aspects of the SCO, while Beijing advocated enhancing trade and economic cooperation, where China had an advantage.

Russia's bilateral diplomacy with the former republics revolved around energy. In Central Asia and the Caucasus, Gazprom, Rosneft, Transneft, and publicly traded Lukoil, along with the electric monopoly Unified Energy Systems, were used simultaneously as economic powerhouses and instruments of statecraft. In Ukraine, the chief transit country for Russian natural gas being shipped to Europe, a running feud over supply and pricing played out in the years after the Orange Revolution. In the winters of 2006 and 2009, Gazprom cut off gas deliveries to Ukraine, sparking fears in Europe about the reliability of Russia as a supplier. Russian authorities claimed it was simply a matter of market pricing—Ukraine was only paying about half of what Europe was charged. Ukrainian President Viktor Yushenko and his Western supporters argued that Moscow was using energy as a political weapon, punishing

Ukraine for its democratic, pro-Western leanings, in particular its efforts to join NATO.

The issue of Georgia's potential NATO membership and its color revolution (the Rose Revolution of 2003, which toppled Eduard Shevardnadze) was another major irritant for Moscow. Russia had supported the break-away regions of Abkhazia and South Ossetia in the early 1990s, stationing troops there as peacekeepers for these frozen conflicts. Russian-Georgian relations deteriorated after Mikheil Saakashvili, a young nationalist with a law degree from Columbia University, succeeded Shevardnadze as President. Saakashvili's pro-Western orientation and his plans to secure NATO membership for Georgia angered the Kremlin, which imposed an embargo on Georgian wines in March 2006. Relations deteriorated further after Tbilisi arrested four Russian military officers for espionage; Moscow responded by deporting hundreds of Georgian citizens from Russia and imposing a blockade on transportation and communication routes.

Tensions came to a head in August 2008, when Saakashvili ordered Georgian troops to launch an attack on Tskhinvali, the capital of secessionist South Ossetia. Russian troops, clearly anticipating a conflict, responded immediately, occupying parts of Georgia proper along with South Ossetia and Abkhazia. Prime Minister Putin flew back from the Beijing Olympics to direct the war from Vladikavkaz, the capital of North Ossetia. President Medvedev, meanwhile, condemned Georgia's aggression and accused Georgian troops of committing genocide. At the Duma's urging, and in contravention to international opinion, Medvedev granted diplomatic recognition to both Abkhazia and South Ossetia. Russian leaders blamed the United States for encouraging Saakashvili to resolve the impasse with military force. The five-day war, the first time Russia had employed military force outside its borders since the collapse of communism, sent shock waves through the former republics, leaving them uncertain whether to cooperate more closely with Moscow, or distance themselves from a newly aggressive Russia.

In relations with Europe, Putin frequently played on the differences between what former U.S. Defense Secretary Donald Rumsfeld had called "Old Europe" and "New Europe." Old Europe—the western part led by Germany, France, and Italy—tended to be accommodative of Moscow and critical of Washington, particularly over the decision to invade Iraq. Old Europe was more willing to work with Russia on the energy supply issue, as demonstrated by Gerhard Schroeder accepting a leadership position with the Nordstream gas pipeline project immediately after stepping down as German Chancellor. The Nordstream line would run from northwestern Russia under the Baltic Sea, bypassing the truculent Baltic states, Ukraine and Belarus, and giving Moscow greater flexibility and clout in its energy diplomacy. New Europe—

the former communist states of Poland, Hungary, the Czech Republic, and the Baltic countries—were far more suspicious of their former colonial master and more willing to go along with American initiatives. Poland and the Czech Republic's support for an American missile defense complex on their soil, putatively targeted at rogue states like Iran, received only lukewarm support from Western Europeans, who feared antagonizing Moscow.

Poland and Lithuania, nervous about their energy dependence on Russia, repeatedly sought to block an economic partnership agreement between the European Union and Moscow, bringing them into conflict with France and Germany. Russia's energy diplomacy divided Europe from within, and widened the distance between Europe and the United States, strengthening Moscow's position. Russian energy firms further augmented their country's influence in Europe by acquiring refineries in Romania, Bulgaria and Italy, gas stations in Cyprus, Finland and Bulgaria, and Serbia's state-owned oil company NIS. In early 2008, Putin concluded the South Stream gas pipeline deal with Bulgaria, undercutting the European-favored Nabucco pipeline that envisioned piping natural gas directly from Central Asia, bypassing Russia.

The one exception in Old Europe was Great Britain, which was frequently at odds with Russia during Putin's second term. A major source of tension was the 2006 poisoning of Aleksandr Litvinenko, a former Russian intelligence officer, in London with radioactive polonium 210. Litvinenko had close ties to the Kremlin's bete noir Boris Berezovsky, and had incurred the Kremlin's wrath by accusing Russian security services of staging the 1999 apartment bombings to ensure Putin's rise to power. On his deathbed, Litvinenko charged Putin with engineering his killing. Russia's government refused to extradite the man British police charged with the murder, Alexei Lugovoi, and ultranationalist Vladimir Zhrinovsky placed Lugovoi's name in second place on the LDP party list for the December 2007 Duma elections, guaranteeing him immunity from prosecution. The incident unleashed a wave of anti-British sentiment: Lugovoi became something of a national hero, Nashi demonstrators harassed British ambassador Anthony Brenton for associating with the liberal opposition, and the Foreign Ministry shut down the British Councils in retaliation for London's July 2007 expulsion of Russian diplomats.

Relations with America deteriorated steadily over Putin's two terms. When he first met Vladimir Putin in 2001, President George W. Bush described the Russian president as straightforward and trustworthy, and famously remarked that he had looked into Putin's eyes and "got a sense of his soul." Putin's wholehearted support of the United States after the 9/11 attacks, and his willingness to provide intelligence on Afghanistan and to countenance American bases in neighboring Central Asia, augured well for a partnership in the war on terror. By 2008, however, when both leaders were ending their terms, Russian-American relations had reached a new post-communist low.

Russia, like much of Old Europe, vigorously opposed the 2003 U.S. invasion of Iraq. The American drive to expand NATO eastward, uncritical support for Georgia and Ukraine, and diplomatic recognition of independent Kosovo all antagonized Moscow. Most galling of all was Washington's unilateral exercise of power, which marginalized Russia and wounded its sense of national pride.

China, like Old Europe, provided a welcome counter to America's unipolar moment. Under Putin, Moscow and Beijing moved closer, both bilaterally in the form of their strategic partnership, and through such organizations as the Shanghai Cooperation Organization. Trade expanded significantly, with Russia providing high-tech weaponry and oil to China in exchange for consumer goods. A rising China, like Russia, resisted the American concept of global hegemony. Moreover, the Chinese, unlike the Americans or the Europeans, tended not to criticize Russia over human rights abuses and its democratic failings. But despite much common ground, tensions were apparent. Russia and China engaged in tough negotiating over energy deals; Russian fear of being swamped by Chinese immigrants did not abate, and Beijing was deeply troubled by Moscow's support for the separatist territories of Abkhazia and South Ossetia. Beijing had far too much at stake in its relationship with the United States to seriously contemplate a formal alliance with Russia.

DEMOCRACY OR AUTHORITARIANISM?

As Dmitry Medvedev completed his first years as Russia's president, it was unclear whether the country would continue on the path toward greater authoritarianism laid out during Vladimir Putin's eight years in power, or whether Russia might resume its fitful journey toward a more democratic system started under Boris Yeltsin. Prospects for the latter seemed doubtful when Medvedev and Putin pushed a constitutional amendment extending presidential terms to six years, and legislative terms to five, through the Duma in record time. Pundits noted that Putin could now run for two additional terms in 2012 (or sooner, were Medvedev to resign), giving him another 12 years in office. Since Putin, not Medvedev, appeared to be Russia's preeminent leader through at least the first year of Medvedev's presidential term, this scenario did not seem too far-fetched. Indeed, many Russians argued that their country was not yet ready for democracy, that an authoritarian government was more suited to Russia's political culture than liberal democracy, and that Putin was the ideal leader.

While Putin was immensely popular in the first half of 2008, by 2009 popular discontent was growing as the economic crisis deepened. The government's reaction was classic Putin: blame the global recession on the United States, assert that Russia's economy was healthy, and pressure the mass media into echoing the Kremlin line. Ominously, protests erupted in the Russian Far East when the government decided to increase taxes on imported cars, and it appeared that Putin's charisma was wearing thin. But the chances for a color revolution in Russia are small. What remains of the political opposition is fragmented, and there is no commanding figure that could challenge the powerful bureaucracy. Putin's legacy—the absence of an independent media, a weak and marginalized civil society, a supine legislature, regional governors beholden to the center, and a state that rules outside the law—is a Russia with few effective constraints on executive power. In his attempt to restore Russian greatness, Putin in actuality created a fragile authoritarian state lacking the flexible, responsive institutions of a democracy. Whether that state can emerge unscathed from a major crisis remains to be seen.

Notable People in the History of Russia

Anna Akhmatova (1888–1966), brilliant poet whose themes of love were greatly admired before the Revolution. Her work was condemned for its "bourgeois decadence" during the Stalin era.

Aleksandr I (1777–1825), Emperor during the Napoleonic wars (ruled 1801–1825). Aleksandr presided over Russia at the height of its influence in Europe.

Aleksandr II (1818–1881), called the Tsar-Liberator because he emancipated the serfs in 1861. His reforms of the 1860s gave way to increasing conservatism in the 1870s, and he was assassinated by Russian terrorists in 1881.

Aleksandr III (1845–1894), reactionary tsar who ruled from 1881 to 1894. He crushed the Russian revolutionary movement. His chief advisor, Konstantin Pobedonostsev, called parliamentary democracy "the great lie of our time."

Aleksandr Blok (1880–1921), leading Russian poet of the early 20th century. Sympathetic to the Revolution, he is best known for his poem "The Twelve."

Aleksei II (Aleksei Ridiger, 1929–2008), Patriarch of the Russian Orthodox Church in Moscow, 1990–2008.

Leonid Brezhnev (1906–1982), General Secretary of the Communist Party, 1964–82. He presided over a period of stagnation and, with Richard Nixon, initiated détente (relaxation of tensions) between East and West.

Nikolai Bukharin (1888–1938), popular Bolshevik revolutionary and Communist Party theorist. He was convicted and executed in the last of the great show trials.

Catherine II (The Great, 1729–1796), tsarina of Russia from 1762 to 1796. She was literate and enlightened, but strengthened the repressive institution of serfdom and the nobles' privileges.

Fyodor Dostoyevsky (1821–1881), brilliant novelist, Russophile, and moralist whose writings included *Crime and Punishment, The Brothers Karamazov, The Idiot,* and *Notes from Underground.*

Sergei Eisenstein (1893–1948), the director of a number of cinema classics. His films include *The Battleship Potemkin* (the 1905 Revolution) and *October* (the Bolshevik Revolution).

Mikhail Gorbachev (1931–), General Secretary of the Communist Party from 1985 to 1991. He initiated reforms that led to collapse of the USSR. Born in the Stavropol region of southern Russia, he was educated as a lawyer at Moscow State University.

Ivan IV (The Terrible, 1530–1584), Muscovite tsar noted for his cruelty. He crushed the power of the aristocracy through his *oprichnina*, a centralized political and military authority.

Aleksandr Kerensky (1881–1970), Socialist Revolutionary lawyer. He was head of the Provisional Government formed after Nicholas II abdicated and was overthrown by the Bolsheviks in November 1917.

Nikita Khrushchev (1894–1971), General Secretary of the Communist Party from 1953 to 1964. He promoted partial reforms and the "de-Stalinization" of the Soviet Union.

Vladimir Lenin (Ulianov, 1870–1924), dedicated Russian revolutionary, political theorist, founder of the Soviet Union, and creator of the Bolshevik Party.

Mikhail Lomonosov (1711–1765), Russian peasant who mastered chemistry, physics, astronomy, and geology. He was also a skilled poet and a talented literary scholar. In tribute to his scientific contributions, Moscow State University bears his name.

Dmitrii Medvedev (1965–), chief of staff for Vladimir Putin, chairman of board for Gazprom, Putin's hand-picked successor, was elected President March 2008

Nicholas I (1796–1855), reactionary tsar whose reign (1825–1855) was guided by the principles of autocracy, Orthodoxy, and nationalism. His resistance to reform contributed to Russia's defeat in the Crimean War.

Nicholas II (1868–1918), the last Romanov ruler (1896–1917), a weak and incompetent figure who could not deal with the growing pressures of modernizing Russia. He and his family were killed by the Bolsheviks early in the Civil War.

Nikon (Nikita Minov) (1605–1681), Patriarch of the Russian Orthodox Church from 1652 to 1658. He initiated the 1667 ecclesiastical reforms that led to the Great Schism, dividing Orthodox and Old Believers.

Boris Pasternak (1890–1960), famous in the West for his novel *Dr. Zhivago.* Pasternak is revered in Russia more for his beautiful poetry.

Peter I (The Great, 1672–1725), tsar of Russia for nearly four decades. He promoted Westernization of Russia, founded the city of St. Petersburg as the new Russian capital, and presided over a major expansion of Russia.

Anna Politkovskaya (1958–2006), journalist who covered the Chechen wars, strong critic of Russian government and Chechen strongman Ramzan Kadyrov, gunned down outside her Moscow apartment.

Vladimir Putin (1952–), Prime Minister of Russia 1999, 2008–; President 2000–2008; re-established strong central control, moved Russia in a more authoritarian direction after chaos of Yeltsin years.

Aleksandr Pushkin (1799–1837), generally regarded as the greatest Russian poet. Pushkin dominated Russia's Romantic Age. An adventurer and womanizer, he was killed in a duel defending his wife's honor.

Gregorii Rasputin (ca. 1865–1916), mystic Siberian peasant who claimed to be able to cure Nicholas and Aleksandra's hemophiliac son. He manipulated Court life during World War I and was murdered by the Russian nobility.

Ilya Repin (1844–1930), leading artist of the Itinerant school, which in the 1860s and 1870s rejected the classical canon of the St. Petersburg art academy to paint realistic themes of Russian life and history.

Andrei Rublev (ca. 1360–1430), masterful painter of religious icons. This monk from the Holy Trinity–St. Sergius Monastery is considered Russia's first national painter.

Andrei Sakharov (1921–1989), physicist and human rights activist, father of the Soviet hydrogen bomb. Banished to internal exile in the city of Gorky from 1980–86, elected to USSR Congress of People's Deputies in 1987.

Mikhail Sholokhov (1905–1984), Cossack novelist of the Soviet era. Sholokhov's stories about his native Don region, written in a (talented) socialist realist vein, earned him the Nobel Prize for Literature in 1965.

Aleksandr Solzhenitsyn (1918–2008), Soviet dissident, winner of the Nobel Prize for literature, and author of a three-volume exposé on the labor camps, *The Gulag Archipelago,* and many other novels and historical essays, including *A Day in the Life of Ivan Denisovich.* He was expelled from the USSR in 1974, but returned to post-communist Russia in 1994.

Joseph Vissarionovich Stalin (Djugashvili, 1879–1953), Georgian revolutionary and General Secretary of the Communist Party. He established himself as absolute dictator of the Soviet Union after Lenin's death.

Peter Tchaikovsky (1840–1893), classical music composer who wrote the *1812 Overture,* the ballet *Swan Lake,* and the opera *Eugene Onegin.*

Leo Tolstoy (1828–1910), a count whose novels included *Anna Karenina* and the monumental *War and Peace.* Tolstoy held a fatalistic view of life grounded in his personal interpretation of Christianity.

Leon Trotsky (Bronstein, 1879–1940), Russian-Jewish revolutionary, gifted orator, and Bolshevik Commissar of War (1918–1925). He was edged out of power, deported, and later assassinated on Stalin's orders in Mexico City.

Ivan Turgenev (1818–1883), novelist during the realist period of Russian literature, and author of *Fathers and Sons.* His collection of short stories, *Hunting Sketches,* humanized the Russian peasantry of the mid-19th century.

Vladimir I (ca. 980–1015), Kievan prince who adopted Orthodox Christianity as the official religion in 988.

Boris Yeltsin (1931–2007), Communist Party functionary from Sverdlovsk. He became an ardent reformer in the Gorbachev era and the first elected President of Russia.

Gregorii Zinoviev (1883–1936), Bolshevik revolutionary and head of the Comintern from 1919 to 1926. He was one of the principal contenders for power after Lenin's death and was executed during the 1930s show trials.

Glossary of Selected Terms

Bolsheviks: "majority" faction of the Russian Social Democratic Party, led by Vladimir Lenin. Later became the Communist Party of the Soviet Union

boyars: nobility of early Russia

Duma: Russian parliament 1905–1917 and 1993–present

Eurasianism: worldview that stresses Russian distinctiveness from Europe

glasnost: "publicity" or "openness"—Gorbachev era liberalization of publishing and speech to provide more information to policy makers

Golden Horde: powerful Mongol khanate, or principality, of the 13th through 15th century, located between the Black Sea and the Ural Mountains, to which Russia paid tribute

Gosplan: Soviet State Planning Committee; organized the Soviet national economy

icons: religious paintings of Orthodox saints and the Holy Family, usually done in tempera on wood

Izvestiia: official newspaper of the Soviet government

KGB: Committee for State Security—Soviet secret police

khanate: Central Asian territory, ruled by a Mongol or Turkish khan

kolkhoz:　Soviet collective farm in which peasants received a portion of the farm's annual income

Komsomol:　Communist Youth League, to socialize youth ages 15–28 with communist values

kremlin:　walled stone fortress in the center of a city. Moscow's Kremlin houses government offices, churches, and museums

mafia:　Russian term for hundreds of criminal gangs that sprang up after the Soviet collapse that have close links to business and government

Mensheviks:　"minority" faction of the Russian Social Democratic Party, led by Pavel Martov

muzhik:　Russian peasant; also used as "a real man"

Narodniki:　19th-century Russian populists who "went to the people"

Nashi:　"Ours"—nationalistic youth group established under Putin to support the regime

Nomenklatura:　list of names held by Soviet Communist Party of individuals who were politically acceptable for appointment to high positions

oligarchs:　wealthy businessmen who exercised political influence in the post-communist era

perestroika:　Mikhail Gorbachev's program of economic and political restructuring

Politburo:　political bureau of the Soviet Communist Party; highest decision-making body of the Soviet era

Pravda:　official newspaper of the Communist Party of the Soviet Union

Presidium:　the Politburo was called the Presidium from 1952 to 1965

Siloviki:　top officials in the power ministries—FSB, military, police—who constituted influential faction in the Putin presidency

Slavophiles:　19th-century intellectuals who held up Russian culture as morally superior to West European culture

soviet:　"council"—revolutionary era radical assembly of intellectuals, workers, and soldiers. Became the basis for Soviet era government organizations

sovkhoz:　Soviet state farm where peasants were paid a salary

sovnarkozy:　regional economic councils, an attempt (1957–1965) by Khrushchev to decentralize economic management

Sudebnik:　law codes of 1497 and 1550

ulozhenie:　a law code of 1649

veche:　town meeting of ancient Kievan Russia

Westernizers: 19th-century intellectual movement that urged Russians to adopt Western political and cultural traditions

zemstvos: local government organizations, 1864–1917

zhdanovshchina: purge of all foreign influences in the late Stalin period (1946–1948), led by Leningrad Party Secretary Andrei Zhdanov. Anti-Western and anti-Semitic

Bibliographic Essay

Literally thousands of books have been written on various aspects of Russia. Nicholas V. Riasanovsky and Mark Steinberg, *A History of Russia: Combined Volume,* seventh edition (New York: Oxford University Press, 2004), is undoubtedly the best survey of Russia's prehistory through the Gorbachev era. Riasanovsky and Steinberg's quite readable work covers politics; society; religion and culture; economics; and foreign policy. Editor Gregory Freeze's *Russia: A History* (New York: Oxford University Press, 1997) is a collection of articles by British and American scholars. The chapters cover the period from Kievan Rus to the present; included are many excellent photographs, drawings, and maps. *The Penguin Historical Atlas of Russia* by John Channon with Rob Hudson (London: Penguin, 1995) is also very useful. This slim volume is filled with color pictures and historical maps, covering Russia from the earliest historical times to the present.

For those interested in early Russian history, Janet Martin's *Medieval Russia 980–1584* (Cambridge: Cambridge University Press, 1995) is a highly detailed, excellent study, but it may be a bit difficult for the lay reader. David Morgan's *The Mongols* (New York: Basil Blackwell, 1986) provides a fascinating account of the conquest of Russia by these fierce nomads. Robert O. Crummey's *The Formation of Muscovy, 1304–1613* (New York: Longman, 1987) is strong on the development and consolidation of the Muscovite state. The most comprehensive study of slavery is Richard Hellie, *Slavery in Russia, 1450–1725* (Chicago: University of Chicago Press, 1982).

Robert K. Massie's *Peter the Great* (New York: Ballantine, 1992) is probably the best study of this towering figure. B. H. Sumner's *Peter the Great and the Emergence of Russia* (New York: Collier, 1962) is a short, readable treatment of Russia's expansion during this period. John T. Alexander, in his *Catherine the Great: Life and Legend* (Oxford: Oxford University Press, 1989), provides an authoritative and very readable history of the Empress; an epilogue discusses the legends and treatment of Catherine on stage and screen. W. Bruce Lincoln's *The Romanovs: Autocrats of All the Russias* (New York: Dial Press, 1981) is a bit dated, but an immensely readable study of the Romanov dynasty from 1613 to 1917. Another of Lincoln's books, *In War's Dark Shadow: The Russians Before the Great War* (New York: Dial Press, 1983), covers the period from 1890 to the beginning of World War I.

Among the accounts of the Russian revolutionary period, one of the most exhaustive is the massive study of Russia conducted from 1905 to 1921 by Richard Pipes and titled *The Russian Revolution* (New York: Vintage, 1990). Pipes was a Harvard University professor and an advisor to President Ronald Reagan. Many books have been written on the Soviet period. Geoffrey Hosking, author of *The First Socialist Society: A History of the Soviet Union from Within*, second edition (Cambridge: MA: Harvard University Press, 1993), provides an excellent introduction to 20th-century events in Russia. A somewhat longer read is Robert Service's *A History of Twentieth-Century Russia* (Cambridge, MA: Harvard University Press, 1998). Martin Malia's *The Soviet Tragedy: A History of Socialism in Russia, 1917–1991* (New York: Free Press, 1994) surveys the evolution and collapse of Soviet socialism.

There are a significant number of works that are more focused on the Soviet period. Robert Service's *A History of Modern Russia: From Nicholas II to Vladimir Putin* (Cambridge: Harvard University Press, 2005) is very good, but has little on the Putin era. Robert V. Daniel's *The Rise and Fall of Communism in Russia* (New Haven: Yale University Press, 2007) focuses on communism as an ideology in Soviet history. Robert C. Tucker's *Stalin in Power* (New York: W.W. Norton, 1990) details Soviet history from 1928 to 1941. Isaac Deutscher's *Stalin: A Political Biography*, second edition (New York: Oxford University Press, 1966), is also very good, but now dated. For a more recent treatment of the great dictator, see Robert Service, *Stalin: A Biography* (Cambridge: Harvard University Press, 2005). Robert Conquest's *The Great Terror: A Reassessment* (New York: Oxford University Press, 1990) and *The Harvest of Sorrow: Soviet Collectivization and the Terror-Famine* (New York: Oxford University Press, 1986) detail the horrors of the 1930s. On the labor camp system, Aleksandr Solzhenitsyn's *Gulag Archipelago 1918–1956* (Boulder, CO: Westview, 1997) is required reading, as is Evgeniia Ginzburg's *Journey into the Whirlwind* (New York: Harcourt,

Brace and World, 1967). On the same theme, the reader should consult Anne Appelbaum, *Gulag: A History* (New York: Random House, 2003). For reporting on Soviet participation in the Second World War, readers should consult Alexander Werth, *Russia at War* (New York: Carroll and Graf, 1984).

Regarding social problems in the Soviet period, Murray Feshbach's and Alfred Friendly, Jr.'s *Ecocide in the USSR: Health and Nature under Siege* (New York: Basic Books, 1992) is a very thorough, albeit depressing, chronicle of abuse of the natural environment and the related issue of neglect in Soviet health care. For the Khrushchev era, an excellent study is William Taubman's biography, *Khrushchev: The Man and his Era* (New York: W.W. Norton, 2003), as well as *Khrushchev and Khrushchevism*, edited by Martin McCauley (Bloomington: Indiana University Press, 1987). For those eager to venture outside of Moscow, John J. Stephan's *The Russian Far East: A History* (Stanford, CA: Stanford University Press, 1994) is a superb study of a fascinating and remote region. Fiona Hill and Clifford Gaddy argue that Soviet central planning seriously misallocated resources by developing Siberia in *The Siberian Curse: How Communist Planners left Russia out in the Cold* (Washington, D.C.: Brookings Institution, 2003). For more scholarship on the Far East, see Judith Thornton and Charles E. Ziegler, eds., *The Russian Far East: A Region at Risk* (Seattle: University of Washington Press, 2002).

On the history of the Russian Empire and foreign relations, Geoffrey Hosking's *Russia: People and Empire, 1552–1917* (Cambridge, MA: Harvard University Press, 1997) is an excellent study. Hosking, a University of London professor, analyzes the development of the concept of nationhood in Russia and its link to Russia's imperial experience. A very readable and up-to-date study of Soviet and post-Soviet foreign policy is Andrei Tsygankov's, *Russia's Foreign Policy: Change and Continuity in National Identity* (Lanham, MD: Rowman and Littlefield, 2006). One of the best histories of the Cold War is provided by John Lewis Gaddis, *We Now Know: Rethinking Cold War History* (New York: Oxford University Press, 1997).

Although Russia has a long and rich cultural tradition, there are few cultural histories suited to the general reader. James H. Billington, now a Librarian of Congress, produced a magisterial study in *The Icon and the Axe: An Interpretive History of Russian Culture* (New York: Vintage, 1970). The book is richly researched and beautifully written, but is now somewhat dated. In a more recent work, W. Bruce Lincoln, *Between Heaven and Hell* (New York: Vintage, 1998), covers 1,000 years of Russian artistic life, with an emphasis on the 19th and early 20th centuries. An excellent, timely study of Russian culture over the past century is conducted by Solomon Volkov in the form of *The Magical Chorus: A History of Russian Culture from Tolstoy to Solzhenitsyn*, translated by Antonina W. Bouis (New York: Knopf, 2008). Two studies cover the more recent period of Soviet and post-Soviet art: Andrei Kovalev, *Between the Uto-*

pias: New Russian Art During and After Perestroika, 1985–1993 (Carlsbad, CA: Craftsman House, 1996); and R. R. Milner-Gulland, with Nikolai Dejevsky, *Cultural Atlas of Russia and the Former Soviet Union,* revised edition (New York: Facts on File, 1998). On Russian customs and culture, Zita Danbars' and Lilia Vokhmina's *The Russian Way* (Lincolnwood, IL: Passport Books, 1995) is helpful. On the Russian Orthodox Church, consult John Garrard and Carol Garrard, the authors of *Russian Orthodoxy Resurgent: Faith and Power in the New Russia* (Princeton: Princeton University Press, 2008).

All the major writers of Russian literature—Pushkin, Gogol, Dostoyevsky, Turgenev, Tolstoy—have been translated into English, as have Soviet authors, such as Sholokov, Pasternak, Akhmatova, and Solzhenitsyn. In *A History of Russian Literature* (New Haven: Yale University Press, 1991), Victor Terras traces the development of literature from the earliest Russian folklore through the Soviet period. This is an excellent resource and a good way to obtain a quick overview of a huge body of literature, but it could be rather difficult for the nonspecialist. Interested readers may also consult *The Cambridge History of Russian Literature* (Cambridge: Cambridge University Press, 1992), edited by Charles A. Moser.

There are several notable books on women in Russian history. One of the best recent works is offered by Barbara Alpern Engel with *Women in Russia, 1700–2000* (Cambridge: Cambridge University Press, 2003). Barbara Evans Clements et al.'s *Russia's Women: Accommodation, Resistance, Transformation* (Berkeley: University of California Press, 1991) contains chapters on women from the medieval period through the Soviet era. Another very useful work is *Russian Women in Politics and Society,* edited by Wilma Rule and Norma C. Noonan (Westport, CT: Greenwood Press, 1996). Coverage of women in the former republics can be found in editor Mary Buckley's *Post-Soviet Women: From the Baltic to Central Asia* (Cambridge: Cambridge University Press, 1997).

There are a number of excellent books on the Gorbachev period. Geoffrey Hosking's *The Awakening of the Soviet Union* (Cambridge, MA: Harvard University Press, 1990) is a very good analysis of the social and cultural factors underlying Gorbachev's reforms in the late 1980s. Another is the study by Oxford University political scientist Archie Brown, *The Gorbachev Factor* (Oxford: Oxford University Press, 1996). One of the most perceptive foreign observers present during these momentous events was the U.S. Ambassador to Moscow, Jack F. Matlock. Matlock was completely fluent in Russian, traveled to every corner of the USSR, and had extensive conversations with Gorbachev and other Soviet leaders. I highly recommend his *Autopsy on an Empire: Observing the Collapse of the Soviet Union* (New York: Random House, 1995). Yegor Gaidar, Yeltsin's Prime Minister in 1992 and a reform economist, has contributed a perceptive analysis of the social and political instability of the Soviet system with his *Collapse of an Empire: Lessons for Modern Russia* (Washington, D.C.: Brookings Institution, 2007).

On post-communist politics in Russia, political scientists Richard Rose and Neil Munro provide a strong analysis of parties, elections, and public opinion in their book *Elections without Order: Russia's Challenge to Vladimir Putin* (Cambridge: Cambridge University Press, 2002). Editor Dale R. Herspring's *Putin's Russia: Past Imperfect, Future Uncertain* (Lanham, MD: Rowman and Littlefield, 2006) provides a good collection of a range of topics from noted experts in the field. On the role of the oligarchs in Russian politics during the Putin period, with particular reference to oil, see Marshall I. Goldman, *Petrostate: Putin, Power, and the New Russia* (New York: Oxford University Press, 2008).

Perhaps the most perceptive observer of contemporary Russian politics is Lilia Shevtsova of the Carnegie Endowment in Moscow. I highly recommend her writings for those who want to obtain a real feel for the Byzantine intrigues of the modern Russian Kremlin These include *Putin's Russia,* revised and expanded edition (Washington, D.C.: Carnegie Endowment for International Peace, 2005); and *Russia Lost in Transition: The Yeltsin and Putin Legacies* (Washington, D.C.: Carnegie Endowment for International Peace, 2007). Also recommended are Anna Politkovskaya's works—*A Russian Diary: A Journalist's Final Account of Life, Death and Corruption in Putin's Russia* (New York: Random House, 2007); *Putin's Russia: Life in a Failing Democracy* (New York: Metropolitan Books, 2005); and *A Small Corner of Hell: Dispatches from Chechnya* (Chicago: University of Chicago Press, 2003). Her bitingly critical accounts of Russia and Chechnya earned her an assassin's bullet in 2006.

On social developments in post-communist Russia, there is Anthony Jones, ed., *Education and Society in the New Russia* (Armonk, NY: M. E. Sharpe, 1994). For those who want brief essays on the nationality groups that comprised the former Soviet Union, a handy reference is *The Nationalities Question in the Post-Soviet States,* edited by Graham Smith (London: Longman, 1996). A good analysis of Russia's economic reform program is Anders Åslund's *Russia's Capitalist Revolution: Why Market Reform Succeeded and Democracy Failed* (Washington, D.C.: Petersen Institute, 2007). Åslund, a Swedish economist, worked in Moscow as an advisor to the Yeltsin administration. Steven Rosefielde has written a comprehensive overview of the Soviet and post-Soviet economies in *The Russian Economy: From Lenin to Putin* (Oxford: Blackwell, 2007). Stephen Handel's *Comrade Criminal* (New Haven: Yale University Press, 1997) is very strong on the Russian mafia gangs and the criminalization of the Russian economy. Also see David Satter's *Darkness at Dawn: The Rise of the Russian Criminal State* (New Haven: Yale University Press, 2003).

Biographies and autobiographies provide important insights into the Soviet and transitional periods. Mikhail Gorbachev's book *Perestroika: New Thinking for Our Country and the World* (New York: Harper and Row, 1987) outlines the former general secretary's plans for reforming the Soviet Union. In Boris Yeltsin's *Against the Grain: An Autobiography* (New York: Summit Books, 1990),

Russia's controversial first president chronicled his career within the Soviet establishment. Vladimir Putin provided a short autobiography in *First Person* (New York: Public Affairs, 2000). Dmitrii Volkogonov, a former Soviet general who had been quietly conducting research for years within the Soviet archives, published three fascinating biographies of major Soviet leaders: *Lenin: A New Biography* (New York: Free Press, 1996), *Stalin: Triumph and Tragedy* (New York: Grove Weidenfeld, 1991), and *Trotsky: The Eternal Revolutionary* (New York: Free Press, 1996). Two excellent biographies of Boris Yeltsin are *Yeltsin: A Revolutionary Life* by Leon Aron (New York: St. Martin's, 2000); and Herbert J. Ellison, *Boris Yeltsin and Russia's Democratic Transformation* (Seattle: University of Washington Press, 2006).

Western correspondents have provided some of the more entertaining glimpses of Soviet and Russian life. Two of the best are by David Remnick: *Lenin's Tomb: The Last Days of the Soviet Empire* (New York: Random House, 1993); and *Resurrection: The Struggle for a New Russia* (New York: Random House, 1997). Remnick, the former Moscow correspondent for the *Washington Post*, a Pulitzer prize winner, and an editor at *The New Republic*, delivers penetrating and humorous portraits of Soviet life and political maneuvering during and after the reform period. Hedrick Smith's *The New Russians* (New York: Random House, 1991) is a perceptive survey of the impact of Gorbachev's economic, social, and political reforms on the Soviet people. This is a remake of his vastly successful 1976 book, *The Russians* (New York: Ballantine), from his three-year stint as Moscow bureau chief for the *New York Times*. Smith, a Public Broadcasting System commentator, also produced a four-part video documentary to accompany his book. In addition to the works of Anna Politkovskaya, journalistic accounts of the Putin era are provided by Steven Levine, *Putin's Labyrinth: Spies, Murder, and the Dark Heart of the New Russia* (New York: Random House, 2008), and Andrew Jack, *Inside Putin's Russia* (New York: Oxford University Press, 2004).

Finally, there are several very good Web sites for those who want to keep up with Russian issues. Johnson's Russia List (http://www.cdi.org/russia/johnson/default.cfm) collects articles from the Russian press, news services, specialists, and the Russian government. *The Moscow Times* online (http://www.themoscowtimes.com/index.htm) and its sister Web site the *St. Petersburg Times* (http://www.sptimes.ru/) have free articles on their daily page, but the archives are available on a subscription basis. Radio Free Europe/Radio Liberty's Web site (http://www.rferl.org/), funded by the U.S. Congress, provides uncensored articles and video. For the Russian government's side of the story, go to the presidential Web site at http://www.kremlin.ru/eng/. The Russian Orthodox Church has its own English-language Web site, too (http://www.mospat.ru). The Carnegie Moscow Center has many excellent analyses by their resident experts, some in English and some in Russian—http://

www.carnegie.ru/en/. The Jamestown Foundation (http://www.jamestown. org/) has policy-oriented articles with a focus on international issues, and it has links to the Eurasia Daily Monitor and the North Caucasus Weekly sites for more specialized reading. Russia Profile (http://www.russiaprofile.org) presents news and analysis; it is published by the Russian news service RIA Novosti, together with Western partners and advisers.

Index

About the Author

CHARLES E. ZIEGLER is Professor and University Scholar in the Political Science Department at the University of Louisville. He is the author of *Foreign Policy and East Asia* (1993) and *Environmental Policy in the USSR* (1987), co-editor of *Russia's Far East: A Region at Risk* (2002) and author of dozens of scholarly articles and book chapters.

Other Titles in the Greenwood Histories of the Modern Nations
Frank W. Thackeray and John E. Findling, Series Editors

The History of Afghanistan
Meredith L. Runion

The History of Argentina
Daniel K. Lewis

The History of Australia
Frank G. Clarke

The History of the Baltic States
Kevin O'Connor

The History of Brazil
Robert M. Levine

The History of Cambodia
Justin Corfield

The History of Canada
Scott W. See

The History of Central America
Thomas Pearcy

The History of Chile
John L. Rector

The History of China
David C. Wright

The History of Congo
Didier Gondola

The History of Cuba
Clifford L. Staten

The History of Egypt
Glenn E. Perry

The History of El Salvador
Christopher M. White

The History of Ethiopia
Saheed Adejumobi

The History of Finland
Jason Lavery

The History of France
W. Scott Haine

The History of Germany
Eleanor L. Turk

The History of Ghana
Roger S. Gocking

The History of Great Britain
Anne Baltz Rodrick

The History of Haiti
Steeve Coupeau

The History of Holland
Mark T. Hooker

The History of India
John McLeod

The History of Indonesia
Steven Drakeley

The History of Iran
Elton L. Daniel

The History of Iraq
Courtney Hunt

The History of Ireland
Daniel Webster Hollis III

The History of Israel
Arnold Blumberg

The History of Italy
Charles L. Killinger

The History of Japan, Second Edition
Louis G. Perez